漢字源流

林西莉

CECILIA LINDQVIST

China

Empire of Living Symbols

Translated from the Swedish by Joan Tate

Foreword by Michael Loewe, Ph. D.

A Merloyd Lawrence Book

Addison-Wesley Publishing Company, Inc.
Reading, Massachusetts Menlo Park, California New York
Don Mills, Ontario Wokingham, England Amsterdam Bonn
Sydney Singapore Tokyo Madrid San Juan Paris
Seoul Milan Mexico City Taipei

Library of Congress Cataloging-in-Publication Data

Lindqvist, Cecilia.
    [Tecknens rike. English]
    China—empire of living symbols / Cecilia Lindqvist ; translated
from the Swedish by Joan Tate.
        p.   cm.
    Translation of: Tecknens rike.
    "A Merloyd Lawrence book."
    Includes bibliographical references and index.
    ISBN 0-201-57009-2
    1. China—Civilization.   I. Title.
DS721.L625   1991
951—dc20   91-26457
                                             CIP

Chinese script in this book by Wang Xiping, Beijing
Maps on pages 10–11 by Anna Erlandsson

The poem on page 102 is reprinted from THE SONGS OF
THE SOUTH: An Anthology of Ancient Chinese Poems,
translated by David Hawkes and reprinted with the kind
permission of Penguin Books Ltd.

Design: Andrea Ydring
Production: Bonnier Fakta AB/Gunvor Grenholm
Typesetting: Ljungbergs
Stripping: Reklam-Montage AB, Eskiltuna
Repro: Litoteam AB, Gothenburg
Printing: Arcata Graphics/Halliday
Paper: 70-lb. Finch Vanilla and 80-lb. Mountie Matte
Typeface: Baskerville 11/13

1 2 3 4 5 6 7 8 9-HA-9594939291
First printing, August 1991

Foreword to the English edition

Michael Loewe, Ph.D.

Needham Research Institute

Chinese civilization can claim to have retained many of its traditional characteristics longer than that of any other culture. This continuity has been achieved along with enrichment from other peoples, and despite the damage that non-Chinese peoples have sometimes inflicted by way of invasion or occupation. In the development of this extraordinary civilization throughout the last three millenia or so, Chinese script has played a central nurturing role, evolving to serve the needs of philosopher and poet, scholar and official, Taoist priest or explorer of the sciences.

The first Chinese book which treated the origin and growth of the written characters was produced in the form of a dictionary in A.D. 121. Early in the twentieth century, major advances in this work followed from the discovery of the oldest written material yet known— dating from 1700 B.C. onwards—and from Bernhard Karlgren's pioneer studies in applying the principles of western philology, phonology, and textual criticism to China's earliest records. In her fascinating book, Cecilia Lindqvist, who studied with Karlgren, performs a notable service both to students of the language and to those whose interest in Chinese culture has been stimulated by recent translations of traditional literature, by visits to the country, and by the political events of a people taking its place in the international field.

This lively work supplements academic studies of Chinese language by explaining the relation of characters to the dynamics of the natural world. It shows how the economic conditions of China's earliest stages are reflected in the graphs that were evolved in those times and how historical developments and technological advances may be traced in the subsequent growth of the written forms of the language. In calling on the wealth of archaeological evidence discovered in recent years, on woodcut illustrations of 18th or 19th century publications, and on photographs of the contemporary scene, the author illuminates many of the basic aspects and activities of the Chinese way of life. In her vivid explanation of the stages and complexities of China's system of writing, she demonstrates how a combination of continuity and evolution has left its characteristic stamp on China's history.

Cambridge, England, 1991

Author's Preface

Why do Chinese characters look the way they do?

That question has fascinated me ever since I started learning Chinese from the great Swedish scholar Bernhard Karlgren in the late 1950s. Karlgren never taught a character without also explaining how it was put together and what was known about its original forms. He gave the characters a history, making them alive and comprehensible. At the time, he had already been a leading expert on the Chinese language for decades, but his love for the characters was still fresh and exuberant. With apparently unquenchable enthusiasm, he reeled off his analyses of characters until clouds of chalk dust whirled around the blackboard.

I studied Chinese at Beijing University from 1961 to 1962, then *gu qin*, the Chinese lute, at the Academy of Music. To my surprise, I found that even highly educated Chinese were unaware of the roots of their own language. From early school to university level, the learning of characters was purely mechanical, with no background or explanations.

When I returned to Sweden in the late 1960s after some years of traveling in Asia and Latin America and started teaching, I found my students reacted exactly as I had—the more I could tell them about the construction and early forms of the characters, the easier it was for them to understand and remember them. The very best was when I could also tell them something about the world from which the characters were drawn: the everyday life of the Chinese of early historic times—the houses, carts, clothes, and tools they used—and the natural setting—countryside, mountains, rivers, plants, and animals.

The more I worked with the characters, the more fascinated I became with the reality they reflected and by everything I had seen as a student but had not actually understood. Why did the Chinese cultivate different crops alongside each other in the fields? Why were water taps called dragon heads? Why did millions of people insist on living in caves in the mountainsides, when they could live in real houses? I was drawn into extensive reading, not least on technical matters, which, as a student of the humanities I'd never found interesting. Time and time again I went back to

China to find out more about everything I hadn't understood.

Each time, the characters came closer.

When I started this book fifteen years ago, I intended to write a short, popular, and informative account of what is known about the pictorial origins of the characters. But I soon found that many traditional explanations had become obsolete, largely as a result of the new archaeological finds of recent decades, which no one had yet worked on from a linguistic point of view. Archaeology is a young science in China. The first proper excavations were carried out in the 1920s, but during the chaotic decades that followed, with civil war and foreign invasion, the work was largely discontinued and not taken up again until the 1950s. This book is the first to discuss the central store of Chinese characters in the full light of the comprehensive archaeological material that has since been excavated.

For a long time I regarded myself primarily as an art historian. It was natural for me to seek the explanation of the characters in pictures and objects from the time when the characters were created. In this archaeological material one often comes across images expressing the same perception of reality as the original forms of the characters. This book is the first to demonstrate this in detail, character by character.

These images, once confronted, can be seen to recur as archetypes throughout the centuries. Chinese culture has a remarkable continuity; in advertisements, popular art, and in everyday life even today, pictures can be seen that perceive and reproduce reality just as the creators of the characters did over three thousand years ago.

This book deals with only a very small number of the nearly fifty thousand characters included in the most extensive dictionaries. Still, they are the main elements of the written language, and like the elements of the periodic table in chemistry, they recur constantly in all the other characters in new and fascinating combinations. Once you have learned to recognize and understand them, to know them, so to speak, as individuals, they provide not only a key to the written language but also to the reality from which they once emanated, as well as to the life of China today.

It is important to point out that a phonetic component to the Chinese written language also developed at an early stage. While the complex relationship between the spoken word and the written characters is not the subject of this book, I have devoted a chapter ('Meaning and Sound') to some of the fascinating questions involved. Once again, the work of Bernhard Karlgren has been vital in reconstructing the phonetic origins of the Chinese script.

At the heart of this book is a *story*—the cultural history of China as reflected in the characters, their origins and development. I have chosen not to tell the story in an academic style, but in my own language, as I came to understand it, through my own experiences and perceptions.

Cecilia Lindqvist

CONTENTS

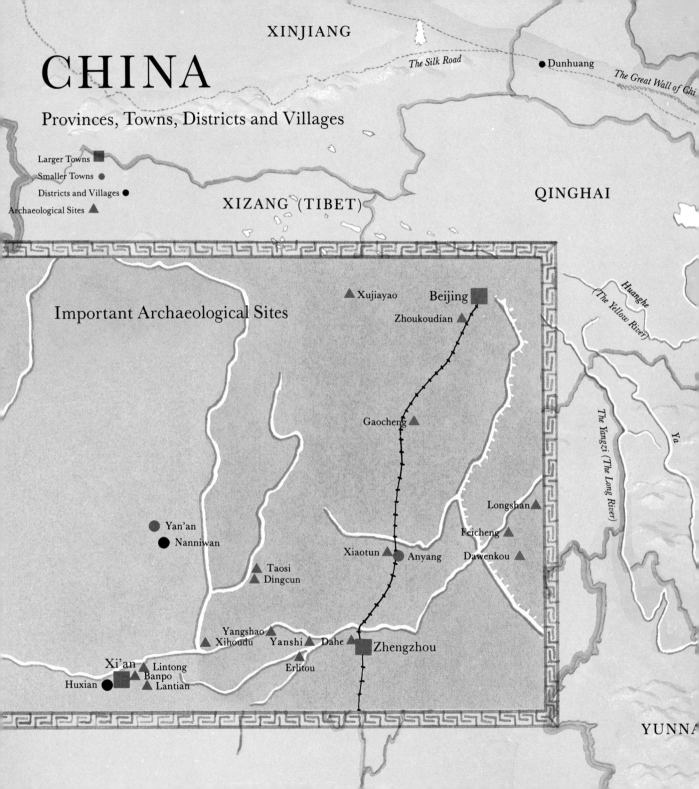

CHINA

Provinces, Towns, Districts and Villages

Larger Towns ■
Smaller Towns ●
Districts and Villages ●
Archaeological Sites ▲

XINJIANG

The Silk Road

● Dunhuang

The Great Wall of Chi

XIZANG (TIBET)

QINGHAI

Huanghe (The Yellow River)

Important Archaeological Sites

▲ Xujiayao   Beijing ■

Zhoukoudian ▲

Gaocheng ▲

Longshan ▲

Feicheng ▲

● Yan'an

● Nanniwan

Xiaotun ▲ ● Anyang   Dawenkou ▲

▲ Taosi
▲ Dingcun

The Yangzi (The Long River)

Ya

Yangshao ▲
▲ Xihoudu   Yanshi ▲   Dahe ▲

Zhengzhou ■

Xi'an ▲ Lintong
Huxian ● ■ ▲ Banpo
▲ Lantian

Erlitou ▲

YUNNA

Oracle Bones and Bronzes

日

This Chinese character means *sun*.
It was originally a picture.

月

This means *moon*.
Originally it was also a picture.

How do we know that?

There are two main sources of knowledge
about the origins of Chinese characters:
oracle bones and bronzes.

Oracle Bones

One summer's day in 1899, Liu E, an author and scholar, went into the Da Ren Tang apothecary to buy medicine for his friend Wang Yirong, who was ill with malaria. The medicine contained an ingredient in common use for centuries called dragon bone. Liu E watched it being ground and, to his surprise, saw inscriptions resembling Chinese characters on the pieces of bone.

As soon as Wang Yirong's attack of fever was over, the two gentlemen set off into the town and bought up every bone they could find in the apothecaries of Beijing. On them, they found a total of 1,058 inscriptions written in strange old characters, older than any then known.

Everything the Chinese knew at the time about the origins of their language, they had acquired from *Shuowen*, a dictionary published in 121 giving current explanations of about nine thousand characters. For two thousand years, with great acumen but also pedantry, Chinese scholars had continued to discuss *Shuowen*'s explanations for the characters with little new source material appearing. Layer upon layer of commentaries had accumulated like a grave mound over the texts.

For the first time, the pieces of bone from Beijing apothecaries now offered direct contact with the past. They revealed that long ago, people wrote *sun* like this:

and *moon* like this:

Chinese civilization was perhaps not the very first. As far as is known, earlier peoples living in Egypt and Mesopotamia kept domestic animals and developed written language. But Sumer, Babylon, and Assyria have long since vanished. China today, on the other hand, is a continuation in direct lineal descent from the culture that arose in the long valley of the Yellow River during the fifth millennium before the beginning of our calendar.

No one today uses Sumerian cuneiform script or Egyptian hieroglyphics. But the present Chinese script is built directly on the first script that arose in China. Many characters are still so similar to the old ones that only a minimum of explanation is needed to understand them.

No wonder Liu E caused a sensation when, in 1903, he published a book on the dragon bone inscriptions.

At the time, nothing was known of where the bones came from or how old they were. But eager scholars of linguistics and no less eager antique dealers soon traced them to Xiaotun, outside Anyang, where the legendary Shang dynasty's last capital was supposed to have been, in the millennium before our calendar.

At Xiaotun there was a mound where poor peasants used to dig for 'dragon bones' to sell to the apothecaries in town. They had been doing this since 500, but no one had ever noticed any inscriptions—perhaps because the peasants, who could not read, used to file away the characters to make the bones smoother and more saleable.

The excavations begun in Xiaotun in 1928 were the first government-sponsored scientific excavations in the history of China. The workers found a wealth of bones and turtle shells, which are now collectively known as oracle bones.

The oracle bones were used when the king of Shang wanted to make contact with the spirits of his dead ancestors who resided in the heavens around Shangdi, the Supreme Ruler. Through the mediation of the spirits, the king was able to convey questions and wishes to him. These concerned campaigns and hunting expeditions, building and sacrificial ceremonies, weather, harvests, illness, dreams, birth, and death.

The diviners polished a piece of bone, often a scapula, or shoulder blade, of an ox or the lower shell of a turtle, and bored or chiseled rows of hollows into it. Then in a loud voice, they called out the king's question to his ancestors, at the same time lowering a flaming thorn or a bronze rod into one hollow after another. The shell cracked from the heat with a clear, sharp sound—the turtle shell was 'speaking,' they said. In the cracks, the diviners could read the answer to the question. Both question and answer were often later engraved with a knife into the bone or shell used. Sometimes whether the prophesy had been verified or not was also recorded, and then the bones were stored.

The hollows were bored or chiseled on the inside of the turtle shell and placed symmetrically in long columns on each side of an imaginary central axis. They consisted of two hollows, one longer and oval, and one smaller and round. The purpose was to make the shell thinner, so that it would crack more easily when the heated bronze rod was inserted in a hollow. This demanded a considerable skill in boring, for the shape of the hollow decided, in its turn, the direction and shape of the cracks. Most importantly, the knife did not go right through the shell. At the bottom of each depression a thin layer of shell a few millimeters thick had to be left, for that was where the ancestors' reply to the king's question was to appear in the form of a crack.

The questions were generally written from the top downward and often started on the right. The Chinese to this day have continued to arrange many of their texts on a page in this way.

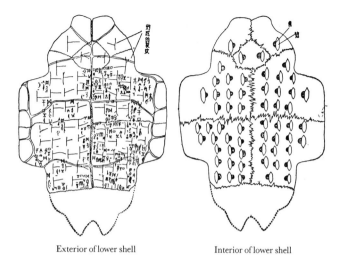

Exterior of lower shell   Interior of lower shell

The king's questions were written on the exterior of the shell, where the cracks can also be seen. The character for *to divine, foretell, predict* shows a crack of that kind. It is still written today almost exactly as it was three thousand years ago. The difference in form is primarily due to the fact that the character is no longer scratched in with a knife, but is written with a soft, flexible brush and ink.

In the distant past, this character was pronounced 'puk'—perhaps that was the sound of the shell cracking and the turtle 'speaking.'

Oracle bone characters provide a clear picture of the thin cracks on the outer side of the turtle shell

divine, foretell

Sometime around the year 1027 B.C. the Shang dynasty collapsed. Archives, ancestral temples, and other buildings decayed, and when the Huan River and the Yellow River later burst their banks, the remains were buried beneath a thick layer of fine yellow silt, where everything stayed hidden for three thousand years.

During the excavations so far carried out in Xiaotun and the surrounding area, according to the latest calculations, about 175,000 oracle bones have been found, of which about 50,000 bear some inscription. The *Jiaguwen bian* dictionary of oracle bone characters, constantly on my desk in front of me, contains slightly more than four thousand different characters, of which a third had already been identified when the

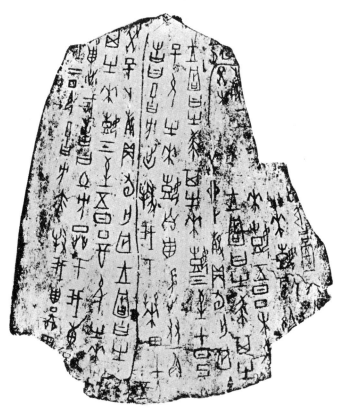

Inscription on a turtle shell.

book was published in 1934. Since then, an additional number of characters have had their meanings confirmed, but even today it is still unclear what half of the known characters mean.

The divining ceremonies and sacrifices to ancestors appear to have taken up a great deal of the Shang kings' time. The year was divided into periods of sixty days, and on every one of the days, sacrifices were to be made to various ancestors according to a definite schedule. To ensure the satisfaction of the ancestor, he was often consulted beforehand.

Added to this were all the divining ceremonies concerning hunting, war, harvesting, and so on. Every tenth day, inquiries were made about what was to happen during the coming period. An inscription from King Wu Ding's rule in about 1300 B.C. contains the king's question, the oracle's answer, and a note on what actually happened:

On the day 'gui-si,' the diviner Que consulted the oracle:

"Will any misfortune occur in the next ten days?"

The king read in the cracks and said:

"Misfortune will occur. Perhaps disturbing news will come."

When it came to the fifth day, 'ding-you,' disturbing news did indeed come from the west. Guo from Zhi said:

"Tufang is besieging our eastern border and has attacked two villages. Gongfang has also plundered the fields on our western border."

The oracle bone inscriptions Liu E published in 1903 were done with a reproduction method usually called rubbings. This is reminiscent of the way, as children, we made paper money to play at shopping. We put a piece of paper over a real coin and ran a soft lead pencil back and forth across the paper until the pattern of the coin emerged. The Chinese also use that method as they tranquilly copy a beautiful inscription they see in a park or a temple. The text is usually carved deeply into the stone, in the same way that the oracle bone characters were cut into the turtle shell and the ox bone in ancient China, and it is easy to make a copy.

When real rubbings are made, however, a moistened piece of thin rice paper is placed over the object to be reproduced and carefully smoothed onto the object to ensure that the paper sinks into every depression. Then a round pad dipped in ink is patted or dabbed over the surface until the ink is evenly distributed. This requires a hand that is both light and steady, and ink that is not so liquid as to run down into the crevices. When the paper is almost dry, it is carefully lifted and the rubbing is done. The inscription then appears in white, surrounded by black areas in which the irregularities of the stone or bone shimmer through.

Most objects with uneven surfaces can be copied in this way—axes, knives, coins, reliefs, even round bronze vessels—but this requires great skill. Reproductions of this kind often depict the object more clearly than a photograph or a drawing, giving the impression that it is right under one's hand. Many illustrations in this book are rubbings of this kind.

All the oracle bone characters in the book are reproduced in their original size.

Rubbings from Liu E's book, 1903.

The Bronzes

The excavations conducted outside Anyang from 1928 to 1937 were primarily aimed at the oracle bones. But bronze objects with a wealth of form, beauty, and strength were also found, and they astonished the world. They had been used in connection with sacrificial ceremonies when the spirits of ancestors were offered meat, wine, and delicacies to ensure their cooperation.

Since the Song dynasty (960–1279 A.D.), Chinese intellectuals had collected antique bronze objects—not least in order to study the inscriptions on them. Up until the finds of oracle bones, the characters occurring on the bronze objects were the only ones that could explain the origins and development of the script. Through the finds in Anyang, scholars for the first time had access to a number of undoubtedly genuine and clearly dateable bronzes. Together with other finds, they made a firm foundation on which it was possible to begin to reconstruct the early history not only of China but also of the Chinese script.

Early bronze inscriptions often consist of only one single character, probably the name of a family or clan. Later ones are often longer and tell of the circumstances surrounding the making of the vessel—who had it made, and in memory of which person or event. According to a study by the scholar Zhou Fagao, there were in the 1970s about five thousand bronzes with inscriptions, and on them almost two thousand different bronze characters for which an equivalent in today's characters could be found, plus about a thousand characters considered to be names of clans and having no modern equivalent.

On the bronzes, the character for *sun* is written like this:

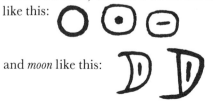

and *moon* like this:

The characters on the Shang period bronzes are more pictorial than those on the oracle bones. Dong Zuobin, the famous scholar who devoted fifty years of his life to the study of early characters, maintained that the bronze script should be regarded as the archaic script and the oracle bone script, which is more simplified, abbreviated, and abstract, as the more modern one.

Other scholars think that an already ancient style was consciously used on the bronzes—just as it is still used when seals are carved or characters are used for decorative purposes. The manner of presentation may also have been significant: oracle bones were whittled down with a knife on a hard piece of bone, while the bronze inscriptions were shaped with a small spatula in the soft clay of the core.

After the fall of the Shang dynasty, the use of divining with the help of oracle bones largely died out. But over the next eight hundred years, bronzes continued to be made in honor of ancestors. During this long period, the form of the bronze characters was also simplified, and toward the end of the Zhou dynasty, the clear old picture had already disappeared in many cases.

All characters in this book taken from bronzes are reproduced in the original size and can be recognized by the fact that they are printed in brown.

On both the bronzes and oracle bones a script can be found that, however primitive it may seem, is already highly developed and must have a long prehistory. But we still have only scattered glimpses of this prehistory. In the village of Banpo, outside Xi'an, pottery fragments with symbols engraved into them have been found, and the similarities to various characters are great. The fragments have been dated, by the process called carbon 14 dating, to the period from 4800 to 4200 B.C. Some scholars are convinced that these symbols are the predecessors of the script on the oracle bones and the bronzes. Others think they are not characters, but signatures or owners'

Pottery fragments on display in the museum in Banpo.

marks scratched into the clay by the potters before firing, so that they themselves and the families for whom the vessels were intended could easily identify them. The puzzle is not yet solved.

Not even the original sites at Anyang have been definitively excavated. In 1976, only a stone's throw away from the ancestral temple, the grave of Fu Hao, King Wu Ding's wife, was found. It is the richest and best-preserved find so far and the only one directly connected to a known historical person.

One summer morning in 1984, I walked out to the grave together with Zheng Zhenxiang, the head archaeologist at the research station in Anyang. There was only a simple little notice on the roadside and in the field where the grave had been; wheat and maize were now flourishing in the humid air. Next to the site some peasants were ploughing.

"It's the middle of the summer," I said. "Why are they ploughing now?"

"We've found another grave," said Zheng, "under this field. It appears to be considerably larger than Fu Hao's and is fourteen meters down. But when we began to dig, we came up against problems. Nine meters down, we found a layer of sand with water running through it. We realized that with the resources we had, we would never manage to divert the water and drain the grave. So now we've just put back the soil."

"Of course, we're curious about whose grave it is," she went on. "It could be King Wu Ding's own. But every day, all the year round, three thousand new archaeological finds are reported to the museums in China and these already reported have to be taken care of first. The grave is still there. One day we're sure to have the chance to excavate it."

Most of Chinese prehistory and early history still lies under the earth, unknown and uninvestigated. But compared with what was known when Liu E went to the apothecary in 1899, a whole new world has opened up: the world of the Chinese characters.

The bronze characters, later referred to as the Great Seal script, became the starting point for the first standard form of writing, what is called the Small Seal script, established in the third century B.C. The First Emperor of Qin had just subjugated a group of states in the area around the Yellow River, and to consolidate his empire and render his government more effective, he had instituted a series of reforms, among them the standardization of the script.

Until that day, characters had appeared in different variations in the different states, but now one single official form for the most common three thousand characters was established. The Small Seal script is beautiful and is often used in decorative contexts, in name stamps, for instance, but for writing in everyday purposes, it was far too rigid and formal. All the strokes were of equal thickness, all characters of equal size, and so on, and this was limiting.

So it was not long before a new, somewhat freer style, given the name *li shu* emerged. This in turn became the starting point for yet another style, *kai shu*, which from the end of the Han dynasty and up to our day has functioned as the so-called normal script in China. The characters for sun and moon, which can be seen on the first page of this chapter, are written in this style, just as are all the other characters I have included.

During the Han dynasty, writing with brush and ink became common. The unparalleled flexibility of the brush that makes it possible, with only a slight change of pressure on the paper, to make strokes thinner or thicker, led to the origin of two even freer styles, *xing shu* and *cao shu*. However undisciplined they may appear, they originate in the normal script and are italicized forms of it.

Not until after the 1949 revolution, when the new government was faced with the gigantic task of teaching hundreds of millions of people to read and write, was a change made to the construction of the script. During the 1950s, slightly more than 2,200 complicated characters with a wealth of strokes were simplified, the first such change since the days of the first emperor of Qin. In many cases, the ordinary abbreviated forms that had been in use for hundreds of years but had never been officially approved were used as the basis of change, and in other cases completely new constructions were made. Many of these new constructions met with considerable resistance, and the old and new forms have continued to exist side by side. Revolutionaries such as Mao Zedong and Zhu De stubbornly kept to the old, unsimplified characters, and many intellectuals did so as well. But among the peasants in the rural areas—the group the character-reformers of the 1950s had foremost in mind—the simplified form was a success.

sun and moon, clear, bright

the Small Seal script

li shu (*the clerical or scribe script*)

kai shu (*the regular script*)

xing shu (*the semi-italic or running script*)

cao shu (*the italic or cursive script*)

Man, Mankind

Many of the oldest and clearest characters are pictures of people and the various parts of their bodies. Let's start with this one, which means **man, mankind, person**. Before I knew anything about the early forms of this character, I thought it showed legs, and I imagined a person briskly walking forward. But I was wrong. Once I found out how the character was written on oracle bones and bronzes, I saw the picture of a person in profile. He is standing upright with his arm hanging down or slightly lifted in front of his body. Occasionally the head is shown, but mostly it is only the body, the way a person is seen slightly at a distance, on the street or in the fields.

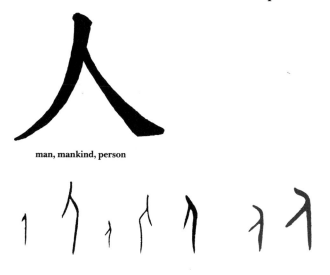

man, mankind, person

The *man, mankind, person* character is included in a great many compound characters, often in a form anyone from ancient China would understand, despite the passage of three thousand years.

The clay figure on the left is slightly older than the characters on the oracle bones, but it also stems from the village of Xiaotun, outside Anyang. It is an ordinary little person standing with his head on one side and an appealing, rather foolish look. His ears are large and his long hair is drawn back from the forehead and fastened in a knot at the back of his head. His long arm, inactive at the moment, hangs down, framing his torso.

This is one of the earliest representations of a human being in Chinese art, almost as simplified as a character.

Note: Oracle bone characters appear in black throughout the book; bronze characters are shown in brown.

Standing man. Clay sculpture from Neolithic times.
Museum of Far Eastern Antiquities, Stockholm. 10 cm high.

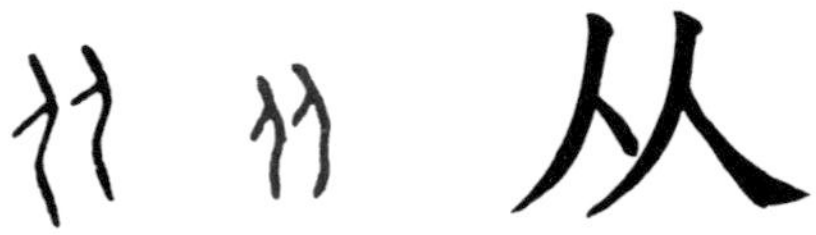

By twisting and turning this character for *man, mankind, person,* and putting it together with itself in various combinations, the ancient Chinese were able to establish many new written characters for words existing in the spoken language. Two people, one behind the other, together form the character for *follow, from.* On oracle bones and bronzes, the two people are sometimes going to the left, sometimes to the right. Before the characters were standardized in the second century B.C., variations of that kind were very common.

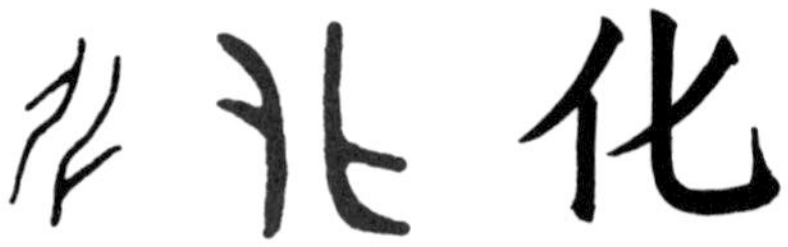

follow, from

Two people, one upside down, as if lying head to foot, means *to turn, change, transform.* The character is included in the composite word for *chemistry*—the teaching of the transformation of substances—and in many other words having to do with transformation or change.

to turn, change, transform

Two people in a row: *to compare.*

to measure yourself against, compare

At the bottom we see two people standing back to back, turning away from each other. The character originally meant *at the back* and *behind,* but in time it also came to mean *north,* because Chinese dwellings and palaces always used to be built with the back facing north. That tradition arose with the beginning of civilization, and the explanation can be found in geographical reality. The icy winter winds from Siberia and the yellow spring sandstorms from the deserts of Mongolia come from the north. To protect themselves, people 'turned their backs' on them. North held darkness and cold, so buildings faced south and the sun. During his audiences, the emperor always sat with his back to the north. And even today, the seat of the guest of honor at a dinner table is on the north side, and that of the host opposite to him on the south.

at the back, behind, north

In the character for **big**, **great**, **large**, a man can be seen standing with his legs apart and his arms held out, like a goalkeeper expecting the ball. Or is he just puffing himself up to impress—showing that he is big?

The same picture with another horizontal stroke at the top forms the character for *grown man, husband*. That top stroke is thought to allude to the long pins that held a grown man's knot of hair together.

big, great, large

grown man, husband

Hairpins were not used only by men, as the character for *grown man, husband* seems to imply. The grave finds from Shang and Zhou show that they were also used by women. The knot of hair and the pins indicated adulthood, just as plaits pinned up around a girl's head once indicated that she was married. Hairpins also indicated status. The more distinguished the person, the more numerous and gorgeous the pins. Fu Hao, King Wu Ding's wife, was given 499 hairpins of seven different varieties to take with her to the grave—enough for a great many elegant coiffures.

For everyday purposes, simple polished bone pins were used, but there were also hairpins for ceremonial use. On these the head was substantially larger and decorated with beautiful carving, often in the form of a bird. Hairpins are among the most common finds in graves from the earliest dynasties. They appear in such numbers and in so many distinctly different forms that they can be used to help date archaeological sites.

Among the almost two thousand artifacts found in Fu Hao's grave were two small jade figures, a man and a woman. They stand on slightly bowed legs, facing forward. The man's hands hang boldly straight down along his thighs; the woman is opening her genitalia to the viewer. Their heads are ornamented with huge hairpins.

Jade figures from the grave of Fu Hao, Anyang. Shang. 12.5 cm high.

The same picture of a man with outstretched arms seen in the character for *big* and *grown man, husband* is also found in other characters, for instance in *to be on both sides of, support, press, in between*. Three people can be seen; in the middle, a big one with outstretched arms, and on either side, two smaller people in profile who are doing their best to support and help.

In the character for *stand, set up, establish*, the man is standing with his legs firmly on the ground, indicated by a horizontal stroke. On the oracle bones and bronzes the picture is clear and easy to understand. But it was distorted at an early stage, and if one has never seen the original form of the character, it probably is difficult to understand why it means just *to stand*.

The same applies to the character for *to cross, intersect*, which was originally a picture of a man with crossed legs. In a transferred sense (see discussion page 349), the character has been used since ancient times for the meaning *contact, exchange, communication*.

to support

to stand

to cross, contact

sky, heaven

Closely related to the characters for *man* and *big* is the character for **sky**, which later also became the name for **Heaven**, the Supreme Ruler over all things in nature and in the world of human beings.

How far back the cult of Heaven goes is still not clear, but the shape of the character on the oracle bones indicated that it may already have appeared during the Shang dynasty. In any event, from the beginning of the Zhou dynasty onward it was in full use, and the king was regarded as the Son of Heaven, whose task it was to rule the country.

In oracle bone characters, the head is drawn as a square or just a stroke, while the bronze character provides a more realistic picture of a large man with a powerful, round head.

The man's eyes are shaped in a very characteristic manner that recurs not only in other sculptures and in the animal masks decorating many bronze objects of the same period, but also in the character for **eye**. The same huge iris and the same long, curved line running toward the bridge of the nose appear.

Along with the standardization of the script in the third century B.C., the eye was made vertical and all the lines straightened. But little imagination is required to see the ancient eye behind today's character for *eye*.

Wild animal mask from a bronze vessel. Early Shang dynasty. Rubbing.

Here is a little man, probably a slave, with his hands resting submissively on his knees. His eyes are large and his gaze is turned inward, as if he had sat waiting there for a long time. The sculpture, which is only 5.5 cm high, comes from the grave outside Anyang where Fu Hao, King Wu Ding's wife, was buried 3,200 years ago with all the equipment she might need in the afterworld—servants, sacrificial vessels, spades, battle axes (she was a famous warrior), jade ornaments, and ivory carvings.

A standing or sitting person and a large eye: *to look, see*.

to look, see

eyebrows

Whiskery lines above an eye: *eyebrows*.

The oldest characters for *eyebrows* are generally limited to the actual eye and eyebrows, but in some oracle bone characters like these, the whole figure can be seen. The person is kneeling, just like the little slave. The body is small, and the large eye and eyebrows reflect the meaning of the character.

A similar picture is repeated in this bronze character, the meaning of which is for some reason considered unknown. I think it must also mean *eyebrow*. All essential details found in the other characters for eyebrows are repeated here. In one inscription the character appears to function as a name. Was the owner of the bronze vessel perhaps given that name because of his unusually handsome eyebrows?

face, surface

The picture of an eye is also the starting point for the character for **face**, **surface**. On the oracle bone one can see an eye surrounded by a blank no-man's-land. Perhaps this empty area is meant as the skin up toward the eyebrows and down to the cheek, perhaps it is simply a surface that stands for the whole face and functions as a background for the eye, the most characteristic detail of the face.

The first time I truly saw the character as a face and realized the brilliant simplicity of the original picture was a day at the research station in Xiaotun, outside

Small Seal script

Human face. Research station in Xiaotun. 1984.

Anyang, where the archaeological finds from the excavations are stored and worked on. In a display case, along with all the other slightly dusty fragments of the life lived in the area over three thousand years ago, was a mask, you can see it above, in its cardboard box, resting on a bed of silk-wool, together with a cast that had been made of it. It is one of the extremely few realistic representations of a human being preserved from the Shang dynasty. A death mask? Perhaps, but of whom is uncertain, perhaps a slave or a page who followed his master into death.

I still do not know why I was so fascinated by that face. Perhaps it was only the surprise of finding a recognizable human being among all the pottery fragments, bronze arrows, and chariot fittings—and he was dead. The moon-pale face with its dreamy, unseeing eyes, its closed mouth and high, arched cheekbones—open and yet completely closed. The picture has continued to captivate me. I have it on the wall by my typewriter, and every day our faces meet over the ages.

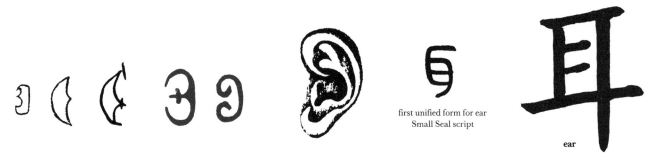

first unified form for ear
Small Seal script

ear

The character for **ear** appears on oracle bones and bronzes in several different, fairly distinctive forms. Some of them seem at first glance to bear only a remote resemblance to an ear, but considering the peculiar design of the outer ear, the pictures are perhaps not so silly after all.

Several of the characteristic lines in the bronze character for *ear*—for instance, the soft curves and the sweep of the upper and lower parts toward the inner ear—are repeated in the picture of the human ear above, taken from a 1905 Chinese reference book.

During the first dynasties, there were certain conventions for the way the many details of reality were perceived and reproduced. Whoever was concerned with formulating them in writing or in pictures started out from a certain way of seeing. The similarity between the different forms of writing and artistic ornamentation is therefore often very great.

Under the First Emperor in the Qin period, the character for *ear* acquired its first unified form. That form differs quite a bit from the oracle bone characters and the bronze characters. But it is from that form that the character for *ear* was derived.

Face on a bronze vessel. Late Shang. Rubbing.

One early summer day, I was cycling up by the Beihai in Beijing and caught sight of a little 'claim' staked out on the pavement. In many areas of the older parts of the city, the houses stand as if on a plinth slightly above street level, and the children often sit out there doing their homework, the old people mend their clothes, and so on. Outside one house, someone had created the most delightful garden, no bigger than a double bed. The roses were fragrant, the creepers winding their way up toward the roof. There were cacti and orchids on shelves, as well as some jars of garlic. Hanging there, too, were some cages of small birds, whose song rang out over the sounds of cars and tinkling bicycle bells.

Every time I rode past this place, I would slowly coast by, enjoying the sight of this Garden of Eden. One day, a family was sitting there on low stools, having their dinner. I jumped off my bicycle, and we started talking about flowers.

"Who made this garden?" I asked.

The man smiled proudly and pointed at his nose. "I did."

In the same situation, most Europeans would probably have tapped themselves lightly on the chest, but in China people point at their nose. And it is more than likely that the gesture goes far back in time, to the character for **self**, which stood originally for **nose**, and is a picture of a nose seen from the front with nostrils and a bridge. Our Western noses generally protrude quite a way out from the head, so it is natural for us to think of a nose primarily in profile. Not so in China, where most people have a nose that undulates with the rest of the face, and for them the characteristic picture of a nose is one seen from the front.

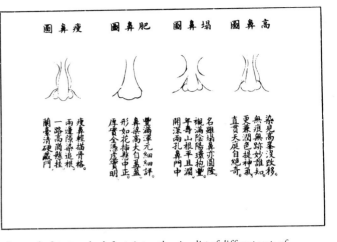

In an 1818 pattern book for painters there is a list of different sorts of noses and their characteristic features — high and narrow, broad, fleshy, wrinkled, short, drooping. They are all seen from the front.

nose, self

mouth

This character means **mouth**, and it once looked like the laughing mouth in a child's drawing. The happy corners of the mouth have now disappeared, and the character looks like any square. In a transferred sense, it means *opening*, *mouth (of a river)* and is included in composite words such as *doorway*, *entrance*, and *exit*.

In old China, when it was difficult to find enough food and children stood hungrily waiting, it was natural for people to think of themselves as mouths to feed. In the language, this remains a memory. When people in China ask how many are in our family, I reply that "we are four mouths"—not just "four" as in most languages. And I see my children standing there hungry and waiting for me to come home with the shopping and start cooking dinner.

Population is called *human mouths* in Chinese. There are now over a billion (thousand million) people in China, a billion mouths to feed. 人口

A mouth with something inside it: *sweet, tasty.*

sweet, tasty

The same stylized way of reproducing eye, eyebrows, and ear found in the early characters is again repeated on this heavy blade of a bronze axe of the same period. The face is barbaric and cruel, fitting for an axe used in connection with human sacrifice. It was found at the entrance of a large princely grave, which also contained forty-eight people who had been sacrificed to follow the dead man into his next life.

Bronze axe from Shang dynasty. Shandong Provincial Museum, Jinan.

The grinning mouth on the axe, with its sparse square teeth, is very like the oracle bone character for **tooth**, **teeth**, but that character was corrupted very early, and after the character reforms of the 1950s, nothing is left of this rather drastic old picture.

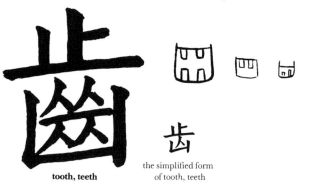

tooth, teeth

the simplified form
of tooth, teeth

心

The character for **heart** as it now appears seems totally incomprehensible. Perhaps that is because we actually do not often see a heart. However much we feel it thumping inside us, as a picture it is abstract. Which of us could draw the exact positions of the different atria, the ventricles, and the aorta?

Our picture of a heart is more like the hearts carved into tree trunks in the spring, often with an arrow through them. For us *heart* means not only love but also yearning, sorrow, and pain.

In China the heart also stands for emotions of various kinds, and it can be found in many compound characters having to do with the emotions and state of mind, as with ideas touching on the inner man, his moral 'heart.'

The oracle bone and bronze characters are not all that dissimilar from our own conventional image of a heart.

Nose and heart: *to breathe, sigh, rest*. Well, breathing can be felt in the nose and heart after strenuously working in a vegetable plot or after climbing flights of stairs.

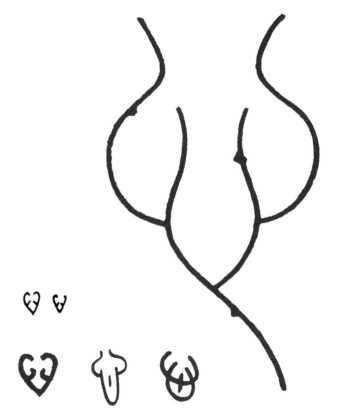

breathe

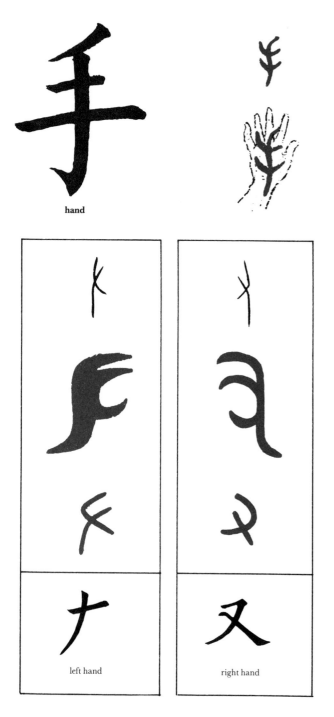

hand

left hand

right hand

Hand. Judging from the bronze characters, the original character may well have been a picture of a hand with its five fingers. But why doesn't it look more like a hand? Why are the fingers spread out like leaves on a stalk? Why can't we see the thumb, which is of such decisive importance to the function of the hand? Of all fingers, that should be indicated.

Our idea of what a hand looks like probably varies. I myself think of it like this, left-handed as I am.

But with a little afterthought, I realize there are numerous ways of depicting a hand, just as natural as my own preconceived idea of what a hand should look like. The hand, man's most important tool, is not so easy to describe in one single picture.

As I sit here at my desk with my own hand and the character for *hand* in front of me, thinking about the relationship between reality and characters, the pictures merge, and I see that the character is not as incomplete as I had first thought. If one looks on the middle finger as the main axle of the hand, the fingers divide themselves equally on both sides of it. My knowledge of how a hand is constructed—bones, sinews, muscles—have led me astray. If I am to understand how people at the dawn of history regarded and represented themselves and their world, I must try to free myself from the conventions stored inside me as a result of my upbringing and education in Europe three thousand years later.

But there is also another way of looking at the matter. As early as in the Shang period the character for *hand* was a written character, not a picture. Like the other characters, it probably had a long history behind it in which simplifications of various kinds had taken place. This can be seen, among other things, from the other existing characters for *hand*.

In the characters here, which originally meant *left* and *right hand*, only three of the hand's five fingers can be seen.

In compound characters,
hand is often written
like this.

friend, friendly

看

to see, look

to grasp

反

to turn over

The *left hand* character has kept its original form all this time, but little remains of the old *right hand* in the character of today. The character, though, still means *hand* in the many compound characters of which it forms a part. Alone it means *again, once again*—perhaps as the hand repeats its movements over and over again during the day's work.

The different characters for *hand* are found in many compound characters. One of them is *friend, friendly*, which originally showed two hands doing something in the same direction, as friends might. Later it was changed so that it looks like a left hand and a right hand meeting—also a nice image.

In another character, a hand shading an eye can be seen, as we often do when the sun is strong and we wish to sharpen our eyes to be able to look fixedly at something far away. The character means *to see, look, observe* but it is also used for *to read* and *to call on, to go to see*. That may seem all too many meanings at once, but if we think about it, we use the word *look* in the same way. We say we 'look' in the newspaper, although we are really reading, and when a neighbor comes on a visit, he says he's only 'looking in' for a moment to ask if he may borrow the hedgeclippers.

In the character for *grasp, take hold of, obtain*, a right hand is stretched out toward an ear as though to grasp it. Hello there! The character was originally also used for *taking a wife*—the picture is here rather drastic—but for that meaning, during the Shang period a new character had already been constructed by adding the character for *woman*, to which we shall soon come.

A hand that bends or turns something over: *to turn over, in the opposite direction, revolt*.

to rap, tap

variant of to hit

father

branch, twig

claw

to bring together

The character for *rap, tap* also shows a right hand equipped with a mattock or axe held high. This never occurs alone, but in many compound characters, with fiercely aggressive meaning: *to strike down, attack, grasp, destroy, disperse, ruin, drive away, stop, castrate, agonizing pain, forcing your way in,* and so on. Before one's eyes rise terrible scenes that must have been enacted before *order* was once again restored—for *to rap* is also included in that character, as it is in *to steer, rule* and *imperial edict.* All power rests on violence, it is said. The way the character for *rap* is used seems to confirm this.

In the original character for *father*, a hand can be seen on the right, but scholars disagree on the other part of the character. It is probably an object representing power and authority, perhaps a weapon, perhaps a symbol for ancestors.

A hand holding a twig or a branch: *branch, twig.*

The character for *claw* was at first a picture of a hand grasping something downward, much like a claw. Alone it means 'the claw of a bird or an animal.' In compound characters it still means *hand.* There it is written like this:

Two hands approaching each other: *to join hands, present with both hands.* The character never occurs alone, but is included in several compound characters.

Hands and arms can be used in a great many ways. These muscular men are caught in an easy, almost dancing struggle. Their thick necks, straight backs, and tensed bent knees, making it possible for the men to gather their strength, are richly and sensually reproduced. The sculpture is from the Zhou period and only a hand high, one of the few existing realistic representations of people from early Chinese history.

When I see these small men, I always think of the old Tian Qiao amusement area down in south Beijing, where Chinese wrestling, that ancient lightning form of various Asian martial arts, attracted as large an audience as the acrobats and conjurors. There was none of that heavy, fleshy shoving and panting that I associate with wrestling in the West. It was swift and playful and went so quickly that you hardly had time to get your breath back before the next man lay on the ground.

Wrestling has been known as a sport in China since the seventh century B.C., and its history most likely goes back even further. These two oracle bone characters resembling simple sketches of the sculpture are the predecessors of the character for **to fight**, **to contest**.

Wrestlers. Bronze statuette from the Zhou dynasty. British Museum.

to fight, to contest

This character originally meant **foot**, and—as can be seen from the early forms—it is a picture of a foot with splayed toes, sometimes the left foot, sometimes the right. The characters on the oracle bones and bronzes are already very much simplified, but some idea of what their predecessors may have looked like can be found on a pottery fragment from Gaocheng, an old trading town north of Anyang. This shard of a jar has been dated to about 1300 B.C. On it the foot can be seen clearly, with the free straight toes of a barefoot walker. Everyone who has walked along a sandy shore or walked with wet feet across a floor will recognize the picture.

foot, stop

The character is now used primarily for **to stop**, **halt**, but in the compound characters it still has its original meaning, *foot*.

A right foot with splayed big toe, followed by a left foot: *to walk*, *footstep*.

to walk, footstep

A foot and a man swinging his arms as if walking at a brisk pace: *to go on foot*. No oracle bone character is as yet known, but there are many bronze characters and they are clear enough.

to go on foot

This character, which today does not in any way look as if it had anything to do with the human body, was also from the start a picture of a foot on its way out of something. Whatever the foot is leaving is indicated with a curved line: *to go out*, *out*.

to go out, out

Everyone agrees that this character means **body**, but the studies say nothing about what kind of body. Perhaps it just shows a universal fat man, with protruding stomach and his hand up?

Being fat has never been considered a good thing in China, and the philosopher Confucius warned against excesses of food and drink as early as the sixth century B.C. But famine was never far away, so the lucky ones who could afford to eat so much and get fat were looked upon with some admiration and envy.

body

What is called the Laughing Buddha, a purely Chinese invention, sitting there with his stomach bulging like rising dough between his legs, has always been particularly loved by the starving lower classes. To think of all the food he must have gobbled to get so fat!

Among simpler people, it is still common to hear the old words of greeting, 'Have you eaten?' which today means only 'Good day,' but bears with it the memory of another and more bitter era when people could consider themselves fortunate if they had food for the day. Another happy greeting is 'How fat you've got!' Today, this just means 'How are you? You look as if things are good for you!' I've never enjoyed that greeting—particularly at times when I'd actually put on a lot of weight.

But what about the character for *body*? Is it simply a picture of a fat person, in general? When the older characters are looked at more closely, it can be seen that a great many—even most of them—have a little dot in the middle of the stomach. Seen as a navel, it is misplaced and more Picasso-like than most of the old characters. But if the character is considered as a picture of a pregnant woman and the dot as a child, then the picture is logical, even beautiful. What could better illustrate the concept of the body? A heavily pregnant woman feels just like this weighty character, filled with kicking life!

If this interpretation is right, it is perhaps also possible to explain this bronze character for *body* (below), which gives the clear impression of representing not only the heavy stomach of a pregnant woman but also her breasts. In ancient times, interestingly enough, the expression 'to have a body' was used for 'being pregnant.'

woman

mother

However dissimilar the two characters for **woman** and **mother** look today, at the start they were almost identical. Both seem to show a person squatting down with the arms crossed in front of her body. Two dots marking the breasts in the character for *mother* are the only differences that distinguish the two characters from each other.

The position of the women's bodies is somewhat unclear. Do the outstretched arms indicate submission, which some scholars think, or are the women shown in the middle of their daily activities on the kitchen floor as they cook food and see to the children?

The former theory has in its favor that over the last two to three thousand years, the women of China have lived a life of oppression. Humbly submissive to their husbands, their only real task in life was to produce sons. Only sons could carry on the family, and most important of all, they were the only ones who could carry out the sacrificial rites through which the living kept contact with their ancestors of previous generations. Daughters were a necessary evil and were often left outside the moment they were born—the most common form of birth control—in the hopes of better luck next time. When asked about the number of children they had, fathers used to answer by giving the number of sons. Daughters did not count. Those girls who nevertheless were allowed to grow up were married off as soon as they had their first period, or before, and in return were expected to produce sons for their new family. In years of famine, they were sold as children to well-off families or to brothels and teahouses. Starting at the end of the nineteenth century, they were also sold to textile factories, where they had to work for their food and the right to sleep under the machines.

Two women: *to quarrel.* There were a great many reasons for quarrels between women in Chinese households in the old days. None had ended up there of her own free will, and they had no rights outside the home. Mothers-in-law took revenge on their daughters-in-law for their own destroyed lives, and, outraged and jealous of any power they could appropriate, however little that was, they all ganged up against the concubines their husbands brought home and installed in the household.

Three women: *adultery, fornication, ravish.* The character is, Bernhard Karlgren says, 'not very flattering to the fair sex.' This is puzzling. Couldn't the three women in the character allude just as well to certain gentlemen's questionable behavior? Such an interpretation may be just as viable, particularly since the character is included in several compound words that mean *rape.*

Woman and hand means *female slave, servant.* Does the hand represent the power of the slave owner—the woman that one has in one's hand, or has power over—or the slave woman's assiduous work in the house?

With a heart added, the character means *anger, rage, fury*—an appropriate reaction to the life many women were forced to live.

to quarrel

adultery,
fornication, ravish

female slave, servant

rage, anger, fury

Adult women were defined in relation to their husbands and sons. They were called, for instance, 'Wang's wife,' 'Eldest son's mother,' 'Her in there,' or quite simply, 'Old prickly.'

Marriage law reform, culminating in the new marriage laws of 1950, gave them the right to a surname of their own; forbade infanticide, bride purchase, and polygamy; and made men and women equal before the law, both in society and in the home. Chinese women today always have a name of their own, which they retain when they marry.

The idea that women were worth less than men goes far back in time. There are inscriptions on oracle bones in which the Supreme Ruler is asked for information on the sex of the child to which the king's spouse will soon give birth, and sometimes there are also comments on the oracle's answer: for son, 'good' is noted; for daughter, 'not good.'

As early as the Shang dynasty, the family system was organized on firm patriarchal grounds. But if we go even further back to the period during Neolithic times when people had just settled, the situation appears to have been different. Many scholars, both Chinese and Western, believe that the oldest Chinese communities were matriarchal and ruled by women. Evidence of this can be found in a passage from *Zhuangzi,* one of China's oldest and most significant books, probably from the year 300 B.C. Speaking about the first settled people, the text says that 'the mother was known and acknowledged, while the father was unknown.' While, for modern anthropologists, this information is insufficient evidence of matriarchy, they attach greater importance to the burial customs of Neolithic times, in which the women often rest alone, surrounded by gifts, in contrast to later periods, when they lie placed to one side and turned toward the dead husband, who was manifestly regarded as the more important of the two.

As further evidence of early matriarchy, anthropologists point to certain ethnic minorities in southwestern China, where extremely ancient customs, practices, and types of tools known in prehistoric China have been retained to this day. In a group of Naxi present-day people, it is the women who organize and administer production. They also run family life. The grandmother is the head of the family, and the children whom she herself, her daughters, and their daughters have borne all live in her house. The women choose among the men freely, and the children belong only to the women. They do not marry. The men make nightly visits to the women but return in the morning to their mother's house, where they live and work. Property is inherited down the female line, and the children take their mother's name. Adult men are called mother's brothers, and the mother and a 'mother's brother' share the care of the

children. However, just as in Chinese prehistoric times, the mother is often 'known and acknowledged,' while the father may be 'unknown.' The fact that the tribe's highest deity is a goddess speaks for itself.

The question of woman's position in China and the possibility of a prehistoric matriarchal system is too complicated for me to go into further here except to say that the subject is vast, exciting, and scarcely elucidated at all. But one interesting observation can be made: a large number of compound characters concerning family relationships on the female side contain the character for *woman*, some being those that denote females such as *mother, dead mother, grandmother, older/younger sister, daughter-in-law, wife of older/younger brother*, and others being those that denote males such as *nephew* and *son-in-law*. The character for *woman* is also included in an expression that brothers-in-law in a family use in greeting one another, as well as in several important characters such as *marriage, wedlock*, and—surprisingly enough—*family name*, or *surname*. There is no corresponding common denominator for the different characters for family relationships on the male side.

The subject would be well worth further study, but for the time being, we must leave the trail there.

son, child

Son, child, that longed-for creature, is represented by the picture of an infant. I am very fond of the oldest forms of this character. They remind me of my own children when they were very small, and my own small brothers and sisters as they lay there with their arms out, or in a basket wrapped in a cotton blanket— the large head and the helpless little body.

The emperor was considered to be the Son of Heaven and so was represented by the character for *Heaven* and *son*: 天子

Woman and child: *good, well*. Were the creators of characters thinking of the person who is well off and owns both a woman and children, or were they thinking of the happiness a woman and her child feel together? Or that the woman who can have children is good, nice, and capable?

Man and child: *to preserve, protect, care for*.

On the oracle bones and bronzes, in some cases we see the child safe in the adult's arms, and other times the child is carried on a back, just as children are carried in China today. When the character was first standardized, the child could still be clearly seen, but during the Han period the character was changed.

good, well

to preserve, protect

Well into the twentieth century, some Western scholars still maintained that the Chinese once emigrated to China from the Middle East at approximately the time that the Indo-Europeans left their homeland south of the Urals and set off toward India and Europe.

A Swedish scholar who refuted this theory and demonstrated that the origins of Chinese culture lay in China was Johan Gunnar Andersson, an internationally renowned geologist. In 1914 he was appointed by the Chinese government to survey the supply of coal and other important minerals with a view toward expanding the coal industry.

During the ten years he spent doing this, he also became increasingly interested in the fossils of extinct animals that he came across during his expeditions, and which under the name of 'dragon bones' were included, as we saw earlier, in so many Chinese medicines. In his search for them, he was led into archaeological studies that came to be highly significant for the understanding of prehistoric China.

In the spring of 1921, he was in Zhoukoudian, forty-two kilometers southwest of Beijing, in order to investigate a fossil-bearing layer in an old limestone quarry. There, and in a few other caves in the mountainside, he and his young collaborator, Otto Zdansky, found a number of petrified parts of skeletons—from hens, deer, pigs, and other animals. He also found angular quartz stones, so sharp that they could well have been used to cut with. The thought struck him that human beings' first tools were naturally not *manufactured*, but were picked up from among the pieces of wood and stones that came their way. He patted the wall of the cave where he had put Zdansky to work, and, as he relates in his book, *Children of the Yellow Earth*, said:

"I have a feeling that there lie here the remains of one of our ancestors and it is only a question of your finding him. Take your time and stick to it till the cave is emptied if need be."

Zdansky took his time. A large quantity of material was sent to Uppsala for further analysis. In that cave Zdansky found a molar and an incisor of a humanlike creature who had lived in the caves about half a million years ago and who was given the name *Sinanthropus pekinensis*, or Peking man.

Six months after the first excavations in Zhoukoudian, 'China Gunnar' was on a journey in the province of Henan in the central reaches of the Yellow River. Near the village of Yangshao, he found not only interesting fossils but also stone axes and jars with geometric patterns in red and black. These finds led him further west to the area of Lanzhou, in the province of Gansu, where, over the following years, he found nearly fifty settlements and a burial ground from Neolithic times—some of the most impressive finds in the world.

The finds in Zhoukoudian, Yangshao, and Gansu—the results of the first archaeological fieldwork in China—showed clearly that people had lived there long before the beginning of historical time. Any notion of immigration from the West was no longer possible.

During the scientific excavations that followed during the 1920s and 1930s, Andersson's finds were verified and complemented. In Zhoukoudian, the remains of forty or so people and about a hundred thousand stone implements were found, many of them of quartz, just as 'China Gunnar' had predicted.

In the autumn of 1941, when it was feared that the war in Asia would spread, all parts of the skeleton of Peking man were packed into two large boxes to be taken away to the United States for safety from the Japanese. Since then, they have vanished without a trace—no one knows what became of them.

All that is left now are the two teeth found by Zdansky and still preserved in Uppsala.

"The reader, however, should not feel too distressed by the disappearance of these priceless objects," the old paleontologist Jia Lanpo says consolingly in his book *Early Man in China*, and he refers to the many finds made since 1949.

Several have been made in the area where the Rivers Wei and Fen join with the Yellow River, and where the provinces of Shanxi, Shaanxi, and Henan meet. This is the actual cradle of Chinese culture. In the village of Lantian, halfway between the site of Andersson's finds in Yangshao and Gansu, archaeologists have found the remains of two people, probably women, which are considerably older than the people who lived in Zhoukoudian. In Dingcun, not far from there, and in Xujiayao, outside Datong, lived people of the same species as ourselves, *Homo sapiens*, as long as a hundred thousand years ago.

From early Neolithic times, when man settled and began to cultivate the soil, there are now also hundreds of excavation sites. Some of them such as Longshan and Dawenkou lie out on the Shandong Peninsula, others inside the original central core area. One of the most important villages is Banpo, which is in the Wei Valley and has been carbon 14 dated to 5000 to 4000 B.C. It is the largest village from that period yet excavated, and the foundations of houses, the clay vessels, and tools found there not only have much to tell about people's lives six thousand years ago but also can help us understand the evolution of the Chinese characters and even life in China today.

Water and Mountains

There is nothing so monotonously flat as the northern plain of China—no hills, no valleys, only vast yellowish-gray flatlands and field after field, bordered by the mountains of Shandong in the east and the mountains of Shanxi, Shaanxi, and Henan in the west. The mountains are not particularly high, but they rise abruptly out of the plain and in contrast appear more impressive than their size actually warrants. Like a major artery in the landscape, the Yellow River flows across the plain, linking the two mountainous areas.

Chinese civilization originated in and around this plain, which still today is more intensively cultivated and more thickly populated than any other part of the country, with, according to statistics, about a third of the population of the whole country living in it. The plain is really one great delta created by the silt of the river, and no other river in the world brings with it so much silt. The Nile contains 1.5 kilos of silt per cubic meter of water, the Yellow River an average of 37 kilos, and there are tributaries in which as much as 760 kilos have been measured. At its mouth, the river creates 23 square kilometers of new land every year.

It is a dangerous river—often called China's sorrow. As long as it flows through the Tibetan highlands where its source lies, all is well. The mountains are rock hard, and the river waters pure and clean. But after a huge sweep up toward the deserts of Inner Mongolia, the river then hurtles due south through the huge loess plateau, where the bedrock is covered with thick layers of finely packed dust easily washed away by the river waters. Through deep, narrow passes, the river presses on down and, after 2,400 miles of winding valleys, comes racing through the last pass and flattens out on the plain for the last seven hundred miles out to the sea, losing speed, widening, while the silt brought with it begins to sink to the bottom.

Over the course of millennia, the Yellow River has not only created the northern plain but, with the help of human beings, has also risen above it. All those layers of silt have raised both the riverbed and the level of the water. To stop the flooding, people have built embankments along the river. And so the cycle has continued: the river has stored its silt, and people have gone on building embankments. The riverbed is now over ten meters above the surrounding plain in many places, and when the summer rains are heavier or last longer than usual, it does not take much for the banks to burst.

But it is not all the fault of the river. One of the worst disasters occurred in 1938, when the leader of the country, Jiang Jieshi (Chiang Kai-shek) had the embankments north of Zhengzhou opened in an attempt to stop the advance of the Japanese. At least 890,000 people were drowned, 12.5 million were left homeless, and the whole region was paralyzed for years. But nothing stopped the Japanese.

There is an old story about a flood that is supposed to have occurred in 2298 B.C.—a Chinese equivalent of the Deluge. Heavy rains made the Yellow River overflow its banks, and the plain and the valleys at the foot of the mountains were under water, food was short, and people were starving. To remedy their wretchedness, every man left his home, and under the leadership of a man called Yu, they dug canals and ditches, built dykes, and opened passes through the mountains. After eight years of hard labor (or thirteen or thirty, the figures vary) they at last managed to divert the water to the sea and could start cultivating the land.

When the work started, Yu had just married. But so occupied was he with his responsibilities to the land and the people, that he passed the outside door of his home three times, once even hearing his son crying, but he did not go inside. The other men thought he should, but he replied: 'If I stop working, then all the others can also do so. How would we then drive the water away?' So they went on working.

Yu, or Yu the Great as he was later called, became the first emperor of the Xia dynasty, earlier regarded as mythical, but now beginning to be taken seriously. The remains of a town with walls and watchtowers have recently been found in the very same place in the Song mountain area, where, according to ancient historical scripts, one of the main towns of the Xia dynasty stood and only a few miles from the place, according to the saga, where Yu had his home.

Since the days of Yu the Great, there have been many more floods. From 602 B.C. onward up to today, continuous records have been kept showing that severe flooding has occurred two years out of every three over the 2,500 years that have passed. They also show that the Yellow River has found it difficult to decide where it is to flow out into the sea. Twenty-six times it has changed course, and no small changes, either. About 2000 B.C., it flowed out up by Tianjin near Beijing, but in 602 B.C., it grew tired of that and moved eighty miles down the coast, south of the Shandong Peninsula. In 70 B.C., the time to change came again, and the mouth opened north of Shandong, where it stayed until 1194 A.D., when it moved south of Shandong again. In this way the river has swung back and forth over the plain like a fan, spreading its silt. After some minor excursions when it took over the course of some other rivers and caused a great deal of trouble there, it calmed down, and from 1324 on, it flowed peaceably out to sea south of Shandong. But in 1855, the peace came to an end, and the river moved north again into the course it now takes. There it is supposed to stay. Over recent decades, a 'Chinese Wall' of embankments has been built for about 1,400 miles to keep the river in its place and to exploit it for energy and irrigation. Two million people are occupied year-round looking after it and keeping it under supervision.

The Yangzi River is not called the Yangzi (or Yangtze) at all; that was a European invention, actually the name of just one section. In Chinese it is called Chang Jiang, the Long River. It is not as unruly as the Yellow River. Though it has also burst its banks innumerable times, it is surrounded by lakes and marshlands on its way to the sea, and they absorb superfluous water and function as a buffer. Most of all, it is not so silt-bearing as the Yellow River, and so does not change its course in the same way.

The Yangzi is in itself an amazing river. It is the longest in Asia and is navigable for oceangoing craft up as far as Wuhan, seven hundred miles from the coast, then another fourteen hundred for smaller boats. Since it flows through some of the richest and most populous provinces in the country, it was particularly interesting to the foreign traders and missionaries who penetrated China in the nineteenth century.

The Huan River where it flows through Anyang, only a few kilometers from the place where the oracle bones were found.

Not so to the Chinese, for them, the Yellow River is the River. And the waters of the river are the Water, not the waters of lakes or the sea. The character for **water** is the picture of a river with its currents, whirlpools, and sandbanks, as one sees when standing on the riverbank looking over the course of the river.

In compound characters, this character is often written simply with three dots—'three dot water,' in Chinese terms.

water

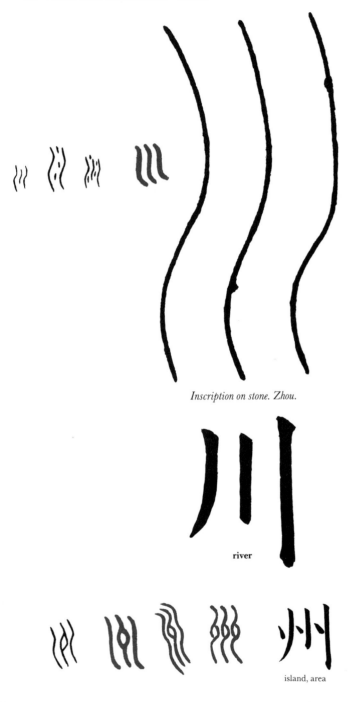

Inscription on stone. Zhou.

river

island, area

Several other characters depict the river in a similar way. The character on the left means **river**, and it is part of the name of the province of Sichuan in western China—the Land of the Four Rivers—through which the Yangzi and three of its tributaries flow.

Perhaps it was largely chance which character came to mean *water* and which came to mean *river*—both start out from the same reality. In another character, a sandbank can be seen surrounded by twisting branches of the river. That character could equally well have stood for the concept of river, for that is just what rivers often look like, but it came to mean *island, sandbank in a river*, instead. Later it also became the name of the Zhou administrative unit, which included 2,500 people. Now it is primarily used for *area, region*.

The river was the center of life for the first settled people. It was a great threat, but also provided huge possibilities. In the attempts to tame and exploit it, a society emerged that is very unlike ours. When referring to the settler in the forest or the lone pioneer on the prairie, we could say that 'alone is strong.' The Chinese would say 'alone is weak'. Thousands upon thousands of hands are needed to dig canals and convey the water out into the fields. With no communal effort, nothing functions.

Chinese civilization grew out of the fertile river silt, and in that same silt, flourishing communities were buried when the river overflowed its banks. They have remained there untouched, deep down beneath meter-thick layers of fine yellow silt. Up on the surface, the peasants have cultivated their millet and maize, and when they have dug out a new canal or well, they have often found amazing bronze vessels, which they have sold to antique dealers in the nearest town. The soil of the northern Chinese plain is full of hidden cities. It is known that they exist and also often known where they are, but as yet there has been time to excavate only a few.

But the river may have met its match. A pearl necklace of power stations, reservoirs, hundreds of miles of new banks, and, not least, tree plantations now line the river on its course down to the sea, to keep it in its place.

The Yellow River on its course south between the eroded mountains of Shanxi and Shaanxi. The waters draw a picture in the soft soil of the valley that can also be seen in the character alongside, which means island, sandbank in a river, area. It is an inscription in stone from the late Zhou period, here given in its original size.

The northern plain where Chinese civilization arose is surrounded by many mountains. No one knows which is the prototype for the character **mountain**, but several resemble it and have been surrounded by an aura of holiness since time immemorial.

mountain

ments of commercialism. For ordinary people Taishan was important because it was where the dead received their final judgment. To receive better treatment after death than one was worth, one could always try bribery, by making a sacrifice in the temple of the East Mountain—such a temple once existed in all northern Chinese towns—but safest was

Taishan rises in the east on the Shandong Peninsula, where the plain extends into the sea. It is the foremost of China's five sacred mountains. There for many dynasties, the emperor carried out the most solemn of all the state's sacrifices to Heaven and received Heaven's mandate to rule the country. There, prayers were offered for good harvests and help against floods and earthquakes.

Very early on, Taishan became an important Taoist center. The height of the mountain, the inaccessibility of the cliffs, the peace and silence of the valleys all held a strong attraction for people who wished to retreat from the wars and wretchedness of the times and live at one with nature. For the Taoists, everything that existed was part of one great whole, in which everything was alive and everything was dependent on everything else. By thoroughly studying the order of nature, they hoped to understand the laws that guided her and to arrange their lives in harmony with those laws. Temples and monasteries emerged, and hermits built their cabins on the cliffs and in the glens.

From the fifth century onward, Buddhists also began to settle there, and the mountain became a universal religious center with a substantial amount of ele-

to make a pilgrimage to the mountain itself and, in accordance with Chinese custom personally, and therefore more effectively, make one's wishes known. Many enfeebled old men had themselves carried up to the top by their browbeaten sons in a last desperate hope of appeasing the mountain and avoiding some of the terrible punishments otherwise inescapably awaiting them.

Even today, a steady stream of visitors climbs the precipitous steps. For even if the religious charge of the mountain has weakened, it is still a dream for millions of Chinese to reach the peak of Taishan once in a lifetime and watch the sun rising out of the mists of the night. At least to take a nice photograph . . .

But the mountain takes revenge if someone unworthy tries to climb it. The first Emperor of Qin, that heavy-handed unifier of China, made an attempt in the second century B.C., wishing to gain the approval of Heaven for his regime, but a raging storm forced him back down. In 1978 I managed to climb just over halfway when a snowstorm came.

Temples, pagodas, and interesting towns of various epochs abound at the foot of the mountain. One of these towns is Qufu, where Confucius was born in

551 B.C. His grave is there and his descendants also live there, now the seventy-ninth generation, from that day to this. But the immense family estate was turned into a museum in 1949 after the revolution, and the forty thousand tons of grain the peasants paid annually in rentals now stays out in the villages where one hopes it is put to better use.

Fourteen miles or so from Qufu is Dawenkou. When a double-track railway line was built in 1959, hundreds of graves from a highly developed culture that flourished between 4500 and 2000 B.C. were found. New finds have since been made at a brisk pace, and now it is known that during Neolithic times the mountainsides were covered with villages. People cultivated the soil with mattocks, hunted with bows and arrows, fished with nets and harpoons, and threw elegant, thin-walled clay pots in black, white, yellow, and pale red ocher.

Among the most interesting finds are some clay vessels and pottery fragments with characters engraved onto them, among the oldest ever found. They stem from different sites, so the images on them are considered characters—not just pictures. In other words, they had acquired a generally accepted form and could be understood over a wide area.

One of the characters shows the sun rising over a cloud or a sea.

Another shows the same sun and cloud/sea above a high mountain with five peaks, not unlike Taishan as it appears from the plain.

According to ancient beliefs, it was from Taishan that the sun started its course over the heavens every day. So the mountain also came to play a part in the worship of the sun that is said to have occurred in Neolithic times, but very little is known about this. Perhaps the clay vessel and the characters ornamenting it had something to do with this sun worship.

The two characters are considered predecessors of *sunrise, dawn*, which later came to be written like this:

sunrise

In Xi'an is a remarkable collection of engraved stone tablets from various dynasties, called Beilin, the Stone Forest. On one of them is a dream version of Huashan, so high, so unworldly and beautiful with its springs, clouds, glens, pines, and valleys, that human beings are pitifully small in comparison. Who would not be seized with a need to worship?

The 1660 engraving taken from a painting by Zhu Jiyi, a poet and painter, one of eight describing beautiful places in and around the town of Xi'an.

If one follows the Yellow River west of Taishan, one comes to Songshan, the Sacred Mountain in the Middle, at the feet of which the oldest finds from Xia and Shang have been made, the place where Yu the Great may have once perhaps lived. It is a long, brooding mountain range, as full of temples as Taishan. There, too, is the famous Shaolinsi—the Temple of the Little Forest—the center of Zen Buddhism in China, where Asiatic martial arts came from, and the Songyang Academy, the most advanced Taoist center in the country since the fifth century.

Still further west is another mountain, Huashan, the Sacred Mountain in the West. It lies just where the Wei River meets the Yellow River as it comes racing down from the mountains and swings eastward toward the sea. Huashan rises straight out of the plain with its three clearly marked peaks, and from them one looks out over the very cradle of China's ancient history, the area where the provinces of Shanxi, Shaanxi, and Henan meet.

Only a few miles away is the place where the Lantian people, predecessors of today's Chinese, lived six hundred thousand years ago. There is Banpo, one of the most important settlements found from Neolithic times. There is Xi'an where the great dynasties of Zhou, Qin, Han, and Tang had their capital cities. There is the grave of the First Emperor of Qin, with his thousands of terra-cotta soldiers—so many remarkable places, it is impossible to list more than a tiny fraction of them.

Huashan overlooks all this, as well as the Tongguan Pass, the gateway to the fertile valley, the pass on which the dynasties depended for their safety.

Early writings tell us that the first king of Shang made a sacrifice on Huashan in 1766 B.C. When his dynasty lost the mandate of Heaven in 1028, the first king of Zhou made a sacrifice there. And that is how it has continued.

Hua means *flourishing*, *splendid*, *magnificent*, and the mountain is said to be glorious. I have never been there, but everyone describes it as one of the most beautiful of all China's mountains. *Hua* also means *China*, *Chinese* and is included in the name of the People's Republic of China.

The character is thought to show the picture of a flower, but there is little of that to be seen after the script reforms of the 1950s.

This character for *mountain*, as powerful as a bronze character, is written by Mi Fei (1051–1107 A.D.), one of China's greatest calligraphers. He was a many-sided and eccentric man, and alongside his more prosaic activities as an imperial official, he was also a poet, author, and passionate collector of ancient paintings and peculiar eroded stones. In addition, he was a painter, and although no paintings remain that can with certainty be said to be by his hand, a great deal is known about his art through the many copies and paintings made by those who came after him. He often painted landscapes and mountains, shrouded in low, dripping greenery and hovering clouds of mist.

Mi Fei has formed the character for *mountain* with a broad brush and thick ink. It is heavy and tangible. The mountain peaks rising out of the mists of the valley in the painting alongside—one of those attributed to Mi Fei—are built up of faint, almost impressionistic patches laid on in separate layers, each darker than the layer below.

Despite the difference in technique, there is an unmistakable similarity between the character for *mountain* and the mountain peaks in the painting, not only in their outward form but most of all in the strength they convey.

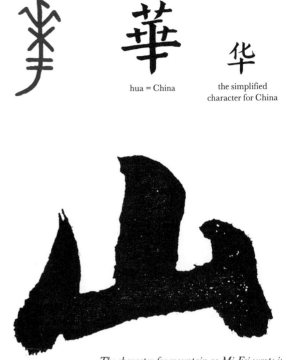

hua = China

the simplified character for China

The character for mountain as Mi Fei wrote it.

Mi Fei's painting of a mountain landscape.

The Taihang Mountains in afternoon mist, as seen from the train on the way up the Fen Valley.

North of Huashan and the Yellow River is the beginning of the Taihang Mountains, which stretch out in a wide sweep, forming a boundary between the northern Chinese plain and the loess plateau in Shanxi and Shaanxi. In ancient times, one of the most important trading routes in China ran along the foot of the mountains, and today the north–south railway line runs along it between Beijing and Guangzhou. There are passes in eight places where people could come down from the mountains to the plain. Several of the oldest towns in China, among them Anyang, lie where these roads meet the great trade routes.

This mountainous area is the setting for the story of Yu Gong, one of the great legends about the determination and strength of the Chinese people. It is about a foolish old man who moves mountains.

In front of his house, two mountains stood in his way. He finally grew tired of all the trouble they caused, and he and his sons started hacking them away.

Then another old man came along and said scornfully: "Huh, you *are* stupid! So few of you can't dig away such huge mountains!"

The foolish old man replied: "When I die, my sons will go on, and when they die, my grandsons and then their sons and grandsons will go on, and so on for ever and ever. Those mountains are high, but they can't get any higher, and for every bit we dig away, they'll be that much lower. Why shouldn't we be able to dig them away?"

And so he went on digging. The Ruler of Heaven was so touched by this determination that he sent two *immortals* who, to everyone's astonishment and gratitude, took away the mountains.

immortal
= man and mountain

In 1945, just before Japan had capitulated and before Jiang Jieshi had been driven to Taiwan, Mao Zedong made a speech in Yan'an, in this area. There the Chinese Communists had their base after the 1934–1935 Long March.

"Today," he said, "two large mountains lie like dead weights on the Chinese people. One is imperialism, the other feudalism. The Communist party of China long ago decided to do away with them. As long as we endure and continue our labors, we will touch the heart of the Supreme Ruler. Our ruler is none but the Chinese people. If they rise and dig with us, why should we not be able to dig away those two mountains?"

It actually is possible to dig away the mountains of Shanxi and Shaanxi. Many of them are not real mountains, but consist of packed, dusty yellow earth brought there by the wind from the deserts in the northwest and settling like a blanket on the ground, in some places over three hundred meters thick. The rainwater has sliced into it and formed ravines and hollow channels; indeed, half the area consists of ravines. The streams carry the dust into the river, which then spreads it out over the plain below. This dust is what makes the Yellow River and the Yellow Sea yellow, and seventy miles or so out from the coast, the water is still yellow from the fine dust of the deserts.

With ordinary mattocks and great patience, in the footsteps of Yu Gong, the peasants have taken down the mountains and filled in the ravines to make fields for their millet. They have also carved out homes in caves on the slopes of the ravines, so their houses would not use valuable cultivable soil, and there—deep down underneath the fields of the high plain and high above the flat fields of the valley—they have lived, and still do live, on narrow ledges in the mountainside. All this has demanded hard labor, and no immortals have appeared to help. Yu Gong and his sons might well have decided to move to another house rather than keep digging away the mountain, but the poor peasants in the loess areas have had no choice. Every extra square meter of soil makes a difference in their survival.

谷

valley, ravine

This character means **valley**, **ravine** and is said to show the opening to a valley.

I only have to look at it to remember my feelings on cold early spring days with clear high skies, when on my way into valleys in the loess area, between yellow, eroded mountainsides of tightly packed soil, fine-grained and soft as pollen. Not a tree in sight, and scarcely even a stem of grass—only a dried-out stream-bed, the slanting walls of yellow dust, and a pervasive smell of artemisia, or wormwood.

A few months later, all of this is transformed. The first downpour of summer turns the stream into a turbulent cataract of yellow, soil-filled water racing down toward the entrance to the valley, bringing everything with it on its way.

Ever since antiquity the character for *valley*, *ravine*, has also been used for *good*, *nourishing*, and in 1958 it displaced a late and complicated similar character for *grain*, *seed*. This is reasonable, for it was in the valleys that cultivation of grain once began, the good and nourishing grain.

Valleys in the loess area of Shaanxi. The deep crevices in the ravines eat their way further and further into the fields. One more downpour and the village will be cut in half.

The character for **cliff**, according to the old *Shuowen* dictionary, is a picture of a steep mountainside where people can live. It is easy to recognize the steep ravine walls of the loess area in the character, with the flat, level surface of the high plain on the top, the precipice down to the bottom of the valley on the left.

However, the form of the oracle bone character can be somewhat bewildering. What is the meaning of that little slanting stroke inside the angle? Is the character perhaps a profile of a cave hacked out of the cliff? As we shall see later, the same stroke recurs in a character that means *cave*.

The character for *cliff* never occurs alone, but it is included in many compound characters, which either have to do with different kinds of mountains, or are a description of different *dwelling rooms* or other spaces such as *kitchen*, *stable*, *toilet*, and *workshop*. For a long time, *cliff* and *dwelling* were one and the same thing.

cliff

stone, rock

The same picture as in the character *cliff* also recurs in the character for **stone**, **rock**. In the present form of the character, the upper stroke is extended somewhat further to the left, but in its earlier form it was written exactly like the character for *cliff*. According to current explanations, it shows a boulder below a cliff. One may wonder how it came about that the 'stone' below the mountain is always written as *mouth* in older characters. Perhaps it is not a fallen boulder we see, but the actual mountainside with one of the caves that are so easily formed there. The character for *mouth* in that case stands for mouth in the *opening*, *mouth (of a river)* sense. Perhaps it is the actual rock we see, with its hollows and depressions.

The pattern book entitled *The Mustard Seed Garden Manual of Painting*, which has been the canon for Chinese artists since it was published in 1679, has a long section on mountains and rocks. When one paints rocks, the book says, one must devote particular attention to the hollows in the rocks and the play between light and shadow over the surface. Rocks can be very different. Before one starts painting, one must have the structure quite clear in one's mind. But that is not enough. Most important of all is to convey the strength embodied in the rock. It must be alive.

The authors illustrate their text with pictures of eroded boulders where time and water have left their traces. Some of them are quite close to the character for *stone, rock*.

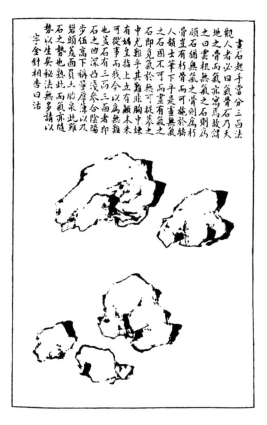

Boulders are much beloved in China, the most coveted being the limestone boulders from the shores of Taihu, the great lake near Suzhou. They are deeply furrowed and hollowed out by the movements of the waves and sand, and as full of holes as Swiss cheese. But there are also remarkable rocks elsewhere—a well-known book on garden planning, from 1634, names, apart from Taihu, thirteen lakes and mountains where suitable rocks can be found. If the holes are not as marked as they ought to be according to Chinese convention, nature can always be helped along by chiseling the holes deeper, then putting the stone back in the lake and leaving it there for a generation or two. Then one has a finished work of art created by man and nature together, with light and air pouring through it like a modern sculpture, ready to place against a wall in a corner of the garden or as the centerpiece of a rock garden with paths, pavilions, small benches for quiet conversation, cool caves, and surprising views over tangles of jasmine and peonies.

Minor defects in a rock can be scoured away with bamboo and pulverized porcelain. To achieve the correct surface, the stone can then be placed under a drainpipe for a year or two, until the rainwater softens the forms. That was often done with stones to be used as ornaments and meditation objects on a desk, or in miniature landscapes together with low-growing bamboo or a little pine tree.

For many Chinese, a stone of this sort, either large or small, functioned as a kind of icon with which they stood in a close personal relationship and with which they needed daily contact. It is said of Mi Fei that every morning he bowed to a large rock in his garden and greeted it with the respectful words, "My elder brother."

A goodly dose of mystery was part of Chinese scholars' relation to nature. What scholars sought, though, was not union with God or any other higher being, but fellowship with all living things. For them, rocks, stones, water, and other things we unimaginative people usually call inanimate were as alive as people, flowers, and animals.

Man was not lord over nature. He was included along with everything else in Heaven and on earth in the Great Oneness (Unity), subject to the same cosmic powers called Yin and Yang. These anticipated each other like day and night, winter and summer, life and death. They were aspects of the same reality and maintained with dynamic equilibrium the harmony in the universe. Everything changed, was transformed, and returned in new constellations in an eternal flow. Nothing was constant except this slow, perpetual change.

The mountains were perceived as Yang and likened to the bones in the human body. Water was Yin and corresponded to the blood. Just as the body could not live without the flow of blood in veins, arteries, marrow, and tissues, mountains and boulders were dependent on water. Through its perpetual trickling, splashing, bubbling, pouring, and flowing, water gave them form. When Chinese artists painted a landscape—or 'mountain and water,' as the Chinese call a landscape—it was not just one motif among others, but the summary of a worldview and a moralistic comment on life.

A painting of a waterfall was not primarily intended to reproduce a whirling scene, in which the misty air of the plateau, the uncompromising height of the mountain, and the clouds around the falling white spray against the cliff wall were designed to activate our senses and put us in a mood of devotion/melancholy/reverence or whatever emotions the painter wished to arouse. Instead, the painter wanted to show us how to live our lives. We are not to preen ourselves, nor strive for glory. Nor are we to act against nature's order, but to try to understand and to live in unity with her laws. We are to acknowledge our place as one of the 'ten thousand things'; to be humble, quiet, and generous; and to make ourselves 'low.' As it says in the eighth poem in the *Dao De jing* (*Tao Te ching*):

> The highest good is like that of water. The goodness of water is that it benefits the ten thousand creatures; yet itself does not scramble, but is content with the places that all men disdain. It is this that makes water so near to the Way.
> And if men think the ground the best place for building a house upon,
> If among thoughts they value those that are profound,
> If in friendship they value gentleness,
> In words, truth; in government, good order;
> In deeds, effectiveness; in actions, timeliness—
> In each case it is because they prefer what does not lead to strife,
> And therefore does not go amiss.

Translation: Arthur Waley

原

spring, origin, source

The basic meaning of this character is **spring, source**. From high above, the water leaps out and falls in soft spray down the cliff wall—a classic motif, particularly in Chinese landscape painting.

I am fond of this character; it gives me a feeling of freedom—water the source, the origin and the beginning of life.

The character is now used primarily in the transferred meaning **origin, originally**. It is included in many expressions, where it functions in the same way as the prefix 'proto' in English, as in, for instance *prototype, protoplasm,* or *protozoon,* and also such words as 'raw,' as in *raw material* and 'basic,' as in *basic color,* or *basic principle*—words that all have to do with origins. It is also used in the words for *open plain, flat level country* and is included in the name for the wide plains surrounding the middle and lower reaches of the Yellow River, where Chinese civilization has its origins, its source.

Spring in the Lushan Mountains in the province of Jiangxi.

Primitive people living in Zhoukoudian, outside Beijing, half a million years ago had already learned to use fire. A cave discovered from this period functioned as a kitchen, the floor covered with meter-thick layers of ash, bits of charcoal, and burnt animal bones. The remains of fires outside the cave indicate that these were lit at night to keep wild animals at bay.

For a long time it was thought that these people were the first in the world to use fire. But in the 1960s, several new finds were made in places including Lantian and Xihoudu, near where the Yellow River swings east, which show that the people who lived there six to seven hundred thousand years ago used fire when they cooked their food.

Presumably none of these early peoples could make fire themselves, but they had acquired it in association with a thunderstorm or a forest fire. They protected it and cared for it very thoroughly. It provided light, warmth, and safety, and perhaps they also used it when hunting. When they moved, they carried their fire with them, a priceless heritage to hand on from generation to generation.

People in China did not learn to make fire themselves until much closer to our own time, approximately nine to ten thousand years ago.

Advertisement for a fire extinguisher, Beijing. Compare the advertisement drawing of the flaring fire with the character for fire on oracle bones.

fire

The character for **fire** in its original form is reminiscent of the character for *mountain*, which at first does not seem to make sense. But if one imagines sitting in front of the fire watching the flames rising in the darkness, the picture seems right: mountain and fire, mountains like solidified flames against the sky, the fire flaring up into mountains from inside the glowing embers.

River waters have caused most of the natural disasters in China. The oracle bone character for *calamity, disaster, misery* quite logically shows the picture of a river racing along with jagged waves.

The modern forms of this character consist of both *fire* and *water,* a graphic description of some of the most terrible misfortunes that can afflict us.

calamity, disaster

Two characters for *fire,* one above the other, mean *flame, flaming, burning hot* and therefore also *inflammation.*

flare, flame,
inflammation

Hand and fire together mean *ash, dust, gray.* Perhaps the hand is carefully raking away the ashes from the falling embers, so that the fire can flare up again. Perhaps it is just gathering together the thin gray dust, the last remains of dry branches and the flames of the fire.

ash, gray

Sometimes when I am feeling really downhearted, when my heart, as the Chinese say, is 'gray,' I think about that character. And I remember some rather bitter lines by Esaias Tegnér, the Swedish poet:

My heart? In my breast there is no heart.
An urn with but the ash of life within.

His words are Byronic and painful. But sometimes they feel exactly right.

灰 心
gray heart
= despair, disheartened, discouraged

Wild animals

Long after people settled along riverbanks and started cultivating the land, they still lived to a great extent on fishing and hunting. Some scholars even maintain that they settled in order to ensure access to all the plant fibers they needed to make nets and lines for fishing and hunting.

In Banpo, numerous fishhooks, harpoons, arrowheads, and net sinkers have been found, along with a whole mass of carp bones in the rubbish heaps, interestingly enough the only species of fish of which any remains have been found. People in Anyang also lived largely on fish, and of the six different species identified in the archaeological material there are four kinds of carp.

Images on early pottery from Banpo.

Fish motifs are common on Banpo pottery. On the oldest vessels, the fish are realistically depicted.

On later vessels, they have been turned into a geometric pattern, in which two fish together form a decorative strip running around the vessel. Sometimes they have been simplified into extended strips of triangles—this is the most common motif on Banpo pottery.

Many of the early fish pictures are so unified in form and size that they almost resemble a character. Pictures of this kind constitute the missing link between picture and character, one of the rare transitions from picture to pictography now to be seen.

The character for **fish** occurs again and again on oracle bones and bronzes, the bronze character being particularly expressive, with a heavy muscular body, scales and fins, staring eyes, and sometimes also a jaw with sharp teeth.

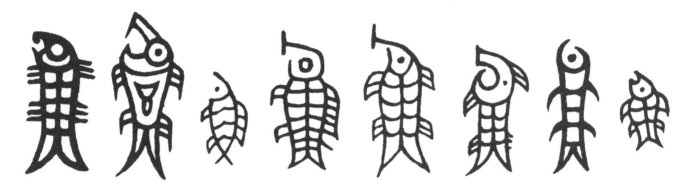

With these pictures in mind, it is easier to understand the character for *fish*, at least as it was written until 1956—although it has now lost most of its old expressiveness.

fish

鱼

the simplified character for fish

For people in Banpo, the fish was probably a totem animal or a fertility symbol. Today the fish is still a symbol of abundance and wealth, and is also used to show that efforts bring their reward. On New Year pictures put up for the Spring Festival, there are often fat little children riding on huge red fish or holding them in their arms like teddy bears.

There is a linguistic pun behind this, as there often is in Chinese writing. The character for *fish* is pronounced in exactly the same way as the character for *abundance*. Just as a picture of a heart to us means love, the Chinese immediately think of abundance and wealth whenever they see a red fish.

Perhaps the Buddhist world of symbols, in which the fish stands for freedom from all hindrances, has been influential. In Buddhist paintings, sculptures, and stone reliefs of Buddha's footprints—a common decorative motif—there are often pictures of fish, and when a monk calls his brothers to prayer, he strikes on a huge wooden fish.

Pools of carp or goldfish are found in many temple courtyards. During religious ceremonies, the devout considered it a good deed to buy a fish from the monks and then release it. Now they are bought from one of the many goldfish breeders sitting by enameled washbasins in rows in the markets, and taken home in a plastic bag to a lonely life in a glass bowl on the chest-of-drawers.

Goldfish and carp are the best-loved fish in China. They are related, and a goldfish that manages to escape its aquarium and return to nature gradually assumes a greenish-brown or gray color and grows to thirty centimeters in length. It quite simply becomes the carp it always was.

Breeding goldfish is a speciality—almost an art— that originated in China. Just how far back in time it goes is not really known. Goldfish are mentioned in scripts from the Jin dynasty (265–420), but the breeding of them does not seem to have spread until sometime during the Song dynasty (960–1279). Since then, 345 varieties have been bred. Like carp, goldfish can grow very old, twenty to twenty-five years being nothing for a goldfish. The best-loved kind are a soft red and have grotesquely protruding, turned-up eyes and huge, feathery tail fins, in English called celestials.

Real carp have been raised for at least 2,500 years. They grow quickly and have no objection to living in cramped conditions—a truly Chinese fish! Carp used to be raised in rice fields, but now the large water reservoirs built after 1949 are often used for fish breeding. Proper fish pools have also been made in many parts of the country.

Many different species of carp can live in the same pond, segregated at different levels yet in total symbiosis. The black carp living in the semideep waters love snails. Their excrement feeds the plankton eaten by silver carp living somewhat further down. Their

New Year picture for the Spring Festival. Boy with large fish, symbol of abundance. Right-hand part of a pair. Shandong, Weifang.

A thousand years lie between the oldest bronze character for fish and this decoration on a bronze vessel from the Han dynasty. And yet it is the similarity that dominates—an example of the continuity in the way of perceiving and reproducing reality that characterize the world of characters and art in China.

excrement, in turn, feeds golden carp and ordinary carp at the bottom of the pool.

Grass carp, as is obvious from their name, eat grass. They are efficient fish, swiftly eating clean an overgrown lake. In summer they eat their own weight per day, and when fully grown, they weigh—and eat—up to thirty-five kilos. Grass carp have been successfully introduced in many places in Sweden, and in Holland they keep the canals clean.

In the village of Baoyang, outside Shanghai, where carp are raised, ten tons per hectare are produced per year. The same yield is achieved over large parts of China, and every day the acreage used for raising fish increases. A great many peasants have often found it more profitable to raise fish rather than to grow grain or vegetables on the acreage they have at their disposal.

Carp is a delicious fish. Steamed with black bean sauce and a little ginger, or fried in batter with a sauce of yellow rice wine, garlic, sugar, and soy sauce—a sweet and fiery taste—it is a treat.

Only sun-dried fish were available inland in the past, although it is really wrong to say 'only', because sun drying is an excellent method of preserving fish, prawns, shrimps, and other shellfish, and is still very common in China. The taste becomes more concentrated, and less is required to enhance the flavor of a dish.

New Year picture of leaping carp.

The carp stands for the rewards of effort and hard work. An old legend says that every year in the third month, the carp try to make their way up the Yellow River and past the Dragon Gate where the plain and the mountains meet. The currents are fierce and few succeed. But those that do are turned into dragons—the foremost of all creatures and a symbol for the emperor. In ancient Chinese society, therefore, the carp became the symbol for the ambitious man trying to pass the imperial examinations—the gateway to honor and distinction in society.

Now the river has been regulated, and the carp find it difficult to make their way, but the really big ones leap up, as in this New Year picture, which depicts the fish in the same way as in the old bronze characters.

In villages where fish are raised, they are often harvested with the help of a seine, a long net laid out slightly offshore and then drawn in a tighter and tighter curve, catching the fish as if in a sack. Such a net functions excellently in shallow lakes, rivers, and ponds where the bottom is even and without stones in which the net could get caught.

Similar nets probably existed as early as in Neolithic times, but what they or other nets looked like at the time is not known, for they were made of plant fibers that have long since decayed. But in all its simplicity, the oracle bone character for *net* provides a good picture of how the nets were once constructed.

In some characters of this kind—predecessors of the character for *fishing*—a net can be seen being brought toward a large fish.

Here two hands are hauling at a net, clearly similar to a seine.

There must have been nets of many different kinds. Nets were used not just for fishing but also for hunting. Some oracle bone characters do not seem to depict the kind of fishing nets with which we are familiar, but rather some construction made of poles to block the flow of water or an outlet, preventing the fish or wild game from escaping from the area. Others look more like fykes or fish traps. One character is reminiscent of the sacks of braided willow or bamboo occasionally seen placed in smaller water courses. The fish are drawn into them by the current and then cannot get out.

I have seen fish traps of a similar kind in use on the Shandong coast, where there is a current very rich with fish. The coastal villagers put out long rows of strong six-by-twenty-meter net traps, which are then emptied every day. The sacks are expanded by the current and float in the water like huge cones. They are crude and the fish have time to see them, but the current is so strong they cannot get away, however hard they try. Many land in the net with tail fins first.

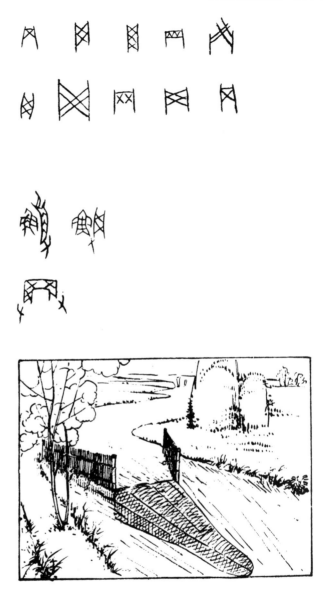

Net sinkers were often found in Neolithic settlements and those of the first dynasties, showing that there were also ordinary fishing nets that hung vertically in the water and were held down by the sinkers, just like the nets seen still in use all over the Chinese countryside.

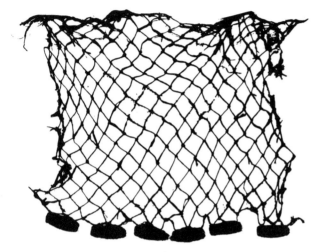

Reconstruction of an ancient fishing net.

Today's character for **net**, reminiscent of both the fishing net and the old characters, is an ancient form that has found favor again in our day. During the Han period, people started using another, more complicated character that lasted until 1956, when the old form was brought back, an excellent example of how clearly many of the oldest characters still reveal their meaning.

net

The character for *fishing* is found in a great many variations.

On the bronzes, a huge fish, its mouth wide open, is trying to escape from two covetous hands. This is a sight often seen today when fish ponds are emptied and the peasants wade around with their trousers rolled up, bringing in the catch.

On oracle bones, apart from the characters already shown, there is one showing a hand holding a fishing rod, a picture any schoolchild could understand.

The most delightful character shows a whole shoal of fish racing through the water.

One variant shows a single fish in the water. When the characters were gradually standardized, this was the one that came to be the character for *fishing*.

漁

fishing

Fishing with bow and arrow was also common. Considerably more is known about the arrows than about the nets—they were made of durable materials such as stone, bone, horn, and bronze. Their form is different from arrows in other parts of Asia, with the shaft not pressed into the arrow, but instead the arrowhead pressed into the shaft.

This may have something to do with the shaft being made of bamboo, the stem of which is soft inside, while the joints are hard. Pounded into a joint, the arrowhead is securely held.

The two bone arrowheads to the right come from Banpo and are probably intended for fishing. The strange bulge on the tang, the lower part of the arrowhead, may have been for slotting the arrow particularly firmly into the shaft, or it could also have served as a fastening point for a line. In that case, the arrow or spear would have been used in the same way as the harpoons that whales and bigger fish are caught with in many parts of the world today.

A group of bronze vessels from the late Zhou period are decorated with hunting scenes. A common motif is archers firing at huge birds. The long ropes fastened to the arrows are perhaps to prevent the bird's flight when it is hit, or perhaps they make the arrow easier to find again if it misses its target.

During the Shang dynasty, arrowheads were generally made of stone or bone, just as they have been since the first use of bows and arrows during the early Stone Age. There were several different kinds, the most common consisting of a flat, leaf-shaped disc of stone with a sharp edge all around. Another kind, made of bone, was triangular and had long, sharp wings down toward the tang, like the arrowheads from Banpo. During the Shang period, arrowheads of bronze became more and more common, but the old forms were retained in the new material.

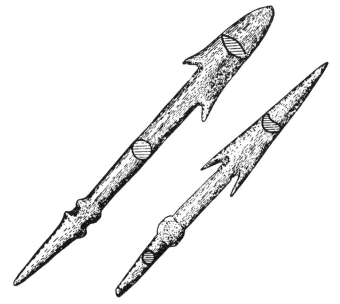

Bone arrowheads from Banpo. Included in the drawing are cross-sections of the arrowheads.

Detail from bronze wine jar from the Zhou period. See whole vessel on page 80.

arrowhead

within

to arrive at

injure, wound, illness . . .

On oracle bones, the character for **arrowhead** was written in several different ways, apparently based upon the types of arrowheads in use during the Shang period. There is a form that bears great similarity to the flat stone discs, and another that is reminiscent of the triangular form with sharp wings proved to have a future ahead of it.

The arrowhead is probably included in two more characters, the basic meaning of which is *within, to enter*. In the oldest forms, they show a pointed object very similar to the upper part of the character for *arrowhead*.

to enter

Arrive at, reach is drawn with the picture of an arrow that has reached its target.

A person with his arms out, as in the character for *big*, is being attacked by an arrow: *hurt, illness, pain, urgent, hate*—a whole story can be read from the different meanings.

In the final form of the character, the arrow is indeed still there, but the person and so also the dramatic event have disappeared almost entirely.

The left-hand part of this character is included in a large number of compound characters. *Mathews' Chinese-English Dictionary* lists 132. They are all concerned with temporary or chronic illnesses.

Manchurian officer, Beijing 1871, and reconstruction of a Bronze Age bow. The bows are the same, despite the three thousand years between them.

The bow has a long history in China. There is archaeological evidence that it was already in use twenty-eight thousand years ago, and as late as the end of the nineteenth century, archers were still the first line of defense in the imperial army, and officers were selected after tests that included archery.

The oldest bow yet found stems from the 'Warring States' period, as the late Zhou era is called. It comes from a grave in Changsha and is made of four bamboo layers, which are thicker toward the middle and finished with end pieces of wood to hold the string. The whole bow is bound with a band of bamboo and silk and beautifully lacquered. It is about 1.40 meters long.

At one time, a measure of length called bow length, which was about 1.65 meters, was used for measuring land. The construction of these bows seems to have been similar to that of the Changsha bow, as shown in particular in the form of the character for **bow** on oracle bones and bronzes.

Chinese Bronze Age bows were of a completely different construction from the longbows used by Robin Hood and European armies of the Middle Ages. They were not made of one single piece, but consisted of thin pieces of wood or bamboo pressed together, on the same principle as modern laminated bows, then reinforced with horn and sinews.

The tension between the various materials made the bows outstandingly strong. According to one calculation, they had a traction force of seventy kilos, which is considerably more than most modern bows. Even if that calculation is not correct, to all appearances the Chinese bows were very efficient weapons. The Inuit of the Canadian Arctic and Greenland and American Indians, like the ethnic minorities of southwestern China up to modern times, used bows of a kind reminiscent of these Chinese Bronze Age bows and made a good living for themselves with the aid of them.

Inscription on a stone drum from the Zhou period.

bow

Bronze wine jar from the 'Warring States' period.

On a bronze wine jar from the same period as the bow in Changsha, bows used for both peaceful and warlike purposes can be seen. The upper part of the jar is covered with lively scenes of people picking mulberry leaves, playing music, preparing for a festival, and target shooting. There is also hunting of large, long-necked birds resembling swans or wild geese.

The lower part depicts violent battle scenes—perhaps the storming of a town—and fighting between two boats on the river, with both men and fish in the waters. At the bottom left are two women in long, frilly skirts. They have drawn their bows to fire and are about to shoot.

A wall tile from a grave of the same period is decorated with the picture of a horseman at full gallop. He has turned around in the saddle and is firing a Parthian shot over the hindquarters of the horse.

The character for **fire off**, **shoot with a bow** is as clear as the picture. The bow and the arrow can be seen, sometimes a hand as well. At the standardiza-

tion of characters in the third century B.C., the bow was unfortunately exchanged for the character for *body*, which in its oldest form bears some similarity to *bow*, and the originally clear picture became distorted.

From bows of the kind used by the horseman on the grave tile, the Chinese developed at the end of the Zhou period the crossbow, which before the introduction of firearms was the most effective weapon in existence. From the Han period onward, and over a thousand years to come, it was the standard weapon of the Chinese army until gunpowder—another Chinese invention—took over.

The crossbow was introduced into Europe as early as the Hellenic/Byzantine period, but it did not come into general use until the eleventh century, when it aroused such terror that in 1139, the Pope and the Lateran Council banned its use—at least against Christians—but that made no difference. All through the Middle Ages and until firearms were introduced, the crossbow was the leading weapon in both China and Europe. As recently as 1521, Hernando Cortés used crossbows as one of his main weapons in the conquest of Mexico.

During Neolithic times and the first dynasties, the climate around the Yellow River was more like that of southern China today: several degrees warmer and considerably more humid. Where today there is nothing but bare mountains and a wide, almost treeless plain, at the time there were forests, rich grazing lands, marshes, and lakes—an environment that provided food and shelter for animals of many different kinds as well as excellent hunting grounds for humans.

In the mountainous regions there were plenty of deer and wild pigs, as well as tigers; the edges of the forest and the fields abounded with pheasant, quail, and

to shoot, to fire off

partridge. There were fish and turtles in the lakes, and flocks of duck, wild geese, crane, and heron rested on the wetlands around the marshes after the breeding season in the north.

Animals not generally associated with China at all were also found, including rhinoceros, elephants, tapir, and peacocks. During the first dynasties, they all lived and thrived around the Yellow River. This is known from both archaeological finds and the characters on oracle bones.

Since then, the climate has grown colder and dryer. Forest clearing, ditch digging, and agriculture have changed conditions for many animals. The deer have disappeared into the forests and grasslands to the north and west. The rhino have totally disappeared. Elephants remain only in the far south, in Yunnan where they are used in forestry. There are still a few tigers left in the area. The rest, long-haired beasts that like the cold and snow of the areas from which they had once migrated, have gone north to Manchuria. Of the four or five different kinds of tortoises and turtles, only one remains, a small turtle often found in local markets. My Chinese friends tell me that it is good made into soup and is excellent roasted whole.

Grave tile from Jincun, near the town of Luoyang on the Yellow River, slightly over one meter high, Han dynasty.

The philosopher Zhuang Zi tells us that the first people in China lived 'among deer and roe-deer.' Just how he could know this is unclear, as he did not live until 300 B.C. But what he says is reinforced by archaeological finds, which show that the early people known as Lantian man and Peking man and all their descendants for half a million years often hunted deer.

Among the finds from Anyang, bones of deer are common, and deer are the animals most frequently found in inscriptions. The present-day character for **deer** is very far removed from the original picture, but the deer on the oracle bones and bronzes stand with their antlers raised, their bodies poised to leap,

deer

and their eyes scanning the plain. Look closely and you can see vivid images of living deer, with the lively curve of their backs, caught in midleap.

Deer not only provided food and materials for tools, clothes, and ornaments but also played an important part in religious ceremonies. Each year the buck loses its antlers. Each year new ones grow, covered with soft skin. Each year a new growing season also starts in nature, and life once again springs out of the bare ground—just as the antlers rise from the deer's head. For people who lived at the dawn of history, the antlers of the deer became a symbol for renewal and the return of life, playing an important part in the magical rites performed to bring out the sun and a new year of growth.

Well into our own day, rituals in which dancers wear antlers have been performed by the fire in many parts of Asia, as well as in Europe and among American Indians. The shamans of China and Mongolia donned deer heads before going into a trance and setting off for the underworld or the heavens to seek contact with earthly spirits and deceased ancestors.

Pictures of deer with great similarities to those on oracle bones can also be found among the jade amulets of the Zhou period, as well as in decorations on bronze vessels.

Deer on bronze vessel. Late Zhou period.

Bronze vessel from Anyang. Shang period.

One of the most impressive bronze vessels of the Shang period, found near Anyang, is decorated with no fewer than eight different depictions of deer, probably sika deer. The front is ornamented with two heads in profile, together forming an *en face* head.

Sika deer come from China. They are quite small and have a white rump and brown-and-white-spotted coat. Their antlers are tall and stately. During the first dynasties sika deer were a very common prey for hunters, and they were also used in various ritual contexts.

One of the profile pictures of the deer from the above bronze vessel is shown by itself below. The similarity between the picture and the character for **head**, **first**, **leader** can be seen quite clearly.

The idea that the character for head, first, leader might depict the head of a deer was put forward only a few decades ago, but it has never really caught on. On the contrary, most reference books still repeat *Shuowen's* now two-thousand-year-old statement that the character is a picture of a person's hair and head.

head

Given the form the character has in the oracle bones, that explanation is not very convincing. In my view, this is the head of an animal, not a person, just as on the bronzes.

But is it a deer? I doubt it. There are other characters providing a considerably more convincing picture of a deer's head. The oracle bone characters below are said to be the name of a town, but unfortunately they lack any equivalent among later characters. They would have fit in well as predecessors to the character of *head* (which is also the first part of *capital* in Chinese). But nothing has as yet been written about this.

The question of the possible significance of the deer head in the formation of the character for *head* has not been answered. But I would stake quite a sum on such a connection. What could represent the concept of head better than a deer's head, with its strong symbolic element and its radiant beauty? What can we human beings produce in comparison with it, at least from the outside?

While the deer gradually lost its religious significance, the associations with resurrection and the life force, even with immortality, remained. It is said that troops during the nineteenth-century civil wars in China used to put a deer at the head of the army to ensure military success and to protect the soldiers' lives with its magical force.

Even today, the sika's antlers are used for medicine, and pharmacists like to use them for their shop windows. With their powerful shape and sleek, silky skin, they are one of the most spectacular ingredients of the Chinese pharmacopoeia.

The antlers are said to contain important substances that are strengthening and edifying. But they have to be 'still alive.' Antlers shed naturally by the deer are useless; as soon as they reach full size, they start calcifying, and their medicinal value—whatever it is—is lost. So the antlers are sawn off sometime in the early summer while the blood still pulses freely in the risen crown.

Ground-up deer antler is supposed to work miracles for men who have trouble with their potency. Antlers from young bucks are considered the most effective, but they are hard to find and very expensive. Every year, China exports considerable quantities of deer antlers to Japan, where the problem is apparently particularly great. Dried aborted deer fetuses are also exported—a macabre medicine that is said to be effective against many female ailments.

The flying lines of the antlers of this deer, on a roof tile from the Han dynasty, hardly seem to depict the closed crown of a sika, but rather the huge open "crown" of the Père David's deer, *Elaphurus davidianus.* This deer, one of the largest and most majestic in the world, also originates in China. In ancient times, it was common in the wet forested lands around the Yellow River, and on the oracle bones are inscriptions telling of hundreds of shot animals.

Père David's deer were eradicated at an early time in the wild, and by the end of the nineteenth century only one herd was left, in the imperial park in Chengde, north of Beijing. During the Western powers' attack on China after the Boxer Rebellion in 1900, those animals were also all killed, except a few that were taken to England. Their descendants have since lived on the Duke of Bedford's estate at Woburn Abbey.

In the autumn of 1985, twenty deer, relatives of those once taken away, were donated to China. A special park for them has been made which recreates, as far as possible, their original environment in the forests around the Yellow River.

Père David's deer.

The three small characters on the right are tortoises or turtles, perhaps seen more clearly when turned horizontally, so that they are obviously on their feet; one can see the huge shell with deep incisions, the protruding head on a thin neck, and splayed toes. The character comes from the oracle bones and means **turtle**, **tortoise**.

At the standardization of characters in the second century B.C., the character for *turtle* and *tortoise*, like so many others, lost its clarity, but it is still possible to recognize the creature. Both shell and feet are still present, however jagged the character appears.

In the script reforms of 1958, the character lost most resemblance to reality.

During the first dynasties, there was yet another way of writing *turtle*. This developed more directly from the shell, the part of the animal most significant to the ancient Chinese, where they wrote their questions to their ancestors and to Heaven. It is possible that the two forms developed from two different kinds of turtle, or had different uses, but the connection has not yet been studied.

Similar pictures of turtles appear as magical decorative elements on Neolithic pottery and on many bronzes from the Shang and Zhou periods, illustrating the central role of the turtle in Chinese mythology. The turtle was thought to have been present at the creation of the world and ever since to have borne the foundation pillars of the universe on her huge upper shell.

The turtle was also closely associated with the ancient concepts of Yin and Yang and the magical square, Luoshu. It was in the cracks of her upper shell that the legendary Emperor Fu Xi found *ba gua*, the three solid and three broken lines, making up the sixty-four hexagrams that for many Chinese to this day still symbolize all natural phenomena and the human state of mind. Through the divination manual, *Yi jing* (*I-ching*), also known as the *Book of changes*, these have spread all over the world.

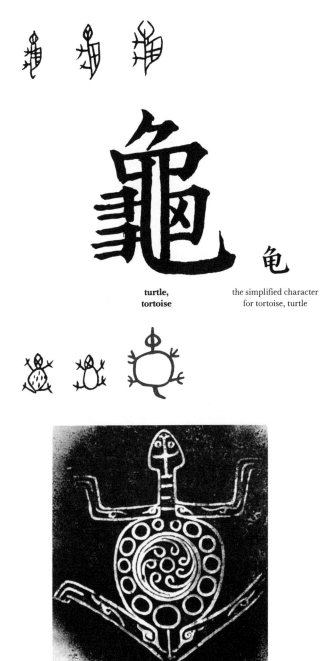

turtle, tortoise

the simplified character for tortoise, turtle

Decoration at the bottom of a deep bronze dish from Shaanxi. Shang.

Turtle in Shaanxi Provincial Museum, Xi'an.

The ancient Chinese saw the turtle as female. Male turtles simply did not exist, which meant that reproduction was something of a puzzle. According to one theory, the turtle saw to that detail herself by thinking—however that worked. According to another, she enlisted the snake. In both cases, proper turtle fathers are lacking. This has given rise to a number of abusive swearwords with degrading sexual associations that are still common today.

Nevertheless, the turtle carries the universe. From that task followed many other weighty and honorable assignments. It is said that the pillars that were to bear the Temple of Heaven in Beijing were placed on living turtles. According to these same legends, the turtles managed without food for three thousand years. They also, it was said, had the magical ability to stop wood from rotting.

Turtles can live to a very old age—some species over a hundred years—and they can indeed manage for long periods without food—if not three thousand years. I remember a tortoise I had as a child. Every winter it hibernated under the writing desk in the living room and did not emerge until the spring. One summer it escaped and we thought it was dead, until one day after the thaw the following year, it slowly ambled into the garden. We never found out where it had been all winter.

It is understandable that an animal of this kind can become the symbol for long life, strength, and endurance, as it is in China. Its very appearance says it all: the shell, that naked, primeval head, and the wrinkled neck—what a granny.

In the dark halls of the old Confucian temple in Xi'an, now a museum, the texts of the thirteen classics are preserved forever, engraved on huge stone tablets. It is like walking in a forest, the shimmer of light briefly freeing the characters from the gray weight of the stone, all in different handwriting by poets and rulers. The knowledge that all classical wisdom is visibly gathered there, close enough to touch, makes it one of the foremost intellectual pilgrimages in China.

Some of the largest tablets are borne on turtles. Heads thrust forward, with appealing, thoughtful eyes, they lie there beneath the weight of wisdom, upholding the concept that eternity exists.

Out on the grasslands of Mongolia, my children and I once came across a turtle of this kind in Karakorum, once the capital of the Mongolian world empire. The stone tablets with inscriptions on them had long since disappeared, and the turtle had become an amusing play sculpture. I cannot believe she disapproved.

Turtle at Karakorum.

*Bronze wine jar,
17.2 cm. Shang.*

elephant

Without the aid of the oldest characters, it is not easy to see that this written character represents an **elephant**, largely because the elephant does not stand on its four feet as we are used to seeing it, but is turned sideways. The simple reason is that many of the characters for animals caused problems for the writers who were inscribing on the oracle bones. They wrote the lines from the top downward and had limited space at their disposal. The long bodies of tigers, tails of dogs, and trunks of elephants threatened to intrude upon neighboring lines. To solve this they portrayed long animals vertically. By just turning the picture, one can see everything: the heavy body, the trunk, and the tail.

There are inscriptions and characters on bronzes that are very clear depictions of elephants, as well as more stylized versions from which the characters of today are drawn.

Many amulets, or small sculptures and bronze vessels, in the form of an elephant, as in the large illustration, have been found in graves from the first dynasties. This one is my favorite, peaceful and pleasing—an elephant as the vessel with its baby on its back as the lid. It is a wine jar from the Shang period. If it is compared with the oracle bone characters on the facing page, one can see how true to nature the figures are.

During the early Stone Age, there were plenty of animals of the elephant family such as the mammoth and the Stegodon elephant. Remains of bones and a few huge whole tusks have been found at certain ancient settlements. By the Shang period, only one kind remained, called the Asian elephant, which has small ears. Now found only in the extreme south of China, in Southeast Asia, and in India, it is used for transport and once also played an important part in war, rather like Hannibal's elephants.

Bird life in China is tremendously rich. There are twenty species of pheasant alone, and all other pheasants in the world stem from one of them, the white-collared pheasant. The cock bird's magnificent plumage and delicious flesh led to the introduction of the pheasant into many parts of the world. They arrived in Europe sometime in the sixteenth century, to the immediate delight of the hunting and shooting upper classes and artists. Think of all the still lifes of dead pheasants in the history of European art. The pheasant was first introduced into the United States toward the end of the nineteenth century—a welcome complement to the wild turkey, by then largely eradicated.

Pheasant, quail, partridge, peacock, and the common hen all belong to the same *Phasianidae* family. They like wooded country, and open fields where they can find grain and the small creatures they feed on. They need bushes and trees to roost in at night, precisely the kind of environment surrounding the Yellow River in ancient times. So it is hardly surprising that of the four species of bird now identified in archeological material, three of them belong to this family: poultry, pheasant, and peacock. The fourth is a type of vulture.

If we turn to the characters, the picture of ancient bird life becomes considerably richer. I searched systematically through *Grammata Serica Recensa*, Bernhard Karlgren's dictionary of the language of the Zhou period, and found over a hundred characters associated with birds, about a quarter of them names of different kinds of pheasant, their plumage, and their calls. Roughly the same number of characters concern waterfowl, mostly names of various wild geese and duck, but there are also characters for *heron*, *crane*, *stork*, and even *pelican* and *cormorant*, the black seabird that can be trained to fish.

Of the remaining fifty, half are names of unidentified birds, the remainder names of small birds such as sparrow, swallow, oriole, kingfisher, jay, and birds of

long-tailed bird

short-tailed bird

the crow family such as jackdaw, magpie, and raven. Added to these are ten or so characters for birds of prey such as hawk, falcon, and eagle.

Apart from special characters for all these birds, there are two general characters, one for **long-tailed bird** and the other for **short-tailed bird**. This division may seem rather primitive to those used to a different classification system, but considering the bird species in the area where the characters were created, it is not at all strange—particularly as the division was made three thousand years ago.

These ancient birds can be seen in all their magnificence on the oracle bones, a festive gathering of wings and feathers flapping in the wind; one can almost hear the screeches and short harsh calls spurting out of their beaks.

The characters for *long-tailed bird* and *short-tailed bird*, predecessors of today's characters, were crystallized out of these flocks during the Zhou period. The flock on the left is considered to be the predecessor of the long-tailed bird; on the right, of the short-tailed bird. Via the forms of the bronze characters, it is possible to follow the development up to their final form.

As far as I know, no thorough analysis of the various characters' relation to one another has yet been carried out, but even from the selection I have made, it is easy to see that there are many borderline cases. Some oracle bone characters now said to be predecessors of one character could equally well be predecessors of the other. Over 10 per cent of all compound characters for different species of bird also appear in two variants—one with the character of *long-tailed bird*, another with that of *short-tailed bird*—pheasant, for instance, and poultry, wild goose, and eagle.

This could perhaps be a way of indicating cock or hen bird, but if that is the case, the method is not consistently carried through.

Some scholars maintain that from the beginning there was only one character for *bird*. The division

into two is said not to have occurred until the end of the Zhou period. At the moment that theory is not accepted, and all we can say now is that there are two characters for *bird*—but no conclusions can yet be drawn about the appearance of the bird simply from the character.

However, it ought to be possible to make some identifications. The characters are based on careful observation of birds and their way of moving. Many of them are so clearly depicted that it should be possible for an experienced ornithologist to identify them. Several oracle bone characters earlier simply allocated to *long-tailed bird* have recently acquired an identity of their own, among them are the following, considered to be the oldest forms for *hen* and *woodpecker*. There can scarcely be any doubt about which is which.

Both characters have their equivalents in bronze inscriptions.

Unidentified characters for clans or families.

Until quite recently, these bird images used to be put together with a group of characters said to be the names of clans or families. Many characters for which predecessors or antecedents have not been found have often ended up there.

Many of them are sure to be names, or perhaps symbolic pictures of mythical birds the clan regarded as their forefathers. But just as names such as Pine, Branch, Hill, Grove, Rose and many others are family names, they also refer to actual phenomena—pine, branch, hill, grove, and rose. The same could apply to the Chinese names and written characters.

As new archaeological finds are studied, more birds are sure to be identified. Some clues are offered by amulets or pendants used by the wealthy of the Shang and Zhou periods to adorn their clothes. Made of thin discs of jade or bone and decorated with engraved lines or reliefs, these reveal silhouettes of birds similar to those on oracle bones and bronzes. Many of them are as simplified as a character.

Amulet.

Amulet.

Adornments such as these amulets are no longer used today, but in many parts of the loess areas around the Yellow River, people still decorate their homes with paper silhouettes or papercuts, as they are often called. From a stylistic point of view, in their way of perceiving and describing reality, they are astonishingly similar to jade amulets from the Shang and Zhou periods as well as to the characters.

The silhouettes are cut out of colored paper, often red or black, then fastened onto white paper windows, on the doors and walls, or high up on the ceiling. To a great extent, this work is done by women. While the children are asleep at midday and it is still too early to start preparing the evening meal, the women sit on the *kang*—the large communal family bed—and make papercuts, just as European women crochet potholders or embroider cloths, or in the past used to cut shelf linings out of white paper to adorn the pantry.

Experienced older women usually use ordinary scissors and cut directly into the sheet of paper without a template. This provides a crude, but uniquely fresh and living, line in which the inspiration of the moment and the willfulness of the scissors are given free rein.

The motifs are everyday animals and plants—oxen and sheep, chickens and pigs, deer and birds, cabbages, melons, and peaches, as well as small daily events occurring in and around the house—two cockerels fight, a horse breaks free and runs away, some birds settle in a fruit tree.

In many parts of China, papercuts have developed into an industry, great numbers being cut at a time by knife or machine. They become identical, and the motifs often have more to do with dreams than daily life: stunning landscapes, floating goddesses in whirling veils, and so on. But in the old, poor areas of Shanxi and Shaanxi, it is still possible to find papercuts similar to the original popular art, a simple and exceptionally cheap means of enhancing everyday life.

The district around the town of Yan'an is famous for its papercuts. The area was an important military, political, and commercial center as long ago as the first dynasties, and it maintained its importance to trade between central Asia and the deserts in the north until the Mongols conquered China in the thirteenth century.

Then decline set in. Communications collapsed when trade ceased, and the whole area stagnated. The valley peoples were isolated from each other by the intractable mountains and ravines, and cultural contacts with the outside world came to an end. Periods of severe famine decimated the population, and when Mao and the Red Army marched in during the autumn of 1935 after the Long March, large parts were uninhabited.

As a result of this isolation, many old customs and practices lived on in the valleys, and the women continued to make papercuts according to the traditions of the area in order to cheer up their gray—though in those loess areas it would be more accurate to say yellow—daily life.

When some of their work was exhibited for the first time in Beijing in 1980, it aroused considerable amazement among archaeologists and folklorists. Forms resembling art objects from the first dynasties were repeated in papercuts done by simple peasant women who had never learned to read or write. How could this be? How much of the ancient art had they seen and been influenced by? Could they have seen the bronzes, the jade objects, and the reliefs and roof tiles of the Han period?

Presumably not.

In the summer of 1987, I went to see some of the skilled older women in the area around Yan'an to learn more about their art. One of them was Ji Lanying, then sixty-four. She lived in a valley outside the town with her sons and their families, in caves with lovely latticed windows. Books did not exist in her world, for neither she nor anyone else in the household could read. The fifteen-year-old grandson had gone to school for a few years, but not long enough to be able to write his grandmother's name. The only writing in the house was the thin booklet in which the tenancy of their land was registered, but no one could read what was in it. Ji Lanying had been to Yan'an, but had never seen a film or television. She knew nothing about the forms of Chinese art during the first dynasties, and she firmly maintained that everything she did know, she had either learned from older women or invented herself.

I had the same impression elsewhere. Only grandmothers and other older women up or down the valley had the interest, patience, and time to bother with little girls when they came and asked what to do to make papercuts. Ji Lanying's mother actively discouraged her efforts to be allowed to make them—the family was poor and there was no money for paper—but she used leaves instead, and finally a neighbor woman took pity on her and taught her some of the old patterns and the way to hold the scissors in order to make such things as the tiny points indicating the down on birds.

I had a great many questions to ask about patterns, shapes, and particularly the symbolism of the different cuts. I was always given an answer, but the answers were rarely informative: "Flowers are beautiful." "Birds are so nice." "Everyone in the village keeps chickens." And so on. When I then went on asking, the answer was often: "I don't really know. We've always done it like this." This was not a reluctance to answer, because we talked openly about most things during the time I was there—about family, money, customs. Ji Lanyang and the others I met quite simply did not know. To them, the patterns were so natural, and had been so since their childhood, that they did not even think about them. They enjoyed the actual craft and the peace that spread within them as they sat on the kang cutting their pictures. They enjoyed the beauty of the frilly patterns as they fastened them to windows and walls or high up in the ceiling of the cave, and that was enough.

How long will this tradition last? As the standard of living rises in the country, other decorations are now taking over. Papercuts are regarded as old-fashioned, and many prefer to adorn their houses with posters of popular singers and film stars—symbols of development and progress. It is presumably only a matter of time before the art disappears.

As far as I know, no proper study of the historical development of papercutting has been undertaken. Perhaps none ever will be. The papercuts are made of perishable material and are often changed once or twice a year, so the evolution of the stylistic tradition is not known. Existing papercuts produced in the loess areas are nevertheless a testimony to the power of tradition and the astonishing continuity in ways of perceiving and depicting reality, so often felt in China.

Bronze character for hen.

Papercuts of birds, all from Yan'an.

Grandmother with grandchild.

Papercut from Ansai, near Yan'an.

A bird in one hand, a rabbit in the other, and two more birds, like pages, holding shirttails out like a skirt. Hair gathered into tufts on the top of the head was common in ancient times and is still seen on many small Chinese children today. A single tuft in the middle for the boys and two for the girls were supposed to protect the children against evil forces. In the papercut the tufts are in the form of birds, reflecting expressions used around Yan'an, where tufts like these are called hens. Or are the tufts in the papercut not intended as tufts at all but as adult hairpins, which are so often in the shape of birds? Chickens, cocks most of all, symbolized the sun and the dawn, when all things dark and dangerous disappear. They also eat insects and small poisonous creatures, and in that way protect both children and adults. In the village of Ansai, women still sew cloth chickens onto children's jackets on the fifth day of the fifth month, as has been done since time immemorial, to protect them from all things evil. They also sing a song that goes:

Hens peck,
tigers watch.
Hens eat poisonous insects,
tigers drive off all evil.

On the fifth day of the fifth month, high summer has just started, the heat increases day by day, and insects proliferate and become more dangerous. As a safeguard, a papercut of a cock that has just caught a huge scorpion is put up.

Both long-tailed and short-tailed birds are included in many characters naming different birds or the movements and sounds of birds. Mouth and long-tailed bird together form the character for *birdcall*, in a transferred sense also used for *sound* and *signal*. In mountainous areas where passes are narrow, there are often notices on dangerous corners or at entrances to railway tunnels—Sound your whistle! Signal!

Short-tailed bird and hand form the character for *one*, *one single*, used when the subject is one single animal of a kind usually found in groups, such as chickens. On oracle bones and bronzes, one can see a right hand held out toward a bird with its wing and tail feathers outspread. The same motif often recurs in papercuts from Yan'an. But although those pictures are often more complete—the whole person can be seen, not just the hand, and sometimes a table, a chair, or a basket as well—it is nevertheless the bird in the hand that is central.

birdcall, sound, signal

one, one single

Birds are one of the most common motifs in papercuts from Yan'an, where they are very often found in mirrored pairs, a natural result of the actual cutting technique—by folding the paper double, two birds can easily be cut out at once. The bronze character for *a pair* looks like an older relative of the papercut. Two birds can be seen beak to beak, their tail feathers curving up, as in the papercuts.

At the first standardization of characters in the third century B.C., the character for *hand* was added for some reason, perhaps to coordinate it with *one, one single*; and in that form, the character was used until 1958. Then the birds were removed, and another character for *hand* was added instead. Now the character lacks any connection with its original form, but two hands convey the idea of a pair just as well.

Above, we see a woman holding her bird, the two calmly looking at one another, the bird's eye gleaming in the same way as on some of the bronze characters.

In another papercut, also from Yan'an, a man has a bird in his arms, obviously a hen. The hen's beak is open as though she is cackling, as hens are apt to when they have laid an egg. The man has an egg in his hand. Next to them is a basketful of eggs, or is it the hen's nest?

a pair

the simplified character for a pair

Small bird, sparrow. The upper part of the character means *small* (this will be dealt with later in connection with abstract characters) and fits well in this context.

small bird, sparrow

Heron. The strange upper part of this character is perhaps explained by the oracle bones. Is it the tuft on the head of the heron? Do the two characters for *mouth* stand for the heron's unusually shrill call?

Herons have an unusual way of flying, letting their long, thin legs dangle freely from their bodies. Is that what we see in the bronze character, or are they feathery wings?

heron

Long-legged, long-necked birds from a bronze vessel of the late Zhou period.

Falcon. "A picture," says Karlgren laconically about this character in *Grammata Serica Recensa*. In his *Analytic Dictionary* he is more explicit: "A bird on some kind of roost: captive falcon."

falcon

Hunting with falcons is a very old pursuit in Asia. The Assyrians used them in the seventh century B.C.—the oldest known example. The character for *falcon* suggests that the Chinese of that time also used them.

The way people set about taming falcons in early times is not known, but during the nineteenth century, they were tied to a stick for three months, the first month with a cloth over their heads, so that they got used to food coming from their caretakers. When at last allowed to fly—at first with a long line attached to one leg—they pursued the prey, and were trained to return it to the hunter in exchange for a tidbit such as the entrails. After the hunt, they were firmly tied to their perches again.

During the Crusades and with increasing trade links in the eleventh century, this old Asiatic form of hunting was introduced into Europe, where it became tremendously popular among the upper classes throughout the Middle Ages.

In the border areas of China, hunting with falcons has continued to this day. I met a falconer once in Mongolia in the 1960s. He came riding along a valley, the wind tossing his earflaps about like dark wings. On his leather-clad arm was perched the falcon, a grave, impressive creature, and the spoils of their hunt, a bundle of hares, were hanging from the saddle.

The character for *short-tailed bird* or *long-tailed bird* is also included in the name for many other compound characters that describe a bird's movements—*swift, elegant, uneasy gaze, birdcall, response, reach high, gather, settle on*—one of the many proofs of the careful observation of nature on which the characters are based. A crass motif for bird-watching appears in the character for *grilled, roasted, burnt*—a bird above a fire.

roasted, burnt

Roasted birds were a great treat. Below is a song from Chu. With tempting descriptions of all the delicious dishes to come, the poem tries to persuade the 'soul' of the dead man to come back to life. Come back, oh soul! The pans are already simmering on the stove, full of delicacies!

> Cauldrons seethe to their brims, wafting a fragrance of well-blended flavors:
> Plump orioles, pigeons and geese, flavored with broth of jackal's meat.
> O soul, come back! Indulge your appetite!
> Fresh turtle, succulent chicken, dressed with the sauce of Chu;
> Pickled pork, dog cooked in bitter herbs, and ginger-flavored mince,
> And sour Wu salad of artemesia, not too wet and tasteless.
> O soul, come back! Indulge in your own choice!
> Roast crane next is served, steamed duck and boiled quails,
> Fried bream, stewed magpies, and green goose, broiled.
> O soul, come back! Choice things are spread before you.
> Four kinds of wine have been subtly blended, not rasping to the throat:
> Clear, fragrant, ice-cool liquor, not for base men to drink;
> And white yeast has been mixed with must of Wu to make the clear Chu wine.
> O soul, come back and do not be afraid!

Translation: David Hawkes

The state of Chu was contemporary with Zhou and near the Yangzi. But the way of cooking and the ingredients the poem so appetizingly describes were also used around the Yellow River, and the same notion—that the best contact with the spirits of the dead was through food—existed in both places. Ancestors were still included in the family, and when the good smells of cooking rose to the skies, they wondered, as did everyone else, What is it that smells so good? In many oracle bone inscriptions, the prince negotiates with his guests/ancestors over the menu—Shall it be ox or sheep? And how many? One? Ten? Fifty?

Birds, particularly chickens, have continued to be an important ingredient in the Chinese diet, and many families fatten them in woven bamboo baskets between bicycles and flowerpots in the yard. Under the eaves there is often also a songbird in a cage.

We keep cats and dogs; the Chinese keep goldfish and birds. And just as we go out with our dogs, they go out with their birds. At dawn as the morning mist slowly gives way, older men gather in parks and on the streets, hanging their bird cages up in the trees or on a line across one of the small, overgrown patches found in an environment that has grown by itself and not been constructed all at once.

The cages are round and stubby like cheddar cheeses, and inside, the birds sing loudly to maintain their territory, mostly larks of various kinds, Chinese robins, and nightingales. The really great singer and favorite all over the country is the yellowish-gray thrush, *Garrulax canorus*, his song making even the nightingales lose all their self-confidence.

The old gentlemen come with their cages every morning, and a certain element of competitiveness enters their gatherings—Which bird sings loudest? Strongest? Longest? But the birds are mostly an excuse for them to meet, and with a bird cage in hand, anyone is accepted.

When the gray light of morning changes to daylight and the stream of bicycles and buses thickens on the streets, the old gentlemen are already on their way home, their cages covered with blue cotton. In the evening they are back again. As the day grows quiet, the same lovely songs resound in the dim light between the trees, and the old men talk about the day that has passed.

pheasant

Arrow and bird together form the character for the ordinary *white-collared pheasant*.

pheasant feathers

This is one of the many characters for *pheasant* and *pheasant feathers*.

feathers

The upper part of the character means **feathers**. It is unclear whether the character shows the tail feathers, the wing feathers, or a plume on the bird's head—scholars disagree—but the issue may not be of great importance. The picture of bird and feathers together evokes a pheasant quite nicely.

The tail feathers of an ordinary pheasant grow no longer than half a meter at the most, but several other kinds can have feathers as long as two meters. During the Zhou period, pheasant feathers were used on many ceremonial occasions, and adorned banners, war chariots, and even musical instruments.

Décor motif from the Zhou period.

With a feather in each hand, the Monkey king laughs after outwitting his opponents in the episode 'Havoc in Heaven.'

Later, during the Imperial period, embroidered pheasants decorated the court dress of some of the highest officials—the golden pheasant for officials of the second grade, the silver pheasant for the fifth. The other officials had crane, peacock, wild goose, egret, duck, quail, flycatcher, and oriole feathers on their costumes—a full array of bird life around the Yellow River in ancient times.

The two-meter-long feathers of the northern pheasant, *Phasianus reevesis*, even today adorn the magnificent headdresses worn by the generals in Peking Opera. Like huge insects or birds, the actors whirl around on the stage and, by guiding the pheasant feathers in various ways, express indignation, decisiveness, unease, and other important emotions. Spectators familiar with character language at once understand what is going on, or is going to happen.

If the actor swings his head around so that the feathers are a swirling crown high above him, everyone knows he is beside himself with rage and bitterness. If he bends his head so far forward that the feathers touch the floor, he is thunderstruck and has to have time to think matters over.

If he lets the feathers glide between his forefinger and middle finger from the fastening right out to the tip, at the same time bringing the feather in a wide sweep in toward his body, then everyone knows he is looking at a distant goal—an enemy army approaching, a town, or a high mountain. If he carries out the same movement with both hands, it is a sign of joy and delight. But if instead, with trembling hands, he brings the feathers with small circular movements in front of his chest, this means he is agitated and uneasy.

These characters undeniably mean **tiger**, standing there with their heavy bodies, their jaws wide open and tails swinging menacingly.

The tigers should really be shown upright, vertically for, as we saw, long four-footed animals are placed in that way on the oracle bones—presumably for reasons of space. These animals are obviously tigers seen in profile, standing on all fours.

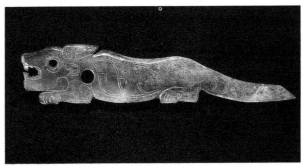

This little tiger of pale brown jade, to the right, is crouching, ready for the decisive leap, ears back and fangs bared. One can almost hear the mortal scream of his prey.

The tiger is a pendant from the Shang period, found in the Fu Hao grave outside Anyang. Ornaments of this kind were common during both the Shang and the Zhou periods, not only in the form of tigers but also of birds and fish. Often hung from the belt, they also functioned as amulets and went with the dead into the grave.

Pendant from the Shang period.

The oracle bone character for *tiger* gradually became more and more stylized.

In certain older bronze characters, the tiger's open mouth, claws, and whipping tail are still there, but then he disappeared into a jumble of strokes.

Without the help of the characters on oracle bones and bronzes, it is almost impossible to see that the present character is a picture of a tiger. But there he is, the Chinese king of beasts.

tiger

Among the many exciting tiger stories in China, one of the most famous is about Wu Song. Drunk as a lord, he comes across a tiger that has long terrorized the neighborhood and kills it with his bare hands. Chinese children all love this rather primitive tale.

The episode is included in a collection of tales known in English as *All Men Are Brothers*, or *Outlaws of the Marsh*, about a twelfth-century gang of robbers plundering western Shandong, one of the domains of the

parks are long, and the booklet about Wu Song is always out on loan.

The tiger is known as a dangerous animal, a man-eater, the most terrible of all. But for the Chinese, the image of the tiger also has a different meaning. Far from being a threat, the tiger also provides protection and security. According to Chinese folklore, it had close ties with the earth, and so also with ancestors— two of the most central concepts in ancient times. It

Tigers from a bronze vessel. Zhou period.

Shang dynasty two thousand years earlier. Their exploits gave rise to a wealth of legends carried on through the centuries by skilled professional storytellers.

I heard the story of Wu Song for the first time in a market in Kaifeng. Storytelling used to be the most common form of entertainment in China. In the past, only a tiny fraction of the population could read, but everyone liked hearing exciting stories. When I was a student there in the early 1960s, there were still storytellers in the markets and amusement quarters. People sat on hard wooden benches in the semidarkness of a simple, unadorned shed, often with a cup of tea in their hands. I shall never forget the breathless attention of the audience and the dry sound of the wooden clappers that the storyteller struck to emphasize the drama of the story.

Today most people can read, but the story of Wu Song and the tiger has not lost its fascination. The queues at the library stands that offer comics in the

was also a female symbol. There are a great many tales about tigers, or rather tigresses, saving people from evil forces and giving their milk to abandoned infants, much like the story of Romulus and Remus and the she-wolf of Rome.

In China, the tiger still has this double face. One of the most beloved toys is a cloth tiger filled with buckwheat seed or rags, with the character for *king* on its forehead. By playing with it, the child is meant to become as strong and powerful as a tiger, as a king, and just as secure. Previously, these tigers were always homemade, like the rag dolls and teddy bears made for our children, but today they can be bought in many sizes in most toy shops.

Even today, little children wear caps and shoes with appliqué tigers on them to protect them from evil —just as the warriors of the first dynasties were protected by wild animal masks on their helmets— and aprons with an image of a roaring tiger across their bellies—just as prehistoric soldiers carried shields

with terrifying paintings of tigers on them, ready to leap onto the enemy with their terrible jaws and tear them to pieces.

A few years ago I found a worn collar for a child in the shape of a tiger skin in a market outside Xi'an, and I suddenly remembered a shimmering green bronze axe from the Shang dynasty, on which a small man, his eyes open, is looking out between the jaws of two huge upright tigers, as secure as the children who ever since have looked out of their tiger caps and tiger collars.

Decoration on a bronze axe from Shang, a child's collar of today, and a Shang warrior in a wild animal helmet.

It is difficult to find a better illustration of the tiger's double face in Chinese culture than this papercut from Ansai, outside Yan'an. The grinning jaws, with their sharp predator's teeth, are as menacing as the tiger jaws on the oracle bones and bronzes. But the face, with its watchful eyes and the character for *king* glowing on its forehead, is the same protective one found on toy tigers.

This tiger was cut out by a woman now eighty years old, who has made paper decorations for her own home and those of her neighbors since she was very young. She comes from a very poor family and was not given her own name, Wang Zhanlan, until she was asked to give a course in papercutting in 1979.

"Children are the future and the hope of the nation," says this poster showing a boy in a tiger cap sleeping contentedly on a tiger cushion. Beijing, 1985.

'Paper tiger.' People all over the world interested in politics will remember the conversation Mao Zedong had in the 1940s with Anna Louise Strong, the American journalist, in Yan'an. It was in the middle of the war, and the situation of the Communists looked anything but bright. But Mao was hopeful. All ruling reactionary groups such as imperialists and dictators were doomed to fail because they were separated from the people. For a time, they could indeed be as terrible as real tigers, which killed and ate people. But, said Mao, in the end they would be rendered harmless and turned into paper tigers, toy tigers.

The animals mentioned so far are highly realistic, but during the Shang and Zhou periods, animals also played an important mythical role. The turtle took part in the creation of the world. The deer, the bird, and the tiger were associated with the seasons of the year, the renewal of nature, and the soil. Ancient people still lived close to nature. They regarded animals as their ancestors, and the lineage of princely families came from them—Yu the Great, the first of the Xia dynasty, stemmed from a bear, the Shang dynasty from a blackbird; and the founder of the Zhou dynasty grew up protected by oxen, birds, and sheep.

Animals acted as messengers between people and ancestors. This contact with them was vital; with their help, people could approach the Supreme Being of Heaven, the ruler over all things, about everything from great events in nature down to health and success in hunting and war for individual princes.

When the cult of ancestors was at its height, many of the ceremonies were carried out under signs of animals. With the skull of a deer or a tiger above his head, the flayed skin a cloak around his shoulders, the shaman led the rites. Sacrificial vessels were covered with pictures of animals, even the vessel itself was often in the shape of an animal.

One of the most magnificent vessels of the Shang dynasty, a wine jar, is in the shape of a tiger with a man clinging to the soft fur of its stomach, just as a baby monkey clings to its mother. The tiger's jaws are open, its great fangs menacingly bared, but the man is calm, his gaze as solemn as that of an infant, quiet and with wonder, but no fear.

But is it a tiger? A closer look at the body reveals that it is composed of animals of various kinds. The tiger's back and tail are actually the head of an elephant with a long trunk and the powerful horns of an ox. Dragons with rolled-up tails swirl around the thighs, and snakes wriggle on the man's trousers. The handle is covered with reptiles and ends in an elephantlike head, and on the lid, on the 'tiger's' head, is a deer. Underneath, invisible to all, is a dragon with horns and two fish.

What are we to make of all this? A child or a slave being sacrificed to wild animals? The birth of a clan's mythical original ancestor, or perhaps the actual intercourse that gave rise to him?

Animal images on bronzes constitute a complex mythological language still far from being deciphered. At present there exist totally different interpretations. But the basic features are becoming clearer. Many of the motifs seem to be a transition from one stage to another, primarily birth–death–rebirth.

Wine jar from the Shang dynasty.

Nature was a threat, but also a source of security; it was in nature that man originated and drew his livelihood. By handing himself over to her protection, man secured his own existence. This symbiotic relationship is expressed in many aspects of early Chinese art. Protected by menacing wild beasts, man was at the same time both a child of nature and master of it.

As man's ability to control nature according to his desires grew greater, the significance of animals declined, says Kwang-Chi Chang, one of the world's leading authorities on the archaeology of China. From mythical representations in which every detail—as in medieval churches of Europe—interpreted and developed the religious meaning, the animal motifs became increasingly purely decorative. The attitude of devotion and respect with which people had previously regarded animals had to give way. Man became the measure of all things.

But in popular art and beliefs, the old images remained, and one can see them even today, the descendants of wild animal masks once embellishing the sacrificial vessels of the Bronze Age.

Rubbing of oracle bone.

The elevated mythical position of animals did not stop man from exploiting them for more prosaic needs. Meat, hide, bone and horn, down and feathers were important raw materials that everyone in the country needed. But the king, and later the emperor, reserved a considerable supply for himself and his court. He had large hunting domains where he mounted hunting expeditions, which also served as a kind of military exercise for his wars with neighboring states.

A high proportion of the inscriptions on the oracle bones—as many as half, according to some calculations—concern hunting. From the carefully recorded results of hunts, it is known there was plenty of game in the forests.

The oracle bone above, from the days of King Wu Ding around 1300 B.C., bears inscriptions saying:

Divined on the day Wu-Wu
Ku made the inquiry:
We are going to chase at 'Ch'in'; any capture:
Hunting on this day, [we] actually capture:
Tigers, one;
Deer, forty;
Foxes, one hundred and sixty-four,
Hornless deer one hundred and fifty-nine ...

Translation: Li Chi

Birds.   *An elephant.*   *Tigers.*   *Wild pigs.*

Among many different methods of capturing animals, nets were often used. Various animals can be seen, above, on their way into nets. (Two similar nets can be seen on the picture with the oracle bone inscription, used in the sense of 'to hunt.') One of the tigers is depicted clearly with jaws alone.

Larger animals were caught in pits, like these two deer.

But there was apparently another hunting method—of a more unusual kind.

The various characters in the row below all mean **wild animal** or **game**. On the right of the character is *dog*, which I will come to later. But what is on the left?

Scholars have suggested *big*, *shield*, *net*, *shovels*, *drum*, *star*, *to assault*, *cicada*, *banner*—in short, they do not know. There are, however, certain new archaeological finds that I think may help solve the puzzle.

In 1976, a Stone Age dwelling place was found near Datong in northern Shanxi, 140 or so miles west of Beijing. It has been dated to about 100,000 B.C. and is interesting in several respects. Parts of skeletons were found—the first people of our own species, *Homo sapiens*, to be discovered on Chinese soil—as well as great quantities of bones from various kinds of deer.

wild animal, game

Painting in the museum in Zhoukoudian, purporting to show the way Stone Age people hunted deer.
Right: Hunting stones from about 4000 B.C. in a display case in the Banpo Museum.

Several tons of astonishing round stones were also found, the smallest only about one hundred grams, the largest, two kilos. Some of them were only half-finished, so tracing the procedure used when making them was easy. The site appears to have been a workshop for making them, the original stones themselves fetched from a nearby shore.

But what could they have been used for? In Yunnan, in the far southwest of China, are two small groups of primitive people, the Naxi and the Pumi, who used an interesting hunting method until only a few years ago. They tied a round stone at each end of a half-meter-long rope and made a noose or a handle of the ends. Then they whirled the stones around in the air and let them fly, swirling across the plain to become entangled in the legs and antlers of the fleeing animals.

The Indians on the South American pampas used the same hunting method until the end of the nineteenth century. Charles Darwin speaks admiringly of their skill with these bolas in his *Naturalist's Voyage Round the World.*

I saw bolas for the first time in 1967, in a museum in Paraguay, showing how the gauchos, the cowboys of South America, lived on the treeless plains with wells lined with knuckle bones and chairs made of the pelvic bones of oxen. They had adopted the Indians' method of hunting with stones. I bought one and took it home, and it lay on my desk for almost ten years as a paperweight, an interesting reminder of an alien world.

Then I went off to Xi'an and visited Banpo Museum, devoted to the first settled people in China. The guide took us briskly through the first hall, in passing mentioning that in one of the display cases barely glimpsed were some round stones that had been used for hunting. I would probably never have taken note of what she had said had I not had my South American stone at home. I went straight back and to my surprise found a stone that could have been an exact copy of mine, except that it was six thousand years older.

Without that experience, I probably would never have noted the strange information I have come across over the years in various Chinese archaeological journals. I read about the Xujiayao settlement on the plateau outside Datong and the great finds made there, as well as in other places in Shanxi, Shaanxi, Hebei, and Shandong, and I realized that these stones were one of the most important hunting implements of the Chinese Stone Age people.

Bernhard Karlgren says in his dictionary of archaic Chinese that the character to the right in the oldest scripts, means *exhaust, carry to the utmost.* But the meaning is not certain, and he has no explanation for what the picture represents. Perhaps the character is only a form of grasshopper, he says, with no further argument than the fact that it is included in the modern form for *grasshopper.*

That is a very odd explanation. But what *is* interesting is that of the twenty-five compound characters listed by Karlgren in which this character is included, eight of them concern *exhaustion, shooting pellets at, fear, fighting,* and *biting.* The other characters, as far as I can see, have no such common denominator.

If it is true that stones were one of the most important hunting implements of Stone Age people, demonstrably used not only by the first members of *Homo sapiens* in China but also by Stone Age people in Banpo six thousand years ago, and by ethnic minorities up until the present day, it is natural that they are included in characters concerning *shooting pellets at* and *fighting.* And what could be more natural than letting these two hunting implements—the stones that make the animal stop and fall and also the dog that catches up and holds it until the hunter arrives—join together to form the character for *game,* the purpose of the hunt?

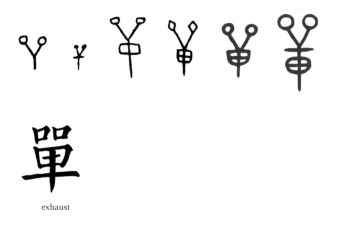

exhaust

Eskimos and several ethnic minorities in China have also hunted birds with stones until the present day, but their stones were no bigger than the marbles played with by European children. A handful of stones were placed in a piece of cloth fastened to the bowstring, and when they flew off, there was always the chance of one of them hitting the bird and stunning it long enough for the hunter to be able to get to it and wring its neck.

Bronze inscription from the Zhou period, probably the name of a clan or family.

Apart from the animals mentioned so far that since time immemorial have contained a strong mythical element, there is one other, purely imaginary (as far as can be made out) creation—the dragon. Some scholars have speculated that the prototype might have been a small crocodile still living in the Long River, or primeval animals like dinosaurs that grazed on the fringes of the swamps once found in what is now Mongolia. But no one really takes those theories seriously. Nor is much attention really paid to Wen Yiduo, the Chinese writer who says that the dragon was originally a snake that over the years acquired increasingly mythical associations. The dragon is part of the conceptual world of the Chinese people to such an extent that what are called natural explanations are regarded as uninteresting, at least to ordinary people.

In Western legends and myths such as those in the Bible, the dragon is usually depicted as a fire-belching, often many-headed monster representing evil. Heroes such as Beowulf, Sigurd, and Saint George fought it to rescue noble maidens and save besieged soldiers from its claws, or to retrieve the immense hidden treasures on which it had been brooding.

Not so in China. There they turned to the dragon and asked for help, not least to make rain. For the Chinese, the dragon symbolizes goodness, strength, fertility, and change. It was thought that he—the dragon was definitely male and one of the leading manifestations of male force—slept curled up at the bottom of the sea or the river in winter. When spring came and the atmosphere was at last again filled with moisture and warmth, he rose into the sky and lived up there through the six months of summer. He whirled around in storm clouds, washing his curly mane in the pouring rain. His claws were the forked lightning across the sky, his voice the thunder and

the storms rustling the dry leaves in the forest and making nature tremble. He was dangerous, certainly, but if people danced in his honor with willow twigs in their hands and asked for help, he might let the clouds huddle round the mountain peaks and the rain fall onto the dry fields.

One of the oldest depictions of this remarkable animal is on a large clay dish, found in Taosi in southern Shanxi, scarcely seventy miles from the Dragon Gate, where the Yellow River descends from the mountains and runs into the great northern China plain. The dish and many other finds made there are carbon 14 dated to 2500–1900 B.C. and so would originate in Xia, China's first dynasty.

The dragon lies curled up and fills the whole inside of the dish, its body muscular as a python's and patterned with broad, sparse stripes. Or are the black shapes stylized scales? That is not impossible—according to later descriptions, the dragon has large, flat scales like those on a carp. Its head is small and crowned with something that could perhaps best be described as a horn, and its mouth spurts fire or perhaps steam. Or is it a long, flickering tongue?

Similar images can be seen in oracle bones approximately a thousand years later. The dragons swing this way and that with powerful motions, their mouths open, their bodies strong. Sometimes, like the dragon on the Taosi dish, they have a kind of horn or crest on their heads that can also be seen in certain characters.

dragon

This joyous, uncomplicated picture of a **dragon** was elaborated during the following centuries with a great many new details. During the Han period, according to public conceptions, the dragon had antlers like a deer, ears like an ox, eyes like a hare, paws like a tiger, claws like a bird of prey, scales like a carp, a stomach like a silkworm, and a head like a camel. It could also perform the most amazing transformations, with no difficulty making itself as small as a silkworm or so big it filled all the space between heaven and earth. It could make itself dark or light, even invisible if necessary. This fabled animal is the main character in many distinctive stories, especially within the traditions of Buddhism and Daoism, in which the dragon often appears in his crystal palace deep down in the darkness of the sea, protected by an army of fish and turtles.

The dragon was not just another mythical animal. It was regarded as the most elevated of all creatures and symbolized China and the power of the emperor. The Yellow Emperor, who, according to legend, ruled the land along the Yellow River, the cradle of China around 2700 B.C., and is considered to be the father of all China, was said to have been the incarnation of a dragon. Rulers of later periods eagerly attached themselves to this concept, and, keen as they were to legitimize their position, they presented themselves as dragons. Their throne was called the Dragon Throne, their bed the Dragon's Bed, their magnificent long silk coats called Dragon Robes, and so on. The gilded pillars holding up the palace roof were adorned with dragons, as were the exquisite porcelain bowls from which their meals were served.

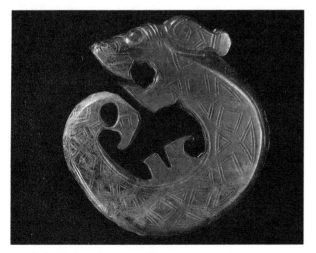

Amulet in the shape of a dragon. Shang.

Dragon in the clouds. Enamel painting on an eighteenth-century dish.

Dragons adorning the emperor's private property were always shown with five claws, while dragons for more ordinary use had to be content with four. That time has now passed. Porcelain can be bought with five-clawed dragons in any shop for household goods, and T-shirts and silk dressing gowns exported to the West are decorated with five-clawed dragons like those which once adorned the emperor's own robes.

For ordinary people, the dragon was once very tangible, and they often referred to themselves as Children of the Dragon. They put paintings and carved wooden reliefs in the form of dragons above their doors and included the character for *dragon* in the names of their sons in the hope that their sons would therefore be gifted, forceful, and dynamic.

Two popular annual festivals are associated with the dragon. The first falls on the fifteenth day of the first month according to the lunar calendar, and marks the end of the Chinese New Year celebrations and the arrival at last of spring. Joyous dragons parade through towns and villages on that day, followed by musicians with drums and cymbals and crowds of little boys letting off firecrackers with a tremendous noise. The dragons consist of lanterns, sometimes several hundred of them, representing the jointed segments of the dragon's body. They are mounted on a pole and worked by dancers moving in a long line behind one another. The first and largest lantern is shaped like a huge dragon head, and behind come the rest, in decreasing size to the very end of the tail and the smallest lantern. As the dancers weave slowly forward, simultaneously raising and lowering the lanterns, the flickering points of light merge together into a luminous dragon wriggling its way through the darkness. The procession is often led by a lone dancer teasingly holding a lantern in the form of a red ball, which the dragon chases in vain, to the delight of the spectators, tossing its head and spouting sparks in its fury.

Another variation for daytime celebrations is the dragon made of paper or cloth and painted with scales, all in bright, glowing colors. It is worked in the same way by dancers with long poles and is often much wilder and more unruly than the dragons made of lanterns, but not so magical.

This dance probably originated in some of the ceremonies carried out at the beginning of the planting season when it was necessary to waken the dragon from his winter sleep and get his help to produce rain so that the growing could get started.

Even today, the character for *dragon* is included in compound words denoting irrigation equipment such as the long chain pumps for pedaling water up into the rice paddies, just as the word for *water tap* is *dragon head* in Chinese.

Perhaps these labels simply come from the similarity with the dragon's long body and head with its protruding jaws, but folk expressions often have a firm

Dragon composed of thousands of potted plants, in front of the gateway to the Forbidden City. Decoration for National Day, 1986.

basis in popular traditions, which seems likely in this case.

The second festival involving dragons falls on the fifth day of the fifth month in the lunar calendar. Boats shaped like dragons compete in rowing races, long, narrow boats holding up to a hundred oarsmen. Musicians sit astern or in the middle of the boat with their drums and cymbals, urging on the oarsmen and coordinating their efforts. Dragon boat races, like dragon dances, are probably associated with rain-making magic but are also linked with a tragic event concerning Qu Yuan (340–278 B.C.), an irreproachable statesman and poet in the Kingdom of Chu, who was said to have been dismissed in a degrading manner from his post and banished. After many years in exile, the bitter news reached him that the capital of his country had been taken and utterly destroyed, thus extinguishing his hopes of returning

one day. So he wrote one of the most poignant sequences of poems in Chinese poetry, filled the long sleeves of his coat with stones, and drowned himself in the Miluo River. On the first anniversary of his death, people began offering cakes of sticky rice wrapped in bamboo leaves to his spirit in the river, and boats rowed back and forth there to keep the demons away.

In our day, dragon boat races are one of the most spectacular of all popular festivals, and on the fifth day of the fifth month, oarsmen compete not only on the Miluo River, but also on a great many other rivers, most of all in southern China. The custom has also spread to Japan and Southeast Asia.

Domestic animals

In the Western world, the dog is 'man's best friend' and on the whole stands for something good, for friendship and loyalty, protection and company.

One would think that the same might apply to China, for the dog has been a domestic animal there for at least eight thousand years and was their very first domestic animal. But when the character for *dog* was created, it seems to have been regarded more as a part of the wilderness than of the world of man.

This is evident from many compound characters using the character for *dog*, in which no tame and faithful creature comes to mind: *mad, coarse, crude, noisy, ruthless. Dog* is also part of a large number of compound characters for wild animals, not just animals such as *wolf* and *fox* of the *Canis* family, but also *badger, otter, weasel*—elongated doglike creatures outside the world of man—as well as for various kinds of *monkeys.*

One of the earliest depictions of a **dog** is on a bronze vessel from the Shang period. With its glistening eye and wide-open, aggressive jaws, it gives a fierce, almost wild impression, definitely no lapdog.

On the oracle bones, dogs seem better–tempered, although animals inspiring respect with long curved tails are also found on them. Some of the dogs are barking so furiously, they might still be heard.

Late bronze characters for dog.

The character for dog often found in compound characters.

dog

A grave sculpture from Luoyang, one of the capitals of the Zhou period along the Yellow River, shows a dog with a strong body and short, powerful legs. A dog lover at once sees a spitz, the clever working dog of the Northern Hemisphere. The pricked ears and energetic curl of the tail over its hindquarters are characteristic features not apparent together in other breeds.

China actually has a native spitz, the chow, one of the oldest breeds, known for at least two thousand years, and many consider it even older. The chow is closely related to the huskies of Greenland, Siberian huskies, and the Lapp and Jämtland dogs of Sweden.

Closest to these, in turn, are some of the Japanese short-haired spitz. There is also a Chinese short-haired chow. Is the old sculpture from Luoyang one of these?

Apart from hunting for birds and small game, in which it functioned as a barking dog to drive them

Rubbing from the Yuan dynasty.

out of trees, the chow was used as a guard dog in temples. Chows were also bred for their fur and meat. The same is done today. In China, dog meat is said to be good, especially the flesh of black male chows, preferably before they are nine months old. There are restaurants in many parts of China that specialize in dog meat, and the further south, the more popular it is. In some places, the dogs are shown to the dinner guests, as trout are in pools in Italy, and the 'little delicacies' leap about expectantly in their cages. Guests choose the one that looks the most tender, which is then cooked according to special recipes.

Pekinese dogs, also of Chinese origin and with a long history, have never been eaten. They functioned as pet dogs in the palace, particularly loved by the idle court ladies, who used to walk around with them in the wide sleeves of their gowns. No one was more enthusiastic about them than the eccentric Dowager Empress Cixi, who ruled China during the late nineteenth century. In her time, the palace was filled with Pekinese of every conceivable color, and the court painters were kept busy portraying her favorites.

After the scandalous pillage by Europeans of the Summer Palace in Beijing in 1860, some of the dogs were taken to Europe with the rest of the spoils, and since then the breed has spread all over the world.

Dogs are not often seen in China today, at least in the towns. In the post-revolution hygiene campaigns, all stray dogs were collected and destroyed, and gradually, even pet dogs were forbidden, largely because of the great shortage of food at the time. After decades of war, food was scarce and people's needs were considered greater than those of dogs. Only working dogs were left, those directly involved in useful work such as sheep dogs and guard dogs.

The first time I went to Shanghai was at the New Year in 1961. A temporary zoological miniexhibition had been arranged down in the Old City, with narrow aisles of cramped wire-netting cages, one of them labeled Dog. The children flocked to it. Ten years after the revolution, few of them had ever seen a dog before.

As the standard of living in the country rose, dogs began to reappear. But since 1981, pet dogs have once again been forbidden in towns, largely for reasons of hygiene.

Dog and mouth: *to bark*. Although some people with Western inclinations started keeping pet dogs in the late nineteenth century, dogs have never been regarded as members of the family in China the way they have in the West. As in European peasant communities of the past, the dog's main task was to guard the house and stop thieves from breaking in. The more alert and aggressive the dog, the better it could carry out its task. Marco Polo writes about the respect incurred by Chinese dogs, and more recent travelers tell of how a town could be located in the dark by the persistent barking, an invisible cupola of sound above the roofs and walls where dogs were guarding the houses of their masters.

Dog and two mouths: *to howl, whimper, cry*.

Dog and nose: *to stink, smell bad*. Is it the dog, with its sensitive sense of smell, noticing a stink? Or is it the dog itself that smells? The majority of Chinese dogs have been thin, roaming, semiwild beasts and never came anywhere near a bubble bath. Indescribably scruffy and the worse for wear, cowardly as well as insolent, the typical Chinese dog roams the streets and rubs his fleas off in the sand, wolflike, evil-smelling, and dangerous.

Classic Chinese village mongrel. Dirty, shaggy coat, upright ears, and tail in an energetic curve across its hindquarters.

to bark

to howl, whimper . . .

to stink, smell bad

Dog and man: *to admit defeat, give up, struck to the ground.* The various meanings of the character demonstrate some of the Chinese attitudes toward dogs.

Give up and *sky* (which also means *day* and *weather*) together make the character *give-up-weather*, which is the expression for the period from the end of July to the middle of August when the heat is at its worst and everyone feels ready to give up.

Dog and four mouths: *vessel, object, tool, capacity.* This character seems an insoluble puzzle, but there are possible explanations. From the late Stone Age to today, the Chinese have stored foodstuffs in large clay jars. Is the dog standing guard over their openings—mouths?

Or is he guarding the openings to the meter-deep cellars under the floors of the houses, where seed corn was kept, together with other valuable possessions such as the vessels used for sacrifices to ancestors? Cellars of that kind have been found in large numbers in the Stone Age village of Banpo and in Anyang, and this method is still used today. It is a very efficient way of storing seed corn in dry areas, says Francesca Bray, a leading agricultural scientist, and it functions best for millet. The storage pit is filled and closed with a tight lid, which makes the space as good as airtight. Carbon dioxide given off by the seed during storage kills any insects and larvae that might be present. In our day, this system has appeared in wheat-producing countries in the form of silos.

to admit defeat . . .

'give-upweather'

vessel, object . . .

Typical pigs from northern China (there are some in the trough, too).

The character for **pig** looks peculiar until it is turned horizontal. Then you see the pig standing there. Chinese pigs are nimble, black, shaggy, and free-roaming, famed since time immemorial for their succulent meat and life-giving manure.

For the Chinese, the pig has always been the most appreciated domestic animal. Unpretentiously, it gobbles up everything it finds—grain, fruit and household waste—as it roots around the houses. In a pinch, it even eats the feces of other animals and people, turning these into meat that is a delight to the palate.

Meanwhile, this little benefactor produces marvelous manure, the most valuable commodity in old agricultural areas. Mao Zedong said a pig was a whole little manure factory, which it certainly is. Every pig delivers a ton of top-quality manure every year, an invaluable contribution without which Chinese agriculture would collapse.

pig

Every part of a pig can be used:
bristles for brushes
intestines for sausage
skin for glue
bones for ash (excellent manure)
blood as base when painting wood
impregnating material for fishing nets

And the meat. Quickly fried in thin slices with bamboo, onion, or dried mushrooms soaked in warm water. A tablespoon of soy sauce, a tablespoon of yellow rice wine and a little ginger—no more is needed.

Given the choice, the Chinese favor pork far over beef, which they regard as coarse and hard, and over chicken, which is also easy and good, but lacks pork's richness and flavor.

They say in China that the quality of the meat is directly affected by the way the pig has been allowed to live. No wonder their pigs are well looked after. Even those kept enclosed live a good life, and buildings holding hundreds may be kept as clean and well-run as stables of pedigree horses.

Pig. Papercut from Huangling,
south of Yan'an.

But then there is also the manure. In a country where so many people have been living in the same place for so long, the soil has to be meticulously taken care of so that it receives the nourishment it needs. River waters and the silt they bring with them are fundamental to the fertility of the soil, and all waste from farming and the household—stems, peelings, and rinse water—goes back into the soil, often via the pig, as well as all excrement, both animal and human.

Night soil in particular is considered to be the most valuable fertilizing element. Everything is carefully collected and composted. In country areas, this is simple, for there they have communal toilets. But in some years, in the 1960s, for instance, when hungry peasants cared more about the productivity of their own plots of land than about the communal fields, I often saw signs along the highways near Beijing with the astonishing message: 'Dont be selfish, use the public toilets!'

In the towns, everything is collected by tank trucks or tanker boats and taken out to composting beds in the country. But even only a few years ago, horse-drawn carts came every morning, creaking and dripping through the alleys of Beijing. 'Honey jars,' they were called. I remember the characteristic cries of the drivers and the sound of gates being opened when people who had forgotten to put out their barrels came rushing out. Never shall I forget the red or chestnut-colored wooden barrels of Suzhou. Then, as now, they stood there in their brilliant colors, gleaming against the green, mossy walls of the houses. But for those who had to sit once a day in the gutters scrubbing the barrels clean, the toilets in new apartment houses must have seemed like pure paradise.

The oldest known picture of a Chinese sheep is on a fragment of pottery about six thousand years old. The horns are full of strength and the eyes, rigidly sheeplike, stare straight out over the millennia.

There are great similarities between that picture and the first written characters for **sheep**, though these are only half as old. Some of the characters are still clear pictures, others have already become stylized characters, in which the intense eyes of the sheep have been reduced to a straight stroke.

Bronze vessel from the Museum of History in Beijing. Shang dynasty.

The people who wrote in this way could well have depicted a sheep in all its realistic strength, had they chosen to. Some of the most handsome sheep in Chinese art embellish a huge bronze vessel in the Museum of History in Beijing, of the same period as the oracle bone inscriptions. Four powerful sheep heads jut out like figureheads just where the vessel is broadest, the characteristic features recognizable from the pottery fragment and the characters: huge horns, high bridge of the nose, and protruding eyes.

sheep

There are many lively, realistic depictions of both animals and people from the Shang period. The spikiness of the written characters is not due to an inability to describe reality. At the time the characters already had a long history behind them and had begun to move away from the pictorial stage. But until now little has been known about the way that development came about.

beautiful

The character is included in several compound characters, with positive associations. One of them is *beautiful*, consisting of the characters for *sheep* and *large*. On oracle bones and bronzes, the character appears to be a man with ram horns on his head—like those worn by priests and shamans in various sacrificial ceremonies and rites. It could also be that *large* simply refers to the size of the sheep: a large sheep, fat and with plenty of wool, a beautiful sight.

lamb

Sheep and fire together make the character for *lamb*. Is this because its young flesh was preferred for cooking?

geng

If the character for *beautiful* is put together with the one for *lamb*, it makes the name for a meat soup or stew called *geng*, described in many texts as early as 500 B.C. The meat was boiled in a little stock with salt, vinegar, spices, and vegetables, often onion or Chinese cabbage—a kind of Irish stew à la Chinoise—and eaten by everyone from princes down to ordinary people, its popularity lasting for one or two thousand years.

Otherwise, in some strange way the sheep has always taken second place.

Sheep have been sacrificed, even up to our own day—but the ox has always been considered more special as a sacrificial animal.

Sheep have always been eaten, but never with the same delight as pork.

Sheep's (and goat's) wool has always been shorn and the wool is excellent, but the Chinese prefer to wear cotton, hemp, or silk clothes. When Pierre Cardin, the Parisian fashion designer, went to Beijing in the 1970s, he was enraptured by the excellent quality of Chinese cashmere and ordered a delivery, delighted with his coup.

Sheep. Broad-tailed and white, they lived in pens by the houses. They have never roamed free except in the 'outback,' the border provinces far from civilization. China has a long border with Mongolia, a livestock country that has lived almost entirely off mutton and horse milk. The sheep was roasted whole, and then each person carved a slice off with a sharp sheath knife. Nothing could be further from Chinese culinary customs. The old word for *Mongol/Tartar* also means *foolish*, *ruthless*, *mad*. Language has its cruelties.

At inns in Mongolia, mutton is still served just like this, and it is considered all the more delicious the more trembling blobs of white fat there are. As breakfast, it makes an extremely heavy meal, particularly for anyone not used to such a diet since childhood.

In the thirteenth century, the Mongols conquered China and built their capital in Beijing. Throughout the barely one hundred years of their rule, a few primitive dishes based on mutton spread all over northern China. Or was a great deal of mutton eaten there before? Scholars have not really been able to decide on the significance of Mongolian rule in the popularization of mutton in the country.

In any case, considerably more mutton is eaten in the north than in the south. There is one dish, however, that has spread all over the country and out into the world. That is the 'Mongolian pot' or 'Genghis Khan stew,' as it is sometimes called for tourists, a kind of meat stew or fondue. Each guest simmers paper-thin slices of mutton in a light bouillon with spring onion and cabbage, which are then eaten with flat, fried sesame bread and a delicious spicy sauce—a more recent and ennobled *geng*.

Dogs, pigs, and sheep were the first domestic animals in China, as is known from the many bones found in middens around the oldest settlements. Cattle of various kinds came later. During the Shang period, oxen were often used as sacrificial animals. They were buried for magical purposes in large sacrificial pits or beneath the pillars of ancestral temples, and it was on their scapula bones that questions to the spirits of ancestors were written, for advice on important affairs such as war, hunting, and harvesting.

Rulers at the time must have had access to astonishingly large herds, for oracle bone inscriptions often mention several hundred oxen, and indeed, one inscription mentions a thousand oxen being slaughtered in a single ceremony.

Ox meat seems to have been eaten in association with such ceremonies, but it was never everyday food, as the meat of other domestic animals was. Some was served to ancestors, the rest consumed by the king and his court.

The bronze vessel used at sacrificial ceremonies was often decorated with pictures of oxen. These two come from a large three-legged vessel used for cooking sacrificial meat, from the Shang period.

This morose little ox adorns a bronze vessel from the early Zhou period. The curve of the horns almost matches the shape of horns found in some settlements from the late Stone Age, as well as from sculptures of oxen from the Kingdom of Dian in Yunnan from the beginning of the Han dynasty.

One of four ox heads on a huge bronze wine jar from the late Shang dynasty. Shanghai Museum.

The character for **ox** in its oldest forms bears great similarities to depictions of the kind illustrated on the left. They are from the same period and were used on the same occasions, at sacrifices and religious ceremonies.

In the later form of the character, the U shape of the horns has been modified, but the high bridge of the nose and horizontal line are still there. Not for a moment do I believe the traditional explanation that the character shows an ox from above with its head, horns, two forelegs, and tail.

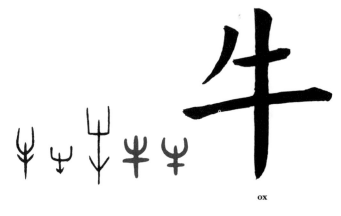

ox

People of the Shang period decorated their homes with animal skulls, a natural reflection of the importance of animals in their lives. Some ethnic minorities in southwestern China still do this. They mount ox heads on their houses as a sign of wealth and power, much as the upper classes in our part of the world used to mount animal heads, and some Indian princes still adorn their rooms with tiger heads. Prehistoric times are not quite so distant as we are apt to think.

But the primary task of the ox was nevertheless in agriculture. Until only a few years ago, the plow was thought not to have been in use in China until 500 B.C., but archaeological finds of triangular stone shares dated 3000 to 2000 B.C. have now, according to the British scholar Francesca Bray, pushed that date back at least a thousand years and there is evidence that ox-drawn plows were in use as early as the Shang dynasty.

Since then, most agricultural labor has been done by oxen and water buffalo—called water oxen in Chinese—just as today. They pull plows, harrows, and simple threshing machines, and agricultural experts say that they offer about as much power as small tractors.

They also have obvious advantages: they do not require oil or spare parts, they run on cheap local products such as maize, stalks, and other coarse fibers, and they produce excellent manure. Today, tractors are used on a large scale, and the days of oxen and buffalo are numbered. It was very different a hundred years ago. When the huge increase in population and innumerable wars made food supplies precarious, the emperor prohibited the slaughter of oxen, and anyone disobeying this ruling was punished with a hundred strokes and had to carry a *kang*, a huge wooden collar, for two months.

In any case, it could hardly have been tempting to disobey this ruling, for a long life before the cart or plow made ox flesh hard and dry and with little culinary promise. Chinese cookbooks today contain few recipes for ox meat.

There were also religious reasons. Taoists regarded the ox as a symbol of spiritual strength, believed that

Lao Zi on his way to paradise.

master Lao Zi had left this world and set off westward toward paradise riding on an ox. For the Buddhists, transmigration of souls was a reality, and in order to escape being eaten themselves, they refrained from eating meat. The ox, particularly the cow, was also a symbol for Earth and therefore taboo.

In the compound character, the character for *ox* is often in one of these two forms.

herdsman ...

Ox and hit – the latter character depicts a hand and a stick – means *herdsman, to herd.*

告

to report ...

Ox and mouth: *to report, notify.*

Karlgren writes that this may possibly refer to an announcement (with sacrifice) made to ancestors in a temple. The explanation seems rather far-fetched, but better than the traditional: "To do with your mouth what an ox does with its horns," i.e., *attack, accuse,* and in a transferred sense, to *inform.*

Whose mouth is calling or giving information? It is possible to imagine the bellowing of oxen as they jostle outside the temple awaiting their fate. Did such a sound 'notify' everyone that a sacrifice was being made?

The character is now included in compound words with such prosaic meanings as *give a lecture, inform.*

Two small jade horses from the grave of Fu Hao in Anyang. Shang dynasty.

The Chinese have never been horsemen in the same way as their neighbors on the steppes to the north and west. Though they have kept horses at least since Neolithic times, in general horses have not been used to pull plows and carts—buffalo and oxen have been used for those purposes. Nor have horses been used as beasts of burden—for that there were donkeys, mules, and camels. As means of transport, there were boats and sedan chairs, and wheelbarrows were considerably more common than horses.

During the first dynasties, the most important job of Chinese horses was to pull the kings' hunting and war chariots. They were buried with their masters so that they could continue serving them in the afterlife. They were used in certain religious ceremonies, but never to the same extent as oxen, and their flesh was not eaten. That taboo appears to have faded with time, but horse meat has never been common in the Chinese diet. Horses are still very rarely seen in China.

Horses of the first dynasties were small. They had big heads with stubby manes and upright ears, short legs, and a long tail with a whisk on the end of it. They are reminiscent of the wild Przewalski horse still found very occasionally in Xinjiang province on the borders of Mongolia, a breed of horses scholars think were tamed sometime during the late Stone Age.

The character for **horse** has gone through a long development before acquiring its present form, and it has changed greatly. When followed step by step from the simple drawing to today's written character, this development seems quite natural.

The little brown horse below is not a character, but a drawing found on what is called a dagger-axe from about 1000 B.C. It shows what the horses of the time looked like, with their large head and short legs.

Here are some oracle bone characters for *horse*. Those on the left are still very realistic pictures of horses as they stand hanging their heavy heads, the mane and tail clearly depicted. In the characters on the right, the horse has already been considerably simplified.

These are bronze characters. Somewhat younger than the oracle bone characters, they are already more stylized. In two, certain details can still be recognized as the muzzle and round eye of the horse. In time, those also vanished. Anyone who has never seen the older forms of the character would find it almost impossible to understand how the strokes of the character came to mean *horse*.

The character below is included in a long inscription on a stone drum, one of the most revered and discussed prehistoric finds in the history of China. The drum was found during the Tang dynasty, together with nine others like it in the Wei Valley just west of

Xi'an. Over the years, many scholars maintained that the inscriptions were made as early as 771 B.C., while others have argued for 422 B.C. The general opinion today is that they were more likely made toward the end of the Zhou dynasty within the area that went under the name of Qin, the state that united China in 221 A.D. The inscriptions celebrate, among other things, the Qin king's hunting expeditions, as well as his horses and chariots, and are written with exceptionally forceful characters. During the time of the first emperor these characters became the prototypes for what is called the Small Seal script, the first standardized form of the Chinese characters. That script developed a few hundred years later into the script still used today as the normal one.

horse

With its ten strokes, the character above was rather lengthy to write, so it began to be simplified privately fairly early. A new character, originating in the handwritten forms, was constructed in the 1950s, and nothing remains of the strong little horse except a few odd strokes that provide little help to the imagination.

马

the simplified character for horse

At the Beijing Zoo, a sorrowful Przewalski horse stands with his heavy head drooping. Perhaps he is dreaming about the wide grasslands up in Xinjiang in northwestern China, where a handful of his relatives still live in freedom, the last descendants of the primeval Chinese horse.

horn

hide, skin

Horn. Above is a broad horn with heavy grooves. The character also has a transferred sense for objects that resemble a horn in form, *promontory*, for instance, and *pointed angle*, and is found in the Chinese name for the Horn of Africa and the Cape of Good Hope.

In the oracle bone character below is an ox and two hands grasping a horn.

Hide, skin is the picture of a flayed hide seen from above, legs splayed, the head and horns at the top. The character also means to *flay*, *take away*, *do again*, and *revolution*—that bitter moment when the ruler lost the mandate from Heaven and was stripped of his power.

cut up, share ...

The hands were later exchanged with the character for *knife* (which I shall come to), a natural change considering the meaning of the character: to *cut up*, *share*, *detach*. The character is included in several compound words having to do with freeing oneself from difficulties and oppression of various kinds—the best known is *The Liberation*, the mainland Chinese name for the 1949 revolution—and it is also included in words with intellectual meanings such as *solve problems*, *arrive at*, *understand*, and *realize*, the result of 'liberating' one's thinking, so to speak.

Carts, Roads, and Boats

The only vehicles in ancient China were the rulers' slender, light hunting and war chariots, their high wheels fixed to an axle on which rested a rectangular basket with space for three men—a driver, an archer, and a warrior with a dagger-axe. During the Shang dynasty, two horses were usually harnessed to the chariot; then later, four or six became common.

The chariots were often buried in the ruler's grave, together with driver and horses, where they lie untouched to this day. Many such chariots were found in Anyang and in different places in Shandong province—which is how we know what they looked like.

One of these chariots is in a simple building alongside the archaeological research station in Anyang. When the door is opened, a strong smell of damp earth strikes the visitor. All wood has long since gone, but before it vanished, it left an impression in the fine-grained soil.

Perhaps *impression* is the wrong word. Over the centuries, the soil became compressed and as hard as the mountains in the loess area. When the woodwork of the chariot and the wickerwork of the basket decayed, they left a hollow space—a firm mold of earth. From this, a cast was made, reproducing the wood and basketwork shapes of the ancient chariot.

The similarities between many of the characters for *chariot*, *cart* and a drawing of the construction of actual ones from the Shang and Zhou periods are amazing—the wheels, the basket, the axle and shaft, even the V-shaped collars over each horse's withers.

War chariot in Anyang, Shang dynasty, and drawing showing the reconstruction of a similar chariot.

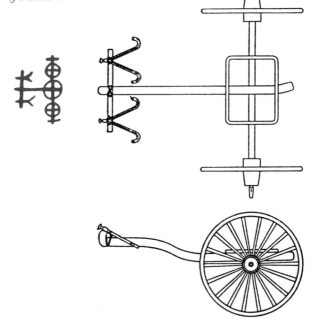

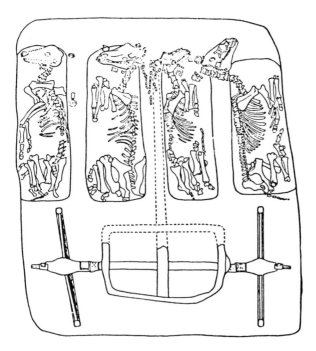

Grave and chariot with four horses from the beginning of the Zhou dynasty.

Bronze character from the beginning of the Zhou Dynasty.

From the reconstruction below, of the four-in-hand it is clear that the two horses in the middle were rigidly harnessed to the shaft of the carriage. The outside horses were able to move considerably more freely, linked to the chariot axle by long reins, with a harness across the horse's shoulders to press against when pulling. Sometimes between 300 A.D. and 500 A.D. a shoulder piece developed out of this, a wooden collar known as a hame, enabling the horse to use all its strength efficiently. A lead rein links each outside horse to the nearest shaft horse.

A reconstruction of what a four-in-hand looked like.

Today, donkeys and mules hauling vegetables, planks, and bricks between the countryside and towns are harnessed along a similar principle. In the middle between the shafts, a few patient donkeys toil away, and in front of them trots a mule on a long rein. At first sight, a vehicle of this kind seems odd, but it has its advantages. The driver steers the cart with the mule, and its brisk pace urges on the donkeys.

The character for **chariot**, **cart** is very common on oracle bones and bronzes. Hunting and fighting were among the most important events in the life of the state, and advice from ancestors on how to act was constantly needed.

Wheels seemed to have been the first to catch the interest of the early creators of script. To inhabitants of quiet Bronze Age villages, the sight of the king's divisions of high-wheeled war chariots, thundering off on one of the great military expeditions against their northern and western enemies, must have been overwhelming.

Inscriptions on oracle bones tell of armies of up to five thousand men during the rule of King Wu Ding in the fourteenth century B.C. On one single occasion, thirty thousand prisoners were taken, then used at sacrificial ceremonies to ancestors, at the king's burial, or when a new palace was being inaugurated—six hundred people on one occasion, eight hundred on another.

There are handsome pictures of chariots speeding off at tremendous speed on some assignment, spokes whirling; and although the three fighting men are not visible, the chariot basket is open at the back so that the men can easily leap in and out when fighting at close quarters began, or when a deer was lying there with an arrow through its chest.

Toward the end of the Zhou period, the crossbow became the leading weapon, and archers gradually disappeared. As the crossbow could only be drawn on firm ground, the war chariot lost its military significance and became an ordinary wagon used to transport people and goods.

chariot, cart

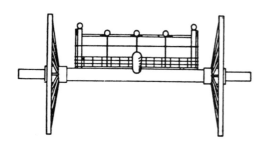

Transport wagons on the Beijing plain during the 1946–1949 civil war.

Wheels had by this time acquired a new and ingenious construction, the spokes no longer level with the rim, but slanted inward, so that the wheel formed a kind of bowl, an important invention that considerably increased the stability of the wheel. This was a big improvement, for when the vehicle of earlier design was overloaded, it could topple over on the uneven roads, and then the wheel often broke.

This improved form of wheel has been common ever since, though it did not come into use in Europe until the sixteenth century, almost two thousand years later. This was true of several other Chinese inventions.

Gradually the cart acquired two shafts instead of one, but since then, nothing much else has happened to it. The carts bowling around the Chinese countryside today would have caused no surprise two thousand years ago, except for the rubber tires that make them so much quieter.

In the long history of China, manpower ('rice-engine') has been the commonest form of power. As late as the 1970s, it was usual to see people harnessed to a plough or cart. The cart seen to the right came along while I was waiting for a bus one day at Beihai in Beijing in 1962.

Haulage teams of this kind are not seen so often today in towns, but out in the country, ordinary carts are often pulled by human power to and from markets and small local factories, noticeably, often by women.

Haulage team at Beihai in Beijing, 1962.

There is an amusing character that means *rumble*, *roar*, consisting of three characters for *cart*, *chariot*, and it is easy to imagine how tiresome the noise of carts must have been for the inhabitants of large trading towns, as well as for those making long journeys across the plains.

rumble, roar

One of the Han emperors was sufficiently annoyed to have the wheels taken off and have his servants carry him. That is how the sedan chair was born, and it lived on until the 1940s. When rich Chinese and foreigners wished to climb Taishan, the sacred mountain, which in itself is no higher than fifteen hundred meters but is precipitous, they usually had themselves carried in sedan chairs. In my old 1924 guidebook, I read that six hours up and three hours down was the calculated time. Sedan chairs were available for three dollars. In comparison, an overnight stay at the hotel in Tai'an at the foot of the mountain was six dollars for a single, ten dollars for a double room.

Rickshaws were used instead on the level ground of the towns, hauled by a running human being. In Chinese these are called manpower-carriages, and the word *rickshaw* is an attempt to produce the southern-Chinese pronunciation for the three characters.

人 力 車   rickshaw

It is said that the rickshaw is a Japanese invention that spread over Asia from the 1870s onward. According to the eminent scholar Joseph Needham, this is not so. He says the rickshaw is a recent descendant of Bronze Age vehicles. There is much to indicate that in the most ancient times, people, not horses, pulled the king's vehicles. A character showing two men harnessed to a vehicle has two meanings, *handcart* and *the emperor's carriage*.

Detail from grave relief. Han dynasty.

handcart, the emperor's carriage

In Hong Kong, tourists enjoy being pulled around by a coolie (the word means *bitter strength*) and in many parts of Asia, as in the old city of Calcutta, the rickshaw is still common as a taxi for the middle classes. The pedicab, (bicycle-rickshaw) in China is also a practical means of transport as long as the traveler is reconciled to seeing the sweat pouring down the back ahead of him while he leans back in comfort.

For the majority of the population of China, over the years, both the rickshaw and other means of transport were of marginal importance. They never traveled, and if they were going anywhere, they went on foot. But in daily life, the wheel played a very important part. For without the wheelbarrow, that ingeniously simple vehicle, they would never have managed their daily lives. It was constructed sometime during the Han period and to this day—in practically the same form—is vital for Chinese peasants and construction workers. In a pinch, it also functions as a means of passenger transport.

The oldest known portrayal of a wheelbarrow comes from a Han dynasty relief dated just before the beginning of our own time. Many similar pictures exist from the following centuries, including some from graves in Sichuan.

What is so ingenious about the Chinese wheelbarrow as it gradually developed is that the weight is placed directly above the large wheel. The barrow can thus carry more and is considerably lighter to handle than if the wheel had been right at the front, as it is on most European wheelbarrows. Five or six people can be transported on such a wheelbarrow without difficulty, for the person pulling it does not carry the load, but concentrates on keeping the barrow balanced and moving ahead.

Dowager Empress Cixi's rickshaw, late nineteeth century.

Han period wheelbarrow, grave relief, and present-day equivalent on village street in Shandong.

Paul Petter and Anna Waldenström. China 1907.

In the spring of 1907, Paul Petter Waldenström, for many years the head of the Swedish Mission Society, and his wife Anna traveled around central China to inspect the activities in which the society had been involved since the 1890s. In his book *To China*, a series of lively travel letters, Waldenström not only describes the life of the missionaries but also everyday life in China and his own and his wife's experiences in this alien environment. A photograph on the endpapers shows the two travelers, each in a rickshaw. They look quite content, but Waldenström writes:

> My wife had made a serious resolution not to be pulled along by people. But already in Hong Kong she was forced to ride. Rickshaws swarmed all around us and we had so far to go, we had to take them. She began in tears. But it couldn't be helped, and out of habit, she soon

thought it rather pleasant, just as I did. Well, as the Chinese were pleased to be allowed to pull us along, why should we be so reluctant to sit there?

Another means of transport is the wheelbarrow, a clumsy affair with one wheel. On each side of the wheel is a screen, so that people can sit on both sides with their back to the screen without being hurt by the wheel... The wheelbarrow is the cheapest means of transport, and in the interior, where there are no carts, it is the only vehicle existing for the transport of people and goods. But one cannot be in a hurry when one travels in this manner. And the Chinese are never in a hurry.

Since the mid-nineteenth century, several new vehicles have been introduced into China, some of them forced meekly to arrange themselves into lesser categories of the primitive cart. The car is called *steam cart*, the train *fire cart*, understandably, in view of the first impressions they must have made—puffing smoke and showering sparks as they chugged through the countryside, the fire from the locomotive glowing. The bicycle, using no power other than the traveler's own, is called a *self-walking cart*.

The character for *cart* also means *machine*. This has nothing to do with foreign, new-fangled machines such as cars and trains, but with the role of the wagon wheel in the Chinese countryside, where cultivation has long been based on irrigation. Farming is hard work, and that is why it was an important step forward when the wagon wheel appeared and could also be used in various types of machines to lift the water out onto the fields. The wheel was also used in mills, bellows, and spinning machines. For this reason, the character for *cart* is included in a large number of names for machines having to do with irrigation or based on the principle of the rotating wheel, as in *mill, spinning machine, lathe,* and *milling.*

Cycle repair workshop in Beijing with the character for cart as a sign. 1985.

All travelers to China via the Trans-Siberian Railway are involved in an hour or two of unusual experiences on the border when the whole train changes wheels at the transition from the wide-tracked Soviet railway line to the narrower-tracked Chinese line. Carriage after carriage is lifted on giant jacks, and new pairs of wheels are rolled in and mounted. Our dependence on standardized systems for communications becomes apparent, as it was, for instance, in the 1870s when Bismarck standardized coinage and weights of German minor states at the time of the unification of Germany.

Linked mills driven by a large waterwheel. From Xu Guangqi's book on agriculture, 1639.

Cart on its way through loess soil ravine near Kaifeng, 1907.

In China, unified weights, measures, and coinage were brought in under the government of the First Emperor of Qin in the third century B.C. when the states of what is today central China were united for the first time. That was also when regulations were brought in for the width of vehicle axles, an important reform, for the ground in the central country of the first emperor consists of soft loess soil, and the wagons and carts made deep tracks. If axle widths varied, the tracks would also vary, and vehicles would have difficulty making their way along the uneven ground.

These reforms were primarily aimed at making imperial control of the country more effective. Good roads meant faster transport of troops, an important matter in the newly established realm. So the emperor had to build a comprehensive system of roads across the country and, via them, throw his troops at the 'barbarians,' as he, like the Greeks, called all those who lived outside the area he controlled. Then he incorporated them into the Kingdom of Qin, and for the first time in history, the area of the Chinese empire approached the borders of today. It is quite fitting that our name for China comes from *Qin*, the name of the realm of the first emperor.

The axle width of carts introduced by the First Emperor of Qin lived on in his own area into the twentieth century. In *Journals from China* (1868–1872), Ferdinand von Richthofen, the German explorer, says that Shaanxi, Shanxi, and large parts of northwestern China had an axle width twenty centimeters wider than that of the eastern provinces. To continue the journey, wheel axles had to be changed quickly at workshops at the 'border,' just as the wheels of today's trains are when they come in from the Soviet Union and Mongolia.

Manzhouli, border station between China and the Soviet Union, 1984.

The character for **road** shows a crossroads, as clearly on oracle bones and bronzes as on a town map. It also means to *walk, act, travel* and *competent*.

The Chinese were indeed competent very early on, when it came to both traveling and roads. The long caravan route between China and the Mediterranean, which von Richthofen named the Silk Road, is familiar, but less well known is the fact that China developed the first road network for everyday use, long before the Persians and Romans, and two thousand years before the Incas, so famous as road builders.

As early as in the Shang period, roads were controlled by a special official, and in the Zhou period, traffic had reached such proportions that regulations were introduced for particularly crowded crossroads and reckless driving was prohibited. Systematic as the Chinese always have been, they are said to have put roads into five different categories: pedestrian roads for people and pack animals, roads for handcarts, roads for single carts, roads on which two carts could pass, and main roads wide enough to take three vehicles abreast.

In the China of today, it is not only the progress of four-wheeled vehicles that needs regulating, although that is beginning to be a problem out in the country where newly prosperous peasants rush around on their tractors with the family on the back. Almost the entire Chinese population rides bicycles, and just along Chang'an, the long east–west main street in Beijing, a hundred thousand cyclists pass every day, many of them astonishingly undisciplined in their attitude to traffic regulations.

We know little about the way transport was arranged in ancient times, but divination records mention extensive flow of natural resources, probably in large part, annual tributes and taxes being delivered to the capital. Trading also went on between the provincial towns. A thousand places of the time are known by name, and many of them are said to be still possible to identify on the map.

Those involved in trading apparently were skillful, for in their day, the traders in Shanxi, one of the main areas of the kingdom of Shang, controlled an important part of all the trade along the Silk Road, and to this day the word *merchant* is the same as *citizen of the Shang state.*

road

Roads were only a minor part of the communication network. A great deal of transport probably was by water. The Shang kingdom was crisscrossed by rivers, and it was along them that life was most vital and bustling.

The rivers in the mountain areas have always been difficult to navigate, the channels rocky, the currents fierce, and water levels varying sharply. For centuries, rafts have been used in these areas, since they glide over the shallows and are not so heavy to haul upstream. Bronze Age rafts were probably made of bamboo, and so are many Chinese rafts to this day. There is hardly a stronger or lighter material than bamboo. Added to that, the hollows in the bamboo stems are divided into segments separated by a thin transverse wall. Should one hollow space be damaged, allowing water to rush in, the bamboo stem is still held up by all the other undamaged hollows, which function as a kind of pontoon or watertight bulkhead.

Rafts of bamboo are almost unsinkable, light, stable, and with a very large capacity. The rafts on the Ya River in Sichuan are famous, often over thirty meters long and carrying seven-ton loads, and yet they lie no more than ten centimeters in the water.

Although there are many other kinds of rafts on Chinese rivers, certain features are common to them all: the bamboo stems are held together by crossbeams, the narrow ends of the bamboo turned forward, the prow upward (bamboo is fairly easy to shape over fire) to enable the raft to glide more easily over the water.

Further down toward the plain, the rivers are more tractable, at least in normal times, but they are never particularly deep, and banks of mud and gravel brought down by the river are always forming. The boats used there are also not much more than ten centimeters deep, lying *on* the water, not *in* it, as ours do.

The boats have a very unusual form, with a flat or slightly rounded bottom and no keel, but a very strong rudder. Prow and stern are straight and slightly curved upward. From the gunwales right down to the bottom, strong cross-partitions divide the boat into different sections, forming the basic framework. This construction does not occur anywhere else in the world.

It is remarkable how close to the earliest characters for **boat** are the characteristic shapes of both rafts and boats today. The straight prow and stern can be seen quite clearly, as can the transverse walls.

Some scholars think the origins of the construction of these boats lie in the bamboo rafts. But there is no real need to go further back than the bamboo itself. If a piece of bamboo is split down its length and put into the water, as Joseph Needham has shown,

it comes close to the prototype for the Chinese boat with its straight prow and stern and its watertight bulkheads.

boat

Boats on one of the canals in Suzhou.

No one knows how long sampans, the small river boats, and junks, the oceangoing craft, have existed as types, but Chinese scholars maintain that they can be traced back to the late Zhou period. They certainly appear to be relics of prehistory, especially the junks. With their clumsy hulls and heavy, dark sails, they resemble strange mothlike insects as they cruise between modern ships of iron and steel in the coastal ports.

Junks in Xiamen Harbor, 1982.

But clumsy is just what they are not. On the contrary, the junk is one of the more efficient craft ever constructed. With its outstanding stability, its swiftness, its great capacity and astonishing ability to cruise and sail against tides and currents and in the shallow river mouths dotted with sandbanks, the junk is unique, marine specialists say. It also exploits the winds better than other crafts.

Boats of this kind are thought to have reached India as early as the year 200 and from 800 until the end of the Middle Ages, the Indian Ocean was as much Chinese as Indian or Arabian. Chinese merchant vessels regularly plied the routes to Southeast Asia, India, Sri Lanka, the Persian Gulf, the Red Sea, and the east coast of Africa. To aid them, from about the year 1100, they had a compass, which, together with the watertight bulkheads, is one of the most important nautical discoveries in history. Both are Chinese.

The Arab world was one of China's largest markets for porcelain and silk, and in that world the Chinese themselves found much-coveted goods such as ivory, pearls, and incense. In the excavations along the African coast from Somalia down to Mozambique, surprisingly large finds of Chinese porcelain and Chinese coins have been made over recent decades, the oldest from the year 600, the majority from 1100 onward.

Not all journeys were for trading purposes. Best known are seven voyages between 1405 and 1433 undertaken by the Chinese eunuch Zheng He on behalf of the emperor. He visited thirty-seven Asian countries to make contact with their rulers and deliver gifts, a kind of diplomatic goodwill voyage, primarily intended to strengthen the prestige of the Chinese emperor and to promote trade. Scientists also traveled with him to collect zoological, anthropological, and cartographical information about the various countries, as well as valuable exotic objects.

The foreign rulers may well have been impressed by this visit of the fleet. The 1405–1407 expedition to the Kingdom of Champa (now Vietnam), Java, Sumatra, Malacca, Sri Lanka, and Calicut in southern India, where the Portuguese first arrived nearly a hundred years later, consisted of over three hundred junks with a total of twenty-seven thousand crewmen. Zheng He's flagship, a flat-bottomed junk, was 147 meters long and 60 meters wide.

The great explorations of the Portuguese and the Spaniards are familiar, and they were indeed great voyages, although their primary aim was not to discover the world beyond their own horizons but to acquire land and raw materials, and to convert the heathens. The history of Portuguese progress along the east coast of Africa is one of ruthlessness and barbarity. When they finally made their way around the Cape of Good Hope in 1498 and with the help of the Arabs reached India, they were confronted with communities that were wealthier, more peaceful, and more orderly than their own, and the boats plying the Indian Ocean were considerably more advanced than the boats the Portuguese were sailing.

The goods and gifts these ships brought with them were laughed at in Asia, and that continued until the early nineteenth century when the English began trading in opium. Then the laughter faded. The Asian countries wanted only gold or silver as payment, the rest they had themselves. The Europeans, to extricate themselves from their inferior position, and with experience of the long religious wars of the sixteenth and seventeenth centuries as a model for the solution of conflicts, took to arms and seized what they wanted by force.

Chinese voyages were of a totally different kind. They were essentially, as Joseph Needham puts it, "an urbane but systematic tour of inspection of the known world." They did indeed trade, and they desired tributes from the rulers. But they never set up trading posts, built any fortresses, made any slave raids, or took any land. They generally showed respect for the faiths of other countries and made sacrifices to the gods of the various countries as a natural courtesy. They brought with them goods no one else had to offer, and what they sought were exotic items that did not exist in China—certain strange animals, remarkable stones, and medicinal plants. They traveled as ambassadors for the mighty Empire of China, so secure in their conviction of the superiority of their civilization that they were able to behave perfectly calmly and politely.

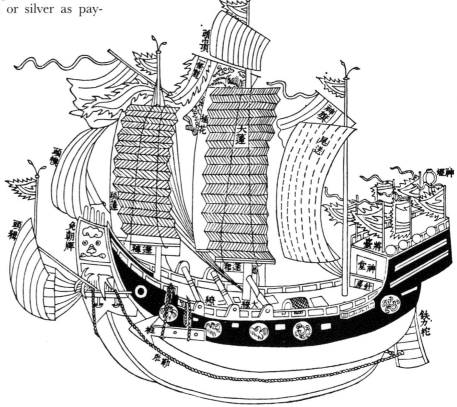

Oceangoing junk. From a Chinese work, 1757.

Boats on their way to the Great Canal. Suzhou.

To this day, a great deal of transport in China is by boat, inland as well. In the Yangzi delta and the great watershed areas of the large rivers that run through the plains, waterways are almost as common as ordinary roads. Sails glide silently past rice and vegetable fields, with no sound other than the wind whistling in the rushes and the water rippling around the steering oar—a surreal experience, at least for Westerners used to traffic fumes and noise as an inevitable part of transport.

In the small town canals, the boats are rowed forward, with a long oar astern, as above, in Suzhou, the most beautiful town I have ever seen, with its camel-hump bridges and walled gardens with pavilions and murky green fish ponds. The canals there are such a lovely sight that Canaletto might have wept with sorrow at wasting his life in Venice.

Just outside Suzhou is the Great Canal, the longest artificial waterway in the world, as remarkable in its conception as the Great Wall. It runs like a giant artery for twelve hundred miles straight through some of the most intensively cultivated areas of the country, connecting north with south. Over twice as long as the Suez Canal, over twenty times as long as the Panama Canal, it starts from Hangzhou, the capital during the Song dynasty, a town almost as beautiful as Suzhou.

上 有 天 堂

In the sky is paradise.

下 有 蘇 杭

On earth are Suzhou and Hangzhou.

The first sections of the canal were built as early as 500 B.C. during the Zhou dynasty, then extended over various periods. In the late thirteenth century, when the Mongols conquered China and moved the capital north to Beijing, nearer their own country, the canal was continued all the way up there. A stream of flat-bottomed sampans and junks carried grain and rice from the rich southern provinces, porcelain from Jingdezhen, silk and sandalwood fans from Suzhou, not to mention the yellow rice wine of Shaoxing.

In the mid-nineteenth century, the canal north of the Yellow River silted up again as a result of the river changing its course, and when the railway then came and took over transport, the canal fell into decay until the 1960s, when it was made navigable again. Several hundred thousand people were put to work carrying the silt away in their small woven baskets and wheelbarrows, then repairing the banks and sluices.

During the 1980s, the canal acquired a new and important role as part of the grandiose and controversial plan to divert some of the waters of the Yangzi northward to the dry plains of Hebei province, where Beijing lies. Fourteen great pumping stations and eleven new sluices are now under construction. Eventually, two-thousand-ton ships will pass between the fields here, and the dry plain will have water year-round.

Boats. Illustration from The Mustard Seed Garden Manual of Painting, *the seventeenth-century pattern book for painters.*

to receive

To receive, endure. Two hands from different directions handling a boat. Or are they, as some scholars have proposed, loading or unloading the goods? The boat is clearly depicted on both oracle bones and bronzes, but during the character reforms brought in by the first emperor, was reduced to the strokes now seen between the hands.

Boat with double-masted Melanesian sprit sail.

Not just boats but rafts as well, and sometimes even wheelbarrows, were equipped with sails to exploit the strong, steady monsoon winds regularly blowing across China.

According to Joseph Needham, the oldest character for **sail** shows a simple, two-masted sprit sail of a type now found only in Melanesia, perhaps a memory of the contacts China had with Southeast Asia and the South Pacific.

To make the character clearer, at an early stage the character for *cloth* was added. With no evidence, this is said to be the picture of a suspended piece of cloth, and that is the form of the character today. The oldest sail, however, to judge from the scripts, was made of bamboo matting, braided straw, or some other cheap material. Sails of cloth represented luxury and abundance.

sail

sail

cloth

There are many handsome characters on bronze vessels from the Shang and Zhou periods showing the craft of the time, hands maneuvering them, and people being transported.

The pictures are quite clear—but what do they mean? No one knows. As far as we can tell, there is no modern form of those particular characters. Many of them appear to be names of families, places, and occupations that had disappeared by the time the characters acquired their definitive form.

Yet they have much to tell us. Several pictures show a man standing in a boat, a carrying pole over his shoulders, with strings of cowrie shells suspended from it. The man with the shells is repeated without the boat in a number of other characters.

Cowrie shells were used as currency during the first dynasties. They are about a centimeter or two long, have a hard, gleaming porcelainlike surface and a wrinkled little 'mouth.' They are found in many places in the Pacific and the Indian Ocean, but along the Chinese coast they are practically unknown today. Whether this was so in early historic times has not been investigated. In comparison with most other shells, they are fairly ordinary, and it is difficult to understand why they were so attractive that they became the first coinage in the world.

Perhaps this was simply because they were hard to come by in inland China, so far from the coast. Perhaps it was because of their similarity to a woman's genitals, which in many parts of the world has given them a magical charge. In Africa, cowrie shells are supposed to bring luck and can protect women, children, horses, and other valuable possessions against the 'evil eye.' They are also linked with fertility, birth, and death, and it seems likely that the prehistoric Chinese had similar associations. Pictures of cowrie shells often decorate Neolithic clay vessels, and real shells have also been found in some graves. During the Shang period they adorned the helmets of foot soldiers, the ruler's horses had their reins and

Clay vessel from the late Stone Age, decorated with painted cowrie shells.

cowrie shell,
expensive, valuable

贝

simplified form

muzzle straps decorated with double rows of cowrie shells, and the dead were often buried with thousands of shells. As an extra safeguard, a few shells were often placed in a dead man's hand or mouth.

The oracle bone characters faithfully reproduce the little shell, the wrinkles around the long mouth reproduced with only a few strokes, but the slanting lines at the top and bottom still there.

The supply of cowrie shells does not always seem to have met the demand, so as early as the Shang period, cowrie shells began to be made out of bronze—faithful copies of real shells—and also out of bone. The latter outwardly resemble real cowrie shells, but the mouth wrinkles less, with only a few horizontal strokes filed across the surface, and those strokes recur in the bronze characters as well as in the form finally given to the character for **cowrie shell**, **expensive**, **valuable**.

Toward the end of the Zhou period, cowrie shells were no longer used as currency in the more developed parts of the country, but they continued to be used in southern and southwestern China. In the account of his journey in the thirteenth century, Marco Polo tells of the inhabitants of what is now Yunnan using cowrie shells brought from India as both currency and adornment. According to other sources, they were in use in the area up to the middle of the seventeenth century.

Two cowrie shells threaded on a string means *to bore through, thread on*. In older literature, it also has the meaning *a string of a thousand coins*.

The basic currency in the Shang period consisted of two strings tied together with ten or twenty cowrie shells on each.

A hand grasping a handsome cowrie shell: *to acquire, get hold of, take*. The character also means *must*—a reminder of the slightly desperate situations most of us experience at some time when for some reason we 'must' try to 'get hold of' some money.

For some reason, the traditional form of the character was expanded with the left part of the character for *road* (which is said to mean *to take a step with the left foot*), but without changing the meaning.

A cowrie shell and two hands: *to acquire, to prepare* and *tool, implement*.

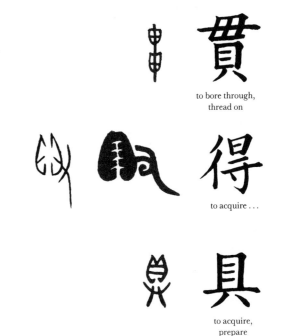

to bore through,
thread on

to acquire . . .

to acquire,
prepare

The character for *cowrie shell* is also included in a large number of characters concerned with trade, value, or wealth. But the shape of coins changed. Bronze coins were made as early as in the second millennium B.C.—naturally in the shape of a cowrie shell—then spade coins and knife coins, small copies of those much-coveted metal tools.

In the state of Qin, round coins began to be made during the third century B.C. They had a square hole in the middle so that they could be threaded onto a string and kept in order, just as had always been done with the cowrie shells. The square shape of the hole may have had something to do with the actual process of producing them, or it was perhaps associated with the Chinese worldview in which the sky is round and the earth square. Scholars' interpretations differ widely.

Round coins prevailed. When the ruler of Qin in 221 B.C. had subjugated his neighboring states and declared himself the first emperor, the coinage was officially accepted all over the realm. Except for minor changes, the Chinese coin remained the same for 2,100 years until the empire fell in 1911.

Over certain periods when the state found it difficult to provide sufficient metal to mint coins, the authorities started reproducing them on pieces of paper made of mulberry bark. The paper was then stamped with their seal, and they vouched that it was worth the same as the coins depicted on it. Even then, however, inflation was high, and paper money lasted for only three years after it had first been issued.

Paper money began to develop in the ninth and tenth centuries B.C., and over the following centuries held a strong position. During the Yuan dynasty, notes were the only legal currency, but the times were occasionally troubled, and the trust between the authorities and the people was not always the best. When the Ming dynasty in the 1450s refused to honor the notes at their coinage value, paper money became worthless and disappeared.

The only valid currency was then the copper coin (threaded on string) or ingots of pure silver, their weight carefully checked by bankers and traders on hand scales before a purchase was completed.

Alongside the native coinage, the so-called Mexican silver dollar played an important role for almost four hundred years. The Chinese wanted payment in silver for their exports of silk and other desirable goods, so the countries with no access to silver themselves had to acquire the silver they needed from elsewhere to be able to trade with China at all. That put Spain in a favorable position.

At the beginning of the sixteenth century, by conquering parts of Central and South America, Spain had gained control of the rich sources of silver in those areas. Somewhat later, the Philippines were also incorporated into the Spanish colonial empire, and direct contact was made between the countries where silver originated and China. Between 1565 and 1820, four hundred million pesos in silver was transported to China, and even in the 1920s the Mexican silver dollar was the most usual means of payment in Beijing, Shanghai, and other large cities.

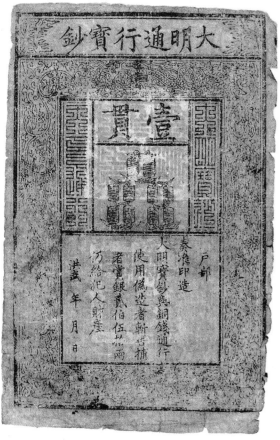

In the middle of this note from the 1350s is a picture of a 'string' of money, consisting of ten units of ten coins in each. The red seal of the emperor vouches for the value of the note. 34 × 22 cm.

So-called tongbao coin issued in 621 A.D.

Farming

Fertile river landscape. "A country as beautiful as brocade and overflowing with rice and fish." Modern painting in classic style.

Look at the painting on the left: from high up on a mountain, we look out over the fertile plain, with boats on a river, a bridge, a cluster of houses, but most of all the square fields of rice and other crops growing in the steaming, humid air.

The fields form a grid, framed as they are by small earthworks. People can walk on the embankments at times when the fields are under water without getting wet, and they can also easily push heavy burdens along them on the one-wheeled barrow, perhaps constructed for precisely that purpose.

The painting was done in 1972, but the landscape is primeval. China has looked like this for thousands of years, a fact underscored by the character for **field**, **pasture**.

field, pasture

On the oracle bones, the character already revealed its definitive form.

But there were other ways of writing it.

One of the oracle bone characters is divided into six fields, like the field on this small grave sculpture from the Han dynasty, which shows five adults and a child working out in the fields. A boat, light as a new moon, is moored in the canal.

During the first dynasties, it was common to sacrifice people and animals and bury them together with the weapons, jewels, and ritual vessels needed by the dead in the afterlife. In the long run, this became very costly. During the Han dynasty, arrangements were rather more practical; instead of real objects, the dead were allowed to take with them small clay figures of everything they needed—like the field and the boat that we just saw. Since the clay figures were simple and cheap to make, the dead were able to take all the more with them.

Nor was there any need now to be limited to real objects small enough to fit in the graves; sculptures of everything needed for a comfortable life could be included: dwelling houses, privies, wells, mills, stoves, grain stores, carts, boats, and the watchtowers required to protect all the servants, acrobats, musicians, horses, dogs, pigs, ducks, and hens living in and around the house.

Many of the grave figures were made from molds and were quick to produce, but many were also made by hand, among them numerous lively and careful depictions. They are probably also, on the whole, correct in their portrayal of what life was like at the time—prototypes for a reality that one day would again come to life.

These grave figures provide a unique opportunity to see everyday life in China as it was lived during the centuries before and after our own civilization began. They also add to our understanding of why the characters look as they do. The characters came about over a thousand years earlier, but developments at the time were not so fast as they are today. Many features typical of the architecture of the Shang period, for instance, are also found in the Han period grave sculptures, and many of these have lived on to this day.

On the walls of graves, mythical events leading to the origins of the particular family buried there were portrayed, as well as the stately processions and ceremonies held in honor of the king and state. Of stone or tile, these reliefs have a great deal to relate about life in the Han period. Several of them will be described in detail later.

It is uncertain whether the character for *field, pasture* is as clear and unambiguous as it first seems. Some scholars maintain that the lines in the character do not indicate embankments and fields at all, but drainage ditches, with which, worthy of Yu the Great, all surplus water was led away. Others think they are canals for artificial irrigation, although there is no evidence that this was practiced as early as the Shang dynasty, when the character first appeared.

Other scholars refer to the fact that the character for *field, pasture* in older texts means *to hunt*, and they say that for developmental reasons this meaning must be the oldest—hunting came before agriculture. What we now see as a field would therefore be an area divided into different hunting grounds, the land being used for cultivation only later.

The character for *field* is included in many compound characters—*boundary*, for instance, which on oracle bones consists of two characters for *field*, sometimes complemented by the character for *bow*.

boundary

The same picture recurs on the bronzes, but with horizontal strokes separating the fields from each other, emphasizing the concept of boundary.

In the late Zhou period, the character was complemented by *earth*, which I shall come to shortly, but the different components are each in themselves explicable. Considering that the character for *field* is also used with the meaning *hunt*, the bow is natural. Hunting often occurred in border areas, far away from habitation, and the main hunting weapon was the bow. When man started cultivating the soil, crops were defended with the help of that same bow; and when the land was measured, the bow was used as a measuring instrument. A bow length was about 1.65 meters.

arable land

The field is also included in the character for *mu*, or *arable land*, the measure used throughout history for land under the plow. The measure has varied; at present it is the equivalent of 0.0667 hectares, or slightly more than the length of two tennis courts. The right-hand part, which has never had any satisfactory explanation, has been removed in the modern character.

The embankments, the level fields, and the straight rows of growing crops all required labor to keep them in order. This appears to have been largely men's work, at least if the character for *man, manly*, consisting of the two characters *field* and *power*, can be believed.

man, manly

For two thousand years, it has been said that the character for **strength**, **force**, **power** shows an upper arm—an ancient symbol—but now that explanation is being questioned. Many newly found characters and new archaeological finds and ethnographical studies indicate that the character is more likely to depict a farm implement. Ethnic minorities such as the Zhuang, Tong, Luoba, and others living in southern China have to this day used primitive farming methods such as burning off of land and ancient implements such as foot plows that disappeared from the central parts of the country long ago.

The foot plow, or tramp plow as it is also called, is made of a curved piece of wood with a crossbar at the bottom, against which the foot is pressed. In that way the plow is driven forward. It does not turn the soil, but provided the farmer is satisfied with making furrows in which to sow the seed, it works well.

Early farmers in the area around the Yellow River worked a light, fine-grained soil in which the clay content is insignificant, and it appears from the oldest characters that they used a plow similar to that used by ethnic minorities to this day.

strength, force
power

Another ancient implement that has also survived among the ethnic minorities is the digging stick. It consists of a straight piece of wood, slightly broader at the bottom, and like the foot plow, equipped with a crossbar to tread on in order to get the stick into the ground.

Digging sticks of this kind are still common among the highland Indians of Peru and Bolivia, where they are called *taclla*.

In some early characters, all from the Shang period, there is a similar implement equipped with two prongs. The crossbar is clearly indicated on several of them. There is also a pair of hands holding the handle, and the foot about to tread down on the crossbar is exaggerated, the big toe splayed out as previously seen on the character for *foot*.

This character is usually translated as **plow**. It might be more correct to call it **digging stick**, since that is what it probably is.

Stone relief from the Han period that shows Shen Nong, the mythical father of Chinese agriculture.
He is using an implement resembling the character for digging stick.

plow, digging stick

earth

The character for **earth** still awaits an explanation. We know what it looked like over various periods, but what it depicts is not clear. Some scholars say it shows a plant breaking up through the ground—a simple and natural picture. Others maintain it is a mound of earth, roughly like the grave mounds still seen around villages everywhere, and the small strokes hovering around some of the oracle bone character would be dust, swirling in the wind.

Karlgren considers the character a clear phallic shape. In that case it would be a picture of an erect penis, which in a transferred sense stands for fertility. Similar concepts are found all over the world, but looking at the shape of the character on the oracle bones, that interpretation does not seem very convincing. The character indeed shows a vertical object. But is that explanation enough?

The bronze characters are equally hard to decipher.

But this character is important. Of the hundred or so compound characters including the character for *earth* in *Grammata Serica Recensa*, 90 percent apply to cultivation or building. There is a handful of purely agricultural terms such as *to sow*, *plow*, *plant*, *earth up* and *drain*, *level out* and *fill in*. But of the others, half of the characters are for all the *embankments*, *walls* and *ditches* necessary for protection against the river waters and for making use of them. There are also two characters meaning *destroy*, *be in ruins*, a reminder of the Sisyphean labors of the peasants in their struggle to survive.

Two people on the earth: to *sit*.

坐   里

sit   village, country

Field and earth together mean *village, country*. During the first dynasties, twenty-five families constituted a village, but the rise in population led to increased pressure on the land, and a village gradually came to contain about a hundred families.

Over the years, families were given increasingly less land to cultivate, which led to more and more intensive use of available arable land. As things are now, according to the Food and Agriculture Organization (FAO), China supports 22 percent of the total population of the world on 7 percent of the arable land. There are only just over a thousand square meters of arable land per person—about the size of a house lot in Sweden. There is as much—or as little—in Bangladesh, a country regarded as disastrously overpopulated. In India, there is two and a half times as much arable land per inhabitant as there is in China. The character for *village, abode* is also used as a measure of length corresponding to *half a kilometer*. Since the script reforms of 1958, the character is also used for *in, inside*.

River waters are the fundamental prerequisite for farming in China. They depend on the rain, which in turn is determined by the climate in Siberia and central Asia.

In winter, when the cold is severe, very high pressure areas form, and icy cold winds are set in motion southward toward the warm Pacific Ocean. These blow in across China via the Gobi Desert and whip up sandstorms, causing a great deal of trouble, but they bring no moisture with them. It is dry in China through most of the winter, particularly in the north. The soil blows, and everything is covered with yellow dust, skin cracks, and people cough and spit.

In May, the weather changes. Siberia and central Asia turn hot, with low barometric pressure and winds that sweep in from the sea in the south and southwest. Saturated with moisture, the rain clouds roll in over China, empty themselves over the fields, and fill the rivers and pools.

In northern China, however, the summer rains are very unpredictable. The less rain an area normally has, the more uncertain the supply—that is the harsh reality. Elsewhere one can be sure the rains really will come, and even the week and day are often known, for the monsoon winds keep to the timetable.

Not so in northern China. One year no rains come, the rivers are empty, the ground is rock hard and cracked. The sun blazes down on the fields, and crops wither away. People search for water in the dry riverbed and try to keep at least a few fields growing.

The next year the rains pour down, the water gushes out of the valleys as if out of a drainpipe, and the rivers overflow. Then it is all suddenly over and people are left with riverbanks collapsed, terraces destroyed, and fields washed away, and a river that now flows in a completely different direction.

In the past, a few years of that sort would devastate whole provinces and drive millions of people to leave their homes and sell their children. They prayed to Heaven and to the mountains where the rain clouds clustered, and they danced rain dances with willow twigs in their hands. There was nothing much else they could do. Since the early 1950s, enormous irrigation installations—canals, dams, and reservoirs—have been constructed all over the country. With their help, floods and droughts may even out between the years. But if no rain comes, there is nothing to even out, nothing more to do.

The character for **rain** shows a cloud, from which hang the coveted drops of rain, suspended beneath the sky. If only it would fall over the dry fields. Just enough, not too much.

But such good fortune is rare. In northern China, over 90 percent of the rain falls in a short summer period and often comes in violent downpours together with thunder, a result of the unstable layers of temperature in the area.

In an apparently endless network of canals, water is carried out to the fields on the plain. The fields are surrounded by embankments where it is possible to walk without getting wet.

雷

thunder, storm

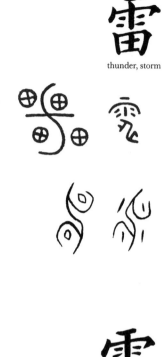

電

lightning, electricity

电

simplified character for
lightning, electricity

The character for *thunder, storm* shows a rain cloud above a field, a clear enough description of the situation. But reverting back to the character's original form, the picture becomes rather more complicated. In the first standardized form of the third century B.C., there is not one but three fields under the rain cloud, and in the bronze character there are four. Moreover, only very occasionally is there a character for *rain* at all. Instead, a long, forceful line is racing away between the fields.

That line dominates as well in the oracle bone characters, surrounded by thin strokes or circles, probably depicting lightning as it streaks across the sky, and the explosions of light and sound that then surround it.

A similar image can be found in the bronze character for *lightning, electricity*. The lower part of that character originally meant *to stretch out, repeat, extend, again and again*, in some texts also *awe-inspiring*. According to old explanations, this shows a flash of lightning. If that interpretation is correct, the disparate meanings of the character at once make sense. What could be more awe-inspiring than repeated flashes of lightning across the sky?

Thunderstorms, however, were not simply regarded as awe-inspiring, especially thunderstorms in the wrong season. Like floods, earthquakes, and other natural disasters, they were seen as signs that Heaven was displeased with the way the ruler or emperor was running the country. People thought they predicted important political upheavals such as rebellion, civil war, and especially the fall of the ruling dynasty.

The great earthquake in Tangshan in 1976, according to official sources, killed 242,000 people (according to unofficial figures, more than double that number) and made 800,000 people homeless. This was at once seen by traditional Chinese as a sign that a change of regime was at hand. And indeed, within a month, Mao Zedong was dead and in less than two years Deng Xiaoping was resolutely taking the country into developments directly contrary to what had prevailed for a generation. It is not surprising that superstitious ideas are cemented when two such remarkable events occur in succession.

The oldest character for *suddenly* consists of rain and three birds. The combination may seem less bewildering if one tries to picture the scene: clouds over a plain, trees, grasslands, and birds calling to each other. Suddenly, unexpectedly, rain starts falling, and a flock of birds rises in a cloud of whirring wings and moves away across the plain. Of the three birds, only one remains in today's character, but the picture is still a vivid one, at least for me.

suddenly

Cloud. The lower part of the character is the original one—two long, resting cloud banks with a loose cloud slowly curling up into a rising current of air.

To emphasize the meaning of the character, as early as in the Zhou period it was complemented with *rain*, and in that form the character appeared for the next two thousand years and more. When characters were simplified in the 1950s, the old cloud picture came back into favor again. Anyone from ancient China would understand it.

'Cloud and rain' is an old poetic expression for *intercourse*. In the past, without rain there was no harvest in northern China. Rain and fertility were connected: the cloudburst that fertilizes the earth.

云 雨

The expression is said to go back to a legend about a prince of Chu, or perhaps it was the king himself. Anyhow, one of these gentlemen was visiting the mountain of Wu. He left his hunting companions,

云

cloud

雲

cloud

grew tired, and lay down to sleep. In his dream, the Queen of the Mountain came to him, and they spent the night together. When she rose to leave him, he asked her who she was and where he could meet her again. "In the morning, I am in the clouds; in the evening, in the rain," she replied, fay as she was, then vanished.

In the character for **air**, **vapor**, **gas** we see not just two but three clouds extended against the sky. The character is usually said to show 'vapors' of damp air rising from the ground and forming clouds. With northern China's summer skies in mind, that explanation makes sense. From the beginning of June and for the next two or three months, the daytime sky is covered with a smooth, white mist that eliminates all shadows and totally exhausts the eyes with its persistent glare. But in the morning and evening, the moisture condenses into clouds, hovering high up in thin parallel layers. According to another explanation, the character shows a picture of the 'vapors' rising out of a saucepan of boiling grain. The character is included in many compound words for *weather* and *atmosphere*, and in Chinese philosophy and medicine it plays an extremely important role, standing as it does for the vital, powerful **regulating principle** pouring through the universe, regulating and balancing the lives of people and nature, their psyche and spirit.

air, vapor, gas
regulating principle

In the enclosed field here on the riverbed, peasants are planting rice, and bundles of delicate leaves can be seen sticking out of the water. The picture is from the famous 1639 work by Xu Guangqi on agricultural techniques.

The book appeared during the last chaotic years of the Ming dynasty, when peasants were worse off than ever before, the country's economy was in total disarray, and peasant rebellions and natural disasters followed one after another. Some areas in southern China were so overpopulated that the slightest trouble with the harvest meant famine, and further north, whole provinces were deserted and uncultivated, in particular from lack of water.

With his book—a summary of about three hundred works on agriculture published in China up to that day—Xu tried to show that with better implements, better varieties of cereal, new crops such as sweet potato, corn, and cotton, and a more efficient use of the acreage, it would be possible to increase production considerably. And should crop failure strike despite everything, all was not lost. About a third of the book is taken up with an illustrated flora of four hundred edible wild plants, on which it is possible to survive. Many of them taste bitter, but that could be improved with a brief decoction. Then all one has to do is sizzle them in a little oil and add salt or soy sauce.

With the picture of the enclosed field, Xu tried to show how practical it is to use odd patches of ground such as part of a broad riverbed during the time of year when the water is only a trickle in the channel. If embankments are built sufficiently high and are stable, the river water finds it difficult to get in, he writes. Even if that should happen, it is easy to pedal it out again with the help of a chain pump. Today's peasants would agree, for that is just how they also use the fertile, sandy soil of the riverbeds. But they no longer pedal away the water, for they have had diesel-driven pumps for some years now.

From Xu Guangqi's book on agricultural techniques, 1639.

grass

Early peasants had neither chain pumps nor diesel pumps, but they would recognize the crops. Look at this character meaning **grass**, **plant**, **herb**.

On the oracle bones, the plant often stands alone—a few thin straws sticking out of the earth—but toward the end of the Zhou period they started doubling it. That form soon developed into something most resembling two small crosses, and they in their turn were simplified even further in the 1950s.

The character is included in a large number of compound ones having to do with vegetation. In *Grammata Serica Recensa*, about a quarter of the characters are names of different *grasses*, *reeds*, and *rushes used for mats*, *brushes*, *baskets*, and *roofing*. Another quarter concern actual cultivation: *to take on a new field*, *plant*, *sow*, *cover over*, *weed*, *mow*. The rest of the characters are names of vegetables such as *spring onion*, *garlic* and *leguminous plants*, and flowers such as *mallow*, *artemisia*, *chrysanthemum*, and a number of *water plants* and *climbers*. There are also characters for *make ready* and *inspect*. Weary farmers can be seen leaning on their mattocks, gazing at the results of their day's labor in the fields where the *growing crop* is thriving.

growing crop . . .

Three plants together form the general term for *herbs*, *plants*.

herbs, plants

The simplified form now introduced has ancient ancestors.

A hand and two plants: *to cut grass*; *hay*, *fodder*.

to cut grass; hay, fodder

The character for *run away*, *in a hurry* does not look very active today, but on the bronzes one can see a man running at top speed across the grass, flailing his arms.

to run away, in a hurry

On the picture of the vegetable field, plants of various kinds are thriving in the shelter of fencing and high trees. Some vegetables have already grown quite high, others are still just sprouts, and the river flows past beside them. It is easy to sense heavy, warm fragrances rising from the field.

In the bronze characters for vegetable field, the field and the crop inside the fencing can be seen quite clearly, but without them it would be difficult to understand the character.

There may be no place in the world where land is exploited as efficiently as in China. Every little patch of earth, even if only a few square meters, is used for cultivation. The plants are looked after with the same care given our city gardens, each one given individual attention, mulched, weeded, tied, and pruned, each one allotted its daily scoop of liquid manure, not a drop more than necessary.

The soil is often used for several different crops at the same time. While the cotton bushes are growing, a quick crop of Chinese cabbage or spring onions is grown between the rows. Between millet plants, beans are grown and are ready before the millet requires all the soil for itself.

In northern China, the nights during the six winter months are cold and frosts are frequent, but vegetables are still grown. A tunnel vault of thin strips of bamboo is stretched across the vegetable plot. Every evening, rush matting is rolled out over it, and every morning, when the sun has warmed up the air, it is rolled back again. If the north wind is particularly severe, the rush matting is rolled only halfway back, giving the plants an effective wind shield and at the same time letting them have some of the sun they need. With the aid of such simple 'greenhouses,' beets, various kinds of white beets, spinach, and

From Xu Guangqi's book on agricultural techniques.

vegetable field

Wheelbarrows of charcoal and vegetables, Anyang.

many other green vegetables are grown all winter. A high proportion of the thousands of tons of vegetables a metropolis such as Beijing requires is produced this way, and the method of growing is said to have been used for over a thousand years.

Along with cereals, vegetables have been the most important ingredient in the Chinese diet for a very long time, particularly Chinese cabbage, spring onions, beans, and quick-growing green vegetables of various kinds. Their rich vitamin and mineral content, iron most of all, and the limited use of animal fats in cooking have meant that for a long time the Chinese diet has been healthier and more nutritious than that of most other peoples of the world. Experts say that even the poor of China ate better than the rich in Europe or America before deep-freeze techniques and air transport came in, at least in those years when there were no crop failures or floods.

An investigation into the Chinese diet in 1930 shows that peasants then got almost 90 percent of their calories from different kinds of cereals, 1 percent from animal products, and the rest from root and green vegetables. Generally speaking, that still applies. Although there are great differences between different regions, between town and countryside, and between different classes of society, cereals and vegetables are still the basics of the Chinese diet.

A change is now slowly taking place. The consumption of cereals is declining while meat consumption increases. Pork, the most favored meat, accounts for most of the increase. So far, however, vegetables are still a staple in the diet.

This character means **well**. In ancient times it was also used for *a system of fields belonging to one village*. The character has always looked the same, but what is it a picture of? There have been many attempts at explanation.

A well with a roof and fence, it says in *Shuowen*, published in 121, because that is what wells looked like at the time, and this can also occasionally be seen in the Han period grave sculptures.

It is the well curb, says Bernhard Karlgren and other scholars, yet archaeological finds made in the twentieth century do not support that theory. They reveal unambiguously that ancient wells were round. The best-preserved one stems from the Zhou period, and it was even lined with half-meter-high rings of pottery. For a long time, no well was found that had a form which could explain the appearance of the character.

But in 1985, results were published of excavations begun outside the town of Gaocheng a decade earlier. Among many remarkable finds were two wells, the earliest found in China to date. They are carbon 14 dated to about 1300 B.C. and so are contemporary with the oracle bones.

In my opinion, their construction may explain the character for *well*. Like all other wells already found, the wells in Gaocheng are round, but—and this is what is exciting—right at the bottom lies a square frame made of logs placed in four or five layers on top of each other. Together, their shape agrees entirely with that of the character for *well*.

But why this wooden frame?

Consider what it is like to dig a hole in a sandy shore. At first the sand is dry and fine, but the deeper one digs, the wetter the sand. In Falsterbo in southern Sweden, where I spent childhood summers, we used to build sandcastles on the shore and surround them with moats and walls. But the problem was always that the deeper we dug, the more water seeped in

well

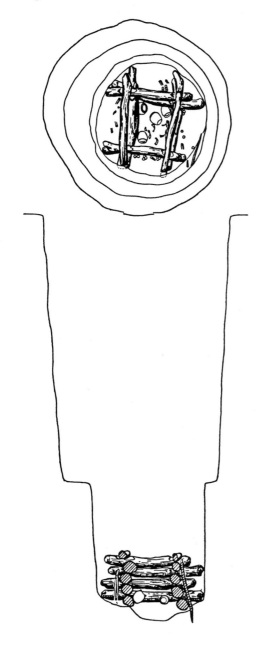

Drawing of a reconstruction of a well from 1300 B.C.
A wooden frame at the bottom.

from below. Eventually the moats swiftly silted up again and the castle collapsed.

Early Chinese well diggers struggled with a similar problem when digging in the soft loess soil. When they at last got so deep that the subsoil water started trickling through, the walls began to be undermined. To counteract this, a frame of logs was placed at the bottom of the well so that the water could continue to surge in without doing major damage.

Once above the groundwater level, the problem was over. Still water does not make the soil collapse. The nearer the surface—the eye of the well—the wider and more open the well could be. The wells in Gaocheng were formed in this way—as can be seen clearly from the reconstruction drawings.

The image of the logs in the depths of the well was one that everyone saw. Fetching water was part of the endless, inescapable daily labor. Leaning against the edge of the well, each person must wait for the vessel to fill slowly with water. Insects scuttle about, breaking the surface of the water, and down in the very depths a square of wood can be seen. A brief moment of quiet, then the surface clears again, and it is time to heave on the rope and haul up the vessel.

One of the wells is nearly three meters in diameter and five meters deep. At the bottom was found not only the wooden frame but also the remains of about twenty clay vessels that had once been dropped by people fetching water from the well. There were also some small bone articles such as spoons and hairpins, easily dropped when leaning too far over the edge.

On some of the bronze characters for *well* there is a dot in the middle. What does that mean? Long before the Gaocheng wells were found, some Chinese scholars maintained that it was the bucket that brings the water up from the well. Considering the new finds, that explanation seems convincing.

But if one draws a frame around the character for *well*, it looks very much like several of the ancient characters for *field*.

Does the character show a field with the well strategically placed in the middle? Some scholars have put forward that idea, referring to the old scripts.

In the works of the philosopher Mencius (374–289) there is a description of a system for dividing up land used at the beginning of the Zhou period. Every piece of land was carefully measured and divided into nine different sections. It was looked after by eight families, each of whom had the right to cultivate one field for their own needs, and together they looked after the middle field on behalf of the ruler, as a kind of tax. When the population increased, new land was cultivated and divided in the same way.

This way of dividing up land is usually called the well-field system because of the similarity to the character for *well*.

It is mentioned in songs and poems as early as 800 B.C., but whether it really existed and functioned as Mencius describes it is one of the most-discussed questions in Chinese history. Was it simply an ideal, or was it a real system for the division of land?

It has been said that, to Mencius, it was probably a utopian dream of a just society in which everyone had his living secured. Then he tried to convince his contemporaries that the utopia had once been reality and could be so again.

In Xu Guangqi's seventeenth-century book on agricultural techniques, the system is presented like this: eight *men*, in the middle the ruler's *public* field.

When Mencius described the system in the fourth century B.C., land was already beginning to pass into private hands. Iron plows and improved use of manure brought with them an increase in the productivity of agriculture, so it was important for the rulers to try to reduce the 'private' land and increase the 'public.' Increased resources could, for instance, be used to build irrigation installations and roads, which would further increase the ruler's power and the opportunity to control the country and perhaps expand it.

But many people fared badly when the power of the rulers increased. In a conversation with Prince Hui of Lian, Mencius said:

> Your dogs and swine eat the food of men, and you do not know to make any restrictive arrangements. There are people dying from famine on the roads and you do not know to issue the stores of your granaries for them. When people die, you say: "It is not owing to me; it is owing to the year." In what does this differ from stabbing a man and killing him, and then saying—"It was not I; it was the weapon?" Let Your Majesty cease to lay

the blame on the year, and instantly from all the empire the people will come to you.

Translation: James Legge, The Four Books, Book I, Chapter 3:5.

To Mencius, a ruler's first duty is to ensure the welfare of his people. If he could not do that, then the people had a right to rebel. Mencius said people must have sufficient resources for a tolerable life; otherwise, society is threatened with disintegration, and then there is no limit to the crimes people may commit. The basic prerequisite for a good society is therefore a just division of land. Everyone must also be given education. Man is by nature good. All he needs is enlightenment.

Developments were not on Mencius' side, at least not at first. In the year 221, the King of Qin subjugated the various kingdoms around the Yellow River and proclaimed himself the first emperor. He started an outstanding expansion of canals and roads, and his people were mobilized to increase his own power as well as that of the Kingdom of Qin.

But the idea of a just division of land lived on, and various reformers continued over the centuries to refer to Mencius when they wished to criticize misrule or justify their own land reforms. Everyone who has read Mao Zedong has heard Mencius speaking to them over the millennia without knowing it:

"It is right to rebel."

"The welfare of the masses is the most important."

Perhaps the ancient well-field system Mencius put forward as an ideal for his own day has also lived on as a memory in the northern Chinese lands. The fields on the plain, particularly in areas once ruled by the Shang and Zhou dynasties, today have an exceptionally clear form. All over the area they have astonishingly unified dimensions and are in regular blocks in a strictly north–south direction.

Referring to three hundred very detailed topographical maps recently made available, Frank Leeming, an English scholar, maintains that this way of dividing up land goes back to what is called the equal-field system that functioned from the fifth century until the middle of the Tang dynasty.

This was a system that had not arisen overnight. The plain was already densely populated, and any new system had to start out from the already existing organization; and that organization was, if one believes the facts Leeming puts forward, the old 'mythical' well-field system that Mencius once described but that was so often dismissed as utopian.

In the 1930s, the plots of land in the Wei Valley around Xianyang, once the capital of the Kingdom of Qin, were generally 332 meters wide. If Leeming is right, they consist of three well-fields in width. The same measure also applied to Shanxi, Henan, and Shandong, and it is also interesting that historical works from the Han period state that the side of the square field each family was allocated during the period in which the well-field system functioned was exactly that length.

But the population kept on increasing. Each family had increasingly smaller plots to cultivate, and land that had previously supported a hundred families gradually had to support five hundred. To manage this, Leeming says, they took away the east–west divisions and retained only the north–south ones. When the authorities wished to regulate land occupation, they had a definite width to start from, and then all they had to do was divide up whatever land there was into as many divisions as necessary.

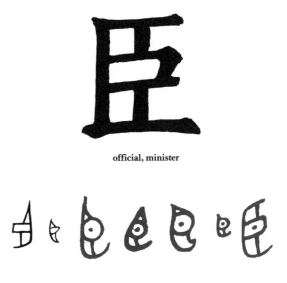

official, minister

During all of Chinese history, income from agriculture has been the mainstay of public income, the state's income. That picture did not change until recent decades, but even today peasants hand over a set quantity of grain (or other raw materials) to the state.

During the first dynasties, the ruler had more direct control over production, and his special officials personally supervised the work in the fields. The character for **official**, **minister** shows a large watching eye—Big Brother is watching you.

But even a minister is subordinate to the ruler, is his *servant*. "A bowing eye," Bernhard Karlgren always used to say, "the eye—*pars pro toto*—a picture of a person bowing low." And he reminded us that the Latin word *minister* also means *servant*.

Field. Irrigation canals. Wells. For 90 percent of our life on earth, human beings have managed without such sophistications. Hunters and gatherers took for themselves everything nature in her abundance had to offer, not least all the wild plants.

For the people who lived in central and eastern China before the dawn of history, life must have been better than in many other places. From a botanical point of view, the area is one of the richest on earth. An unusually large proportion of the plants survived the Tertiary period and the various ice ages. While there are only about five thousand different original plant species in Europe, there are over thirty thousand in China.

This botanical wealth probably had something to do with the early arrival of agriculture in China. Just when or how people became domiciled and started growing their food, is not yet known in detail. It is said to have happened some seven to eight thousand years ago, according to the latest archaeological finds and carbon 14 datings.

There are legends that attempt to explain this great transitional process. A key person in several of them is the mythical emperor Shen Nong, said to have ruled around 2800 B.C. Under his reign the population increased so rapidly that it was difficult for people to survive as gatherers and hunters. Shen Nong constructed a plow, and when millet rained down from the skies, he collected the seed and taught his people how to plow and cultivate the soil.

While myths cannot be regarded as historical fact, they often contain some symbolic truth, a memory of earlier events, before the advent of writing. Who knows, with the speed at which the early history of China is now being unrolled, perhaps Shen Nong may one day be shown to have plowed the yellow soil of the Wei Valley.

It is significant, though, that Shen Nong is not only said to be the father of Chinese agriculture but also the father of the Chinese pharmaceutical arts. He is thought to have been able to differentiate between hundreds of varieties of grass and herbs, and he knew which illnesses they could cure.

A list of 365 medicinal plants supposedly drawn up by Shen Nong (before the arrival of writing?) was the basis of the first known book on herbal medicine. It was published in the second century A.D. and has had hundreds of successors. Most significant of them, Li Shizhen's impressive work *Ben cao gang mu* (*The Great Pharmacopoeia*) was published for the first time in the years 1552 to 1578, but it has been reprinted over and over again, the latest edition in 1981. The book contains an account of 1,893 important substances, most of them herbs, and 8,160 recipes. It is still a textbook for medical students.

For a barbarian from Europe, where important knowledge of herbs has largely been lost, at least to ordinary people, it is a strange experience to walk around a Chinese herb garden. I shall never forget the medicinal plantings around the People's Liberation Army's hospital in Shijiazhuang in northern China. The head doctor, in a cap with a red star on it—this was 1976—showed us around and explained the use of some of the seven hundred plants. These included lovage, mint, fennel, lemon balm, and mustard, which in our part of the world are regarded simply as flavorings, although we know they are ancient medicinal plants. But there were also quantities of ordinary garden plants I have in my own garden at home, such as forsythia, honeysuckle, aconite, harebell, mullein, yarrow, and even weeds such as plantain on which I am constantly waging war.

"I have some of them in my garden," I said with astonishment.

"I would be surprised," she said in a rather superior tone. "These are medicinal plants. We never have them in a garden."

But when I was back home in Sweden, I sat down with my flora and the Chinese dictionary of medicinal plants I had bought in Shanghai and went through my garden, and it was just as I had said. A large number of our garden plants and weeds are medicinal plants in China.

But would I dare use pulverized seed capsules of forsythia when I have a high temperature?

Should I start gathering coltsfoot to save for the winter when the children start coughing?

A friend of mine is a pharmacist. He laughed.

"I don't know anything about forsythia," he said. "But coltsfoot is often included in cough mixtures. The kind I gave you last time is called Coltsfoot Mixture, didn't you notice?"

In China, knowledge of herbs survives and children at school have to learn the most important medicinal herbs in the area where they live. I saw this in the autumn of 1978, when I spent a few weeks on the farthest tip of the Shandong Peninsula in a little fishing village called Dayudao. One day Class 6b was to go up the mountain behind the village to pick three different sorts of medicinal plants. I went with them. One of the village doctors also participated and joined the picnic when work was over.

Afterward, the children handed the plants over to the barefoot doctors in the cottage hospital, where they were cleaned and dried. These three particular plants inhibit inflammation and are included in medicines for various bronchial and lung ailments. One of them was also a remedy for diarrhea.

Later, I went to several large Chinese hospitals where since the mid-1960s they have been doing research on the chemical composition of traditional herbs and comparing their effects with those of Western preparations. Many herbal medicines have been shown to function equally well, if more slowly, and side effects are few.

In cases of serious illness, doctors use a combination of Chinese herbal medicines and Western drugs such as penicillin, streptomycin, and so on, purchased from a drug factory in Shijiazhuang, not far from the hospital with its medicinal garden. The factory is one of the largest in Asia and supplies not only China but several other neighboring countries with high-class penicillin at a cheap price. The Chinese are a practical people.

Over the millennia, China's plant world has, of course, primarily functioned not as a pharmacy, but as a larder. In bad years, as when drought and floods have destroyed crops and the fields are bare, people have returned to being gatherers, their knowledge of wild plants a necessity of life.

The character for *herb, plant* has already been described, and here is another small plant, perhaps one of the many edible seed-bearing grasses found in northern and northwestern China, or one of the many wild vegetables. The straight stroke at the bottom is said to indicate the earth. The character comes from an oracle bone.

fresh, raw ...

Many bronze characters are almost identical with this oracle bone character. Others have another pair of leaves, but over the years these have been reduced to just one straight stroke.

Then we are not far from the standard form of the character for **fresh** (as in vegetables), **raw**, **produce**, **feed**, **live**, **life**.

This character means a type of **onion** and stands primarily for the slightly garlic-flavored flowering Chinese chives *Allium odorum* or *Allium tuberosum*, a very common ingredient in northern Chinese cooking.

The character does not appear in either the oracle bones or the bronzes, despite the fact that this type of onion has clearly been part of the Chinese diet since time immemorial and is mentioned in the *Book of Songs*, the oldest parts of which go back to the early Zhou period around 1000 B.C.

The *Book of Songs*, the oldest collection of poems in China, is a gold mine of information about everyday life in ancient China. The first section consists of lyrical love poems and popular songs, full of concrete descriptions of changes in nature and the various tasks of the year.

The golden oriole sings, and girls take baskets to pick mulberry leaves for the silkworms. Mallow and beans are boiled, hemp put to soak, cherries eaten, dates dried, millet harvested to make wine and rope. When autumn comes and house crickets are hibernating under the bed, the rats are smoked out and the north window sealed to keep out the icy wind.

Industrious scholars have gone through the poems and found forty-six different vegetables mentioned. Most are considered to have been found growing wild in the area where the songs came from, several of them even originating there.

Many of these vegetables are still part of the characteristic ingredients of Chinese cooking: bamboo shoots, Chinese cabbage, spring onion, garlic, water chestnuts, lotus root, radishes, turnips, and various kinds of beans—a well–filled larder.

It is strange that not one of them appears on the oracle bones and only a few on the bronzes. One explanation could be that the character has still not been identified among the thousands of existing inscriptions. The most likely explanation is different. Vegetables were not cultivated, but grew wild everywhere and in such quantities that there was no need to worry about them. The beans and radishes the women picked along the river—just as women in the Mediterranean pick dandelion leaves for salad—were really not worthy of a consultation with Heaven.

The millet harvest, hunting, military campaigns, the king's toothache, and the child the king's wife was expecting—Would it be a son?—those were questions of a quite different and serious category. On them depended the power and continued existence of the state.

This character is usually translated as **grain**. To the European ear, the word is apt to mean wheat, rye, oats, and barley. To the Chinese, it is millet and rice.

The character really ought to be translated as **millet**, for in areas where the character was created, millet has for several thousand years been the dominant grain, as is clear from archaeological excavations. To this day, it has been the basis of the northern Chinese diet.

There are a great many characters for *millet*, often appearing on both oracle bones and bronzes, and alluding to the various kinds of millet collected or grown, primarily *Setaria italica* and *Panicum miliaceum*. The wealth of varieties soon led to a certain terminological confusion that has continued to this day, but the character usually translated as *grain* seems to be the oldest. Botanists maintain that it alludes to the varieties of wild *Setaria* millet that grew all over northern China during the Neolithic period, and still does. It is in fact one of the most troublesome weeds there. But millet is a nourishing cereal. It contains as much protein as wheat, but a much higher content of phosphorus, magnesium, potassium, and several important B-vitamins.

The characters are clear. The heavy spadix, like a tassel, characteristic of *Setaria* millet, appears quite clearly.

grain, cereal, millet

Setaria italica, foxtail.

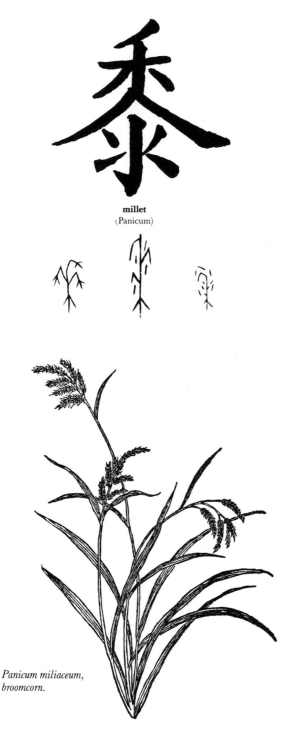

millet
(Panicum)

Panicum miliaceum,
broomcorn.

Panicum miliaceum, the other ordinary variety of millet grown continuously in China since Neolithic times, has no firm spadix of seeds, but loose panicles.

The oracle bone character is very close to the wild variety. Do all those small strokes show seeds on their way to the ground?

That is not impossible. The primitive varieties of millet matured very unevenly, so they had to be harvested panicle by panicle. If not taken in time, the tiny seeds fall to the ground, where they are lost.

Millet was made into soup or porridge, and wine was made from it; and at ceremonies to ancestors, millet was included in the food and wine offered to the spirits of the dead. During the Song dynasty (960–1279), a ceremony still existed in which a special kind of millet was offered. Although it was no longer used as food, it was grown for these important offerings to ancestors, for that was the porridge and wine they had been familiar with during their time on earth.

To Europe, millet is largely something fed to cage birds—those long, firm stems with yellowish-brown seeds hung up for budgerigars. But in northern China, as in Africa, millet is a much-favored cereal. In the countryside around the Yellow River, it is still common to start or end the day with a bowl of millet soup, just as was done at the dawn of history. Small salt shrimp, and pickled cabbage with red peppers to chew, are eaten with it, or as *xià fàn,* as the Chinese say, 'to get the food down.'

Over the centuries, an almost inconceivable variety of millet has appeared. On the Shandong Peninsula alone, where millet is of no particular importance, two thousand different kinds of millet were collected in the 1950s and 1960s, and they turned out to belong to six hundred totally different varieties.

There are varieties of millet for practically every kind of soil and climate. It survives drought and heat surprisingly well, but it also flourishes in marshy ground and on thin-soiled mountain slopes. In difficult cultivation areas such as Shanxi and Shaanxi, the peasants often plant two different varieties at once in the hopes that at least one will survive to harvest.

Millet and mouth together make the character for *peace, harmony*, that good moment of the day when all have been fed and peace descends on the household. Or perhaps it is the harmony felt when it is known that a full supply has been laid up for the winter.

The character for *fragrant, aromatic* is now written with the character for *millet* and something that resembles *sun*. But 'the sun' was from the beginning the character for *sweet* and, as we have seen, shows a mouth, perhaps with something delicious on the tongue.

Were those who made the character thinking of the millet porridge slowly simmering on the hearth and filling the room with its sweetness? Or perhaps of the aromatic wine they brewed from the millet? Who knows, but it does seem to have been good. The character often appears in names for particular dishes, sweets, and in commercial products such as toothpaste, where it is important for the name to have pleasant associations. It is also found in the first part of the name of the city of Hong Kong—'Fragrant Harbor.'

Detail of a gravestone (stele) from the Han dynasty. Below, a peasant plowing with two oxen. Above, a row of millet. Shaanxi Provincial Museum, Xi'an.

peace, harmony

fragrant, aromatic

year

Millet is included in the character for *year*. At first this meant *harvest, to harvest*. The character consists of man and millet, which is hard to see today, but the old characters are clear enough.

Millet and fire form the character for *autumn*. The connection seems obvious; the glowing mature crop is one of the signs of early autumn.

autumn

Or has the combination to do with the way the stubble was burned after the harvest, a simple method of fertilizing still used, also making the field easier to work for the next sowing?

It is tempting to speculate about the origins when the character is so clear, but unfortunately the part now written as *fire* appears in several different guises in the oldest characters, and what it stands for remains uncertain.

The character for *autumn* is also used in the sense of *harvest, harvest time*. According to the old calendar, autumn began on the seventh day of the eighth month—that was when harvesting began and autumn had come. As soon as the millet harvest was over, the winter wheat was sown. Never a moment's pause for the Chinese earth. But with natural manure of various kinds—waste from animals and humans, mud from pools and canals—the soil has supported harvests over the millennia, as long as there was enough water.

A hand grasping a millet plant means *a handful* in the oldest texts. Later the character became a *cubic measure for grain*, then finally acquired the meaning *grasp, hold, maintain*. It is included in expressions for political power and control.

This is again a reminder that peasants' taxes over a very long period of Chinese history were delivered in the form of grain. Agriculture was the basis of the state's economic life. He who had a 'grasp' on the grain also had political power in the land.

to grasp . . .

The character for **wheat** shows a straggling plant. On the oracle bones and bronzes, it was already close to its definitive form, and the first standardization simply tidied up the strokes. Then nothing happened for two thousand years.

In 1958 a simplified form was introduced, the advantage being that four strokes were saved every time *wheat* was written. At the same time, something was lost—the contact with generations who lived and wrote in China over 3,500 years. Is this worth four saved strokes?

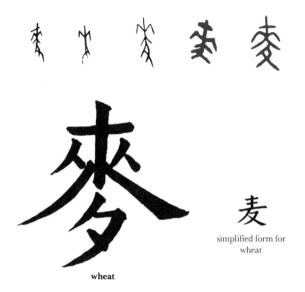

wheat

simplified form for wheat

small wheat = wheat   large wheat = barley

Wheat is generally called *small wheat* in contrast to barley, which is called *large wheat*. Both are winter crops and thus can alternate perfectly with the traditional Chinese grains of millet and rice, grown during the six months of summer. This soon led to very effective crop rotation, to the great advantage of both the soil and people's livelihood.

For a long time, wheat led an obscure existence in China, grown there since prehistoric days—brought in from the Middle East—but for several thousand years regarded as poor-man's food and inferior to millet and rice. It was considered to be coarse, "but can still your hunger," says, rather wearily, the author of a book from the Han period. When famine in 194 A.D. drove prices sky high, the price of millet rose to two and half times that of wheat, although millet was in better supply. Millet was what people wanted, not wheat. But at about the same period, more effective stone mills began to be used, which could grind the wheat into a fine flour. This led to a change in diet, for one could do more than simply boil the wheat, and many other delicious dishes could be made.

At that time, the empire of the Han dynasty had reached so far west that it touched on the eastern Roman Empire's outermost provinces. Trade along the Silk Road between east and west experienced its first flowering. Perhaps it was somewhere up on the high plateaus in the old original wheatlands that the Chinese learned to mix wheatflour, and water into a thin dough and make *baozi* and *jiaozi*, those delicious little dumplings filled with meat and spring onion that Western cookbooks in their ethnocentricity are apt to call 'Peking ravioli.'

Perhaps the Chinese had learned these skills from the caravan drovers of central Asia when they came down from the deserts to the thickly populated areas of China and cooked their homeland's wild food in their camps inside the city gates. Those small dumplings are made all over Asia, either round or half-moon shaped, but nowhere so delicious or in such a rich variety as in China. With them, a whole new chapter in the culinary history of China was introduced.

A spicy filling of pork and spring onion is the most common. But in the coastal provinces, the dumplings are often filled with prawns or crab, and one of the most delicious kinds with a mixture of both pork and prawns. The dumplings are eaten steamed or simmered, in soup or dipped in a sauce of soy and vinegar, perhaps with a pinch of sugar. If there are any left over, they are fried lightly the next day, and then taste almost better.

There are sweet varieties too, filled with a sticky mixture of red beans and dates.

Some restaurants specialize in these dumplings. In northern China it is a common social custom to meet and make jiaozi together. This is not difficult, but rather time-consuming, so it makes an ideal prelude to a good dinner in the company of good friends. There is time to grow really hungry.

Fried spring rolls, rather like small crêpes, are also made with a thin wheat dough, as is thin, flat sesame bread with spring onions and pepper. And *mantou*—steamed, unsweetened, and unsalted wheat buns, slightly larger than Ping-Pong balls, eaten instead of rice. At first they taste bland to those used to crusty bread, but their mildness seems the perfect complement to the various flavors and spices of other dishes.

Most wheat flour goes to make noodles, which in northern China play the same role as rice in the south—the staple dish of the meal. Noodles come in many forms and flavors and are cooked in several ways. They can be boiled in thin chicken soup, with celery and mushrooms, or served with pork, kidneys, and mushrooms. Or . . . the variations are endless.

Because of their length, noodles have become one of the many symbols for a long life, the most sought-after prize in old China. When Mao Zedong was eighty, I happened to be in Shanghai, where noodles are not so common as further north. I asked a friend if there were to be any official festivities. No, the birthday wasn't to be celebrated at all. Chairman Mao had declined all tributes. "But," she giggled, "we're going to have noodles for dinner to celebrate."

In the past, whole-grain flour was always used for all these dishes, but Western white flour has now begun to come in. It is considered grand, and the dishes are white and beautiful, but they lose both taste and nourishment.

Our type of bread never used to be found in China, except among people with foreign connections. But now it is coming in, recently as small loaves sold from stalls in town parks to hungry strollers walking between temples and rock gardens. They are eaten hungrily, just as people in the West eat potato chips or popcorn. There are hamburger stands in several places now, with the usual buns, on license from the United States.

The prestige of wheat rises day by day, although it is considerably more labor-intensive than millet. It is also more susceptible to insects and various diseases, the crop yield is smaller per acre, and it is more difficult to store. Wheat also requires a lot more manure—the Chinese have little manure, as they have never kept livestock on the scale that Western farmers have. But artificial fertilizers and pesticides are now widely used. Wheat will no doubt soon take over.

The character for **rice** is annoyingly clear. But what are we seeing?

A picture, says Bernhard Karlgren, laconically.

Of course, but what of?

Grain, says *Shuowen*. Millet.

Four piles of rice on a threshing place, says another book of characters, referring to the form the character has on certain oracle bones.

Hardly, say those who have in mind other oracle bone characters. Naturally, it is the ear of the rice plant. The horizontal line is the stem. The dots are the rice grains.

Quite wrong, say others. The horizontal line is the flail used for threshing.

None of these many explanations seems really convincing, and yet the character does seem to portray something concrete. It is always translated as *rice*, but also means *seed*, which fits well. The great encyclopedia *Cihai* says: "Seed of a variety of grain or other plant. When the husk is removed, it is white."

大米   小米
large seed = rice   small seed = millet

In everyday speech, rice is often called *large seed*. In contrast, millet is called *small seed*, and it is certainly small, no more than a couple of millimeters. In a transferred sense, the character for *rice* is also used for small, seedlike objects such as peanuts and the dried shrimp that embellish the dishes of coastal regions. 'Shrimp-seed,' these are called. Dried, they are not much larger than a grain of rice. But what a taste!

Most Westerners think the basic food in all of China is rice, but that is not so. Ever since Neolithic times, there have been two quite clearly defined agricultural traditions in China, mainly millet and wheat north, and rice south of the Yangzi.

The explanation is that millet and wheat survive the fierce climate of northern China and its uneven supply of water, while rice is considerably more demanding and requires both warmth and plenty of water. Except for the mountain variety, rice grows only on land regularly flooded either by tidal waters or by irrigation, environments found only in the valleys, marshes, and deltas of southern China.

Rice has been found in early settlements around the Yellow River, and given that the climate of the time was both warmer and wetter, rice growing was probably possible. But was rice really grown there? The question is controversial and opinions sharply divided.

Reference books usually tell us that rice came from India, where it has been known since 3000 B.C. But now that so many new finds have been made in China, that theory perhaps no longer holds. In any case, there is carbon 14 evidence that peasants in the marshes of the Yangzi delta grew great quantities of rice as early as 5000 B.C. When the Neolithic village of Hemudu was excavated in 1976, remains of rice were found everywhere. The layers in the garbage heaps full of grain, husks, straw, and leaves are half a meter high. That this rice was actually cultivated is demonstrated by the huge number of mattocks and other agricultural implements found.

These finds of rice are at present the oldest known in the world. Even if rice did not come from China—as certain scholars still maintain—it is known that people in the villages around the Yangzi grew rice at as early a time as people are known to have grown millet around the Yellow River.

Rice is actually a marsh grass, but one of the existing seven thousand varieties of rice has adapted to growing conditions away from marshlands. Mountain rice survives with less water and in poorer soil, and it ripens considerably faster than other rice. Although it does not taste as good, it is hardy and reliable.

This variety was introduced to the province of Fujian on the south coast in 1027 in association with a long drought. People were starving, and the emperor, not receiving the grain deliveries he had reckoned on, distributed seed for mountain rice from the Kingdom of Champa (now Vietnam) as an experiment to stimulate production.

The new variety spread quickly all over south China. Before that time, it had been grown only in the valleys where the supply of water was certain. New possibilities then opened up, and only two centuries later the mountainous area south of the Yangzi was transformed into terraces, and on these rising green ladders, fields of rice gleamed in the humid air. This scene has become one of the classic images of China.

Ordinary rice needed 150 days to mature after being planted; the Champa rice needed only 50 to 100. Over the years, peasants experimented with new local varieties suited to the soils, rainfall, and prevailing temperatures, and in the mid-nineteenth century the days to maturity were down to 30. By then at least two crops a year were grown—even three furthest south—and often a vegetable crop in between.

The food-supply situation changed radically for the better. If one crop failed, there was another chance later in the year. The population increased rapidly. The center of the country moved south; and although, with brief exceptions, China has been ruled from Beijing since the thirteenth century, the economic center of the country has been in the south ever since. Rice has played an important part in that change.

Luffa cylindrica,
loofah cucumber.

Cucumis melo,
honey melon.

melon, pumpkin, gourd

Western botanical texts tell us that pumpkins, gourds, cucumbers, and melons were introduced into China sometime just before our calendar begins, but that is no longer correct. Archaeological finds of the 1970s show that they have existed there far longer.

Seeds of gourds have been found in the Neolithic village of Hemudu, which takes us, in only a few brisk steps, back five thousand years before the beginning of our calendar. Many of the clay vessels found in the village are also clearly in the shape of gourds, and other finds show that the melon existed in Shaanxi about 700 B.C., and it is mentioned in the *Book of Songs* of the same period. At the excavations in Qianshanyang, carbon 14 dated to 2750 B.C., remains of melons were also found, though that dating is still controversial.

In any event, plants of the cucumber family (*Cucurbitaceae*) such as melons have clearly existed in China for a very long time. As further evidence, one of them can be seen quite clearly in the bronze characters.

On the other hand, they do not appear in the oracle bones. However fresh and thirst-quenching it may be on hot summer days, the melon was perhaps not of such central significance for the future of the state that it was necessary to consult Heaven as to its sowing and harvesting.

The character for **melon, pumpkin, gourd** is included in the name for all the many plants of the *Cucurbitaceae* family.

Melons, pumpkins, and cucumbers are among the favorite vegetables and fruits in China. Everyone grows melons around the house, if at all possible. Many of my friends in Beijing had the whole front of their houses and a large portion of the roof covered with these plants in the summer. The large, strong leaves create a green shade over the edge of the roof and fill the rooms with a gentle green glow—restful to the eye in the strong summer light. And the melons—when tapped, resounded like muffled bells.

Wine and Jars

Wine has been produced in China since time immemorial. The poems of the Zhou period and the oracle bone inscriptions seethe with inviting descriptions of various kinds of wine, and wine played a very important part in society during the Shang period, most of all in association with sacrificial feasts in honor of ancestors. Few characters recur so often in the inscriptions as the character for *wine, spirits*.

The Chinese language does not differentiate between the low alcoholic content of wine and the high content of spirits. The same term is used for all intoxicating drinks, regardless of their strength, and wine was the only alcoholic drink for several thousand years. The raw materials were millet, wild berries, and fruit such as plums and peaches, later also wheat and rice. The method of distilling wine to produce a drink with a higher alcohol content was probably not developed until around 1000 A.D.

Not much is known about how the wine was produced, but among Shang period finds in the trading town of Gaocheng, made known in 1985, is a fifteen-meter-long building that apparently was some kind of factory for the production of wine, the oldest of its kind yet found. In one jar was a grayish-white dried-up mass the archaeologists think is the remains of yeast. Many clay jars in various forms were also found. Some are broad, open vessels, well suited to the first stages of the production process when the grain or the fruit is fermenting. Others are narrow and tall. Most of them are decorated with cord and basket impressions, horizontal lines and bands.

These jars and their predecessors are prototypes for the character for *wine, spirits*.

Neolithic clay vessel.

wine

According to *Mathews' Chinese-English dictionary*, this character means **wine** *made of newly ripe millet in the eighth month*, the wording going back to *Shuowen*. The character is also used to mean 5–7 P.M. It shows a picture of a wine jar.

wine, spirits

The general concept of *wine, spirits*—'the joy and misfortune of mankind,' as *Shuowen* expresses it—started out with the picture of the wine jar, then was complemented with the character for *water, liquid*. When wine began to be distilled around 1000 A.D. the new varieties of spirits were simply included under the old character.

Wine made with grapes has never been common in China. It did appear as early as during the Tang dynasty, but even today it is unusual except in certain wine-producing areas in the deserts of the west and in circles with foreign contacts. The fermented mare's milk of the Mongols—however refreshing it might be—has never caught on outside Mongolia.

The best–known Chinese wine is the yellow rice wine, particularly from Shaoxing. Amber-colored, mild, drunk hot from doll-sized porcelain cups, it goes straight into the bloodstream. This wine has been made for 2,300 years and is famous far beyond the country's borders.

Without rice wine, a feast is not a feast, and it is indispensable at weddings and funerals, as it has always been at important ceremonies in China. In the past, when a daughter was born, a jar of wine was buried and not dug up until she was to be married off. Then guests and ancestors were offered the wine, and the bride took the rest with her as a valuable gift for her new home.

There are, however, stronger drinks that can really be called spirits, with an alcohol content around 65 percent, sometimes flavored with medicinal plants, fruit, or more exotic additions such as snake and lizard. The fiercest of them are distilled twelve times.

The character for *to fill in, fullness (abundance)* has nothing to do with mouth and field, although that is what it seems made up of now. As with the character for *wine*, it represents a long-necked vessel seen from the side. On the oracle bones, the character is also used for *happiness, prosperity*. This transference of meaning is understandable, for the vessel was the most important form of storage, not just for wine but also for dry goods such as grain. When filled, they gave rise to such a feeling of prosperity and confidence in the future.

to fill in, fullness (abundance)

Neolithic clay vessels.

To separate the two meanings, the original picture of the wine vessel was soon complemented with the character for 'prophecy, omen' when *happiness, prosperity* was intended. That character had to do with auspicious and inauspicious signs and unusual natural events that might influence people's lives. It is sometimes said to be a picture of an altar on which offerings were made. Would the harvest be good? The stores filled? Would happiness and prosperity reign, or were disasters impending?

happiness, prosperity

Chinese of later periods came to the conclusion that there were five kinds of happiness: long life, wealth, health, virtue, and a natural death. During the Chinese New Year, street doors were decorated with inscriptions on red paper requesting that in the coming year the home would have its share of the five blessings. That custom has largely disappeared today, and any inscriptions have more to do with tradition than religious belief or superstition.

The character for *happiness, prosperity* also appears as decoration on furniture and cloth, as it does on porcelain, sometimes including the five visions of happiness in the form of five bats—a rebus of the kind the Chinese love. The character for *bat* is pronounced exactly like the character for *happiness, prosperity*.

jug, pot, jar

This character means **jug**, **pot**, **jar**. During the first dynasties it indicated the jugs used for hot wine. Now it is the generic word for *vessel for hot drinks* and is included in words such as *teapot* and *water jar*.

The character often occurs on the oracle bones, showing jugs with tall, heavy bodies standing sturdily on a plinth. Some of them have an elegant neck with small handles to make them easier to move. This was probably very necessary, for the actual jugs were often half a meter high and scalding hot when in use.

There are some problems not yet solved surrounding these jugs and their relation to the character. One concerns the lid. All the images of vessels on the oracle bones and bronzes have lids, but the vessels themselves preserved from the same period very often lack them. This earthenware vessel from the Zhou period is not really representative of the jugs preserved, yet the character must have originated from similar vessels.

Lids have an irritating habit of breaking, particularly if they are pottery. But many of these were bronze vessels, and if they usually had lids—as the character maintains—then numerous examples of lids ought reasonably to have been found among all the vessels excavated. But that is not the case. Lids on these jugs did not appear to become common until long into the Zhou period, some hundreds of years after the character was created, and those lids that have been found are flat.

Wine vessel in hard-fired earthenware from the Zhou period.

There are, however, other wine vessels from the Shang period with a form closely agreeing with the oldest characters which always have lids with a clearly marked knob on top. The only real difference is the handle. Occasionally, similar handles are also found on the wine jug of the type already shown.

The wine vessel below is half a meter high and dated to the middle of the Shang period, its surface covered with a forceful pattern of wild animal masks and swirling clouds. The jug was found in 1982 when a factory was being built close to the city wall in Zhengzhou, one of the leading towns of the Shang period. Is this not fundamentally the same jug seen reproduced in the early character for *jug, pot*?

But instead it is called

Bronze wine vessel from the Shang period. Zhengzhou.

Why is it that vessels, which from a typological viewpoint, are very similar and have the same function, have different names, while other vessels that are obviously different, have the same name?

As far as I know, the question has not been properly studied. Perhaps it is all a mistake on the part of the scholars in the Song period classifying bronze vessels without sufficient archaeological material. In itself, the answer is not of decisive importance, but it is annoying not to know. One day someone will be sure to find out, perhaps with the aid of new archaeological finds constantly pouring in.

Sometime after I had written this, I was sitting reading the *Book of Songs* and got stuck at a line of a poem. When I went to Bernhard Karlgren's translation, I found that the character for *jug* at the beginning of the Zhou period, when the poem was written, meant *gourd*.

Could it be that the gourd, with its practical shape, was the first 'jug,' and that the name had then become the term for the jugs later made in pottery and bronze?

There are many equivalents to this in all other languages. Plumbers, whose name comes from the fact that they once worked with lead (as in 'plumb'), now are likely to work in plastic, and many words describing an article once made of quite a different material are still in use today. We call our steel knives and forks silverware. And the output of car engines is still measured in horsepower.

Characters evolved in a similar way. When they acquired their form, the model was the object then in use. While the objects—as time went by—gradually changed appearance, the characters maintained their original form. Their meaning had already been accepted.

Since the days when people first settled down, gourds have been used as storage vessels, as rhythm and string instruments, as flutes, scoops, cages for crickets, and so on, and most of all as water jugs. Although the gourd is a plant in the cucumber family, its shell is hard and impervious. Shapes vary—some have long, slender necks, others hourglass waists. When ripe, their curvaceous bodies are filled with thousands of seeds. Over the centuries, gourds have played a prominent role in creation myths in southern and eastern Asia—according to one legend, the first people originated from a gourd—and they often appear in rites concerned with fertility, at weddings, for instance.

Neolithic clay vessels in the shape of gourds. Xi'an.

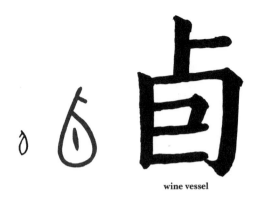

wine vessel

But what about this character, which also means **wine vessel** and has never been explained? It's the same thing—a picture of a gourd. A glance at the early character makes it clear as daylight.

Perhaps a name for vessels that was used in some particular way or came from a particular place? Or a dialect word?

A great many different vessels must have been used for fetching water. There is one type with a very unusual construction that can perhaps be explained by geographical conditions along the Yellow River. Banpo and other settlements were situated on high banks along the river. Every time water was fetched, the problem was how to get the jar, suspended on its long rope, to tip over and start taking in water. Anyone who has tried to draw up water from a boat knows how difficult it is. These jugs solve the problem. The handles for the rope are low down on the body, making the jars top-heavy, so that the opening dips under the surface and starts taking in water. When full, they straighten up of their own accord, and all one has to do is to haul them up.

Clay vessels of various kinds are still very common in the countryside, where so much food has to be stored by individual families after harvest. Corn hangs in bunches from the kitchen ceiling, grain is stored in huge vessels in the main house, and soy sauce, spicy and dark, is kept as always in meter-high lidded jars out in the yard. Many jars from the first dynasties, even from Neolithic times, would not seem out of place today in any country kitchen in China.

The character for **food**, **eat** shows a sturdy vessel with feet and lid. According to *Shuowen*, the lower part alone means *fragrance of grain, feast*—a rather clear hint.

The character also means *eclipse* and is included in the words *eclipse of the sun* and *eclipse of the moon*. I found this confusing until I once witnessed an eclipse of the sun and saw how clear the metaphor is—the moon actually 'eats up' the sun.

food, eat

*Burial urns in the Banpo Museum, from about 4000 B.C., used for
small children, who used to be buried just outside the house. This is still
done in many places, including the Wei Valley, where Banpo is situated.
The very similar vessels on the previous page are six thousand years
younger.*

Two very similar characters in their oldest forms show a lid over a mouth, an *opening*, an *entrance*:

To shut, **to close**, **to fit together**. The character is found in many composite words concerning collaboration—in business, singing, and life.

Together, **alike**, **same**. This is found in the word *comrade*—a friend who is easy *to agree with*, as he thinks like you.

It would take too long to describe all the characters originating from the early vessels, but there is one more that I am much attracted to, one of the oldest, which has a construction apparently unknown in other parts of the world. It is called *li*.

This vessel stands firmly on three hollow legs, each tapered at the ends, as in the jugs used for water and wine. One theory is that this type of vessel arose from three of the pointed vessels, fastened together so that they would stand more firmly on the hearth. That may be. Under any circumstances, the vessel is clearly superior to most in terms of fuel economy, because the surface in contact with the fire is so much larger. The food cooks more quickly, and less fuel is used.

Also interesting is the shape of these 'legs.' On closer look, they resemble female breasts, round and full. On many of them the nipple is even drawn out, as though after nursing an infant. The older the vessel, the clearer the resemblance to a breast.

This similarity is no matter of chance. In the earliest communities, women held a central position. While the men came and went, often away hunting for long periods, the women were responsible for continuity. They not only gave birth and fed the children but also cooked the food for the whole clan. They saw to the crops and gathered plants, and scholars say they made the clay vessels needed for everyday life as well as those used for the various ceremonies and rites performed for the powers of Heaven and Earth.

Sitting with the soft clay in their hands, often with a child at the breast, in a way it is quite natural that the women potters gave their vessels the shape of a breast, that unique container of life and delight. Was there perhaps some strong sense of self-esteem in those women, some joy and satisfaction in their own bodies, in their ability to give birth to and feed so many? Would they otherwise have made such vessels?

They could just as well be the udders of cows or ewes, I hear someone objecting irritably.

I don't think so. Milk has never been part of the Chinese diet, nor have butter and cheese. No one milked. Milk was for calves and lambs, just as women's milk was for children. And for better or worse, human beings see themselves as the center of the world. As women's milk gave nourishment to their children, so the food in the three-legged—or three-breasted—vessels was nourishment for the rest of the family—a benign form of magic that is easy to understand.

This vessel shape occurred as early as in the Neolithic period and during the Shang dynasty achieved its complete development. During that period it was the most common food vessel and in some excavations constitutes three-quarters of all the pots found. They are nearly all sooty and black and bear traces of long use.

After that the shape went into rapid decline and by the beginning of our time had disappeared completely.

Circumstances had changed, for as hunting lost its importance and agriculture developed, the men increasingly took over production and began to dominate village life. During the Shang period, women's position was apparently still strong. King Wu Ding, who reigned about 1300 B.C., made his three wives 'feudal lords' over an area each. Other wives functioned as officials, even as leaders of military expeditions against neighboring states. But as leaders of life in the villages, the women were on their way out.

When the potter's wheel—practical, but heavy to work—became common, the men took over pottery production as well, as evident from fingerprints in the clay. Food vessels changed shape, and the clear connection with a woman's breast vanished, leaving nothing but hollow 'legs.'

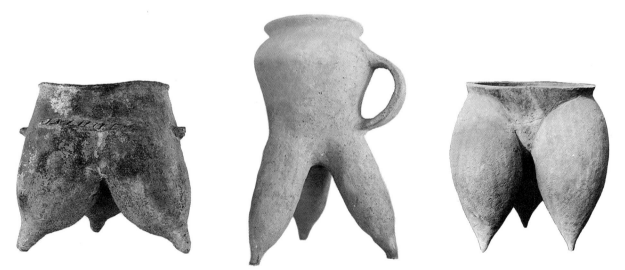

The li *vessel, with its three hollow legs in the shape of breasts, is unique to China. The two examples on the left are from the Neolithic period, the one on the right from Xia, China's first dynasty.*

What about the character for **li**? It remains as clear as can be.

In itself, it must have been one of the most practical vessels ever constructed, but that is not all. Another vessel with a perforated base was placed above the opening, and the heat from the food cooking in the swelling legs rose, steaming the vegetables and other food above—all in one pot. Nothing was lost, neither heat nor flavor.

This combination of two vessels is usually described as a 'rice cooker' or 'steam cooker,' suggesting that the rice was cooked in the upper part, as is sometimes done in the West.

But this is not very likely. First, rice was not particularly common in the regions where vessels of this kind were usually found—considerably more millet was eaten there. Besides, both rice and millet grains are so small that they would immediately fall through the fairly large holes in the perforated base. The staple diet in Chinese households during Neolithic times as well as the first dynasties was a thick soup of grain and meat requiring lengthy cooking to acquire the right consistency. So it seems much more likely that this soup simmered down in the round legs, while vegetables and other more lightly cooked ingredients were steamed in the upper part. That interpretation is also supported by an inscription on a vessel stating that it is intended for use on journeys 'when soup of rice and millet is cooked.'

li

Neolithic steam cooker from Buzhaozhai near Yangshao.

During the Shang dynasty, more ordinary vessels began to be cast in bronze for use when making offerings to ancestors, and *li* also became one of the most common vessels in bronze. Another vessel, which like the *li* had ancestors in the late Stone Age, is called *ding*. At first it was round and had three legs, then later became square and was given another leg. It grew in size and importance. From being a cooking vessel for ordinary people, it became a revered sacrificial vessel and a symbol of the power of the state. The largest round *ding* yet found weighs 226 kilos. The largest square *ding* weighs 875 kilos and is 133 centimeters high—about the height of a Shetland pony.

The story about Da Yu and the great flood that is said to have led to the origin of the Xia dynasty in 2205 B.C. is relevant here. After years and years of hard work, when Da Yu at last managed to divert the waters to the sea and people could start cultivating the soil, he divided the land into nine provinces and had nine great bronze vessels cast, each a symbol of one province. Together, 'The Nine Ding' represented the power of the king and the state. Just over four hundred years later, the Xia dynasty lost the mandate of Heaven, and the nine valuable bronze vessels were handed over to the victorious Shang dynasty, which in its turn, according to historical documents, handed them on to Zhou when that day had come.

The deep, heavy Shang cauldron at the top of this page, with its massive pointed legs, is a good example of the earliest bronze ding vessels. They are simple and austere. So are the bronze characters of the same period.

Gradually, the vessel acquired a somewhat lighter appearance, and the legs were decorated with protruding flanges, 'embroidery' in bronze. This development continued.

On many of the Zhou vessels, the legs seem to be the most important feature, often shaped like birds or other animals in profile.

From these vessels came the character for **ding**.

ding

During the Neolithic period, clay vessels were fired in a kiln set in a hollow in the ground. A fire was lit a short way away and at a slightly lower level to create a draught, and through a covered passageway the heat was directed to a perforated 'shelf' on which the pots to be fired were placed. Above the kiln was a roof, presumably rebuilt after each firing.

The eastern part of Banpo village functioned as a center for the making of clay vessels. Six different kilns have been found there. Inside one were vessels for some reason never fired.

At the museum by the dwelling place, the kilns are explained with the aid of this picture. In the front, the unfired vessels are being carried up and put into place—flames already rising through the holes—and firing is already in progress in the background. The inset is a cross-section of the kiln.

pottery, earthenware

Kilns of this kind were in use late into the Shang period, perhaps also during the Zhou period, and it seems possible that this kind of kiln can be seen in the character for **pottery, earthenware**. In that case, the lower part of the character would stand for the hollow or the opening into which the clay vessels to be fired were placed. But what the pictures represent is not quite clear, especially in the bronze characters.

Reconstruction of a kiln. Banpo Museum.

Hemp and Silk

Above we see two bundles of **hemp**, a plant with very long, thin, and tough fibers, made into rope and nets for at least six thousand years in China. To get at the fiber, the outer layer of the stalk must be removed. The hemp is either left hanging on drying racks out in the field after the harvest and exposed to wind and rain, or the stalks are soaked to break them down more quickly, then hung up to dry. This process may be reflected in the character.

There are several kinds of hemp. Some grow two or three meters high, the kind from which rope, nets, and sacks are still made. They become coarse and hard. Perhaps that is why the character for hemp also means **coarse**, **raw**, **uneven**.

The low-growing kind is well known in the West under its Latin name, *Cannabis*. It has been used in China as a sedative for various illnesses since long before the beginning of history, though not, as far as we can tell, as a general intoxicant. I don't know why.

This plant thrives in the dry, sunny high steppes, but also likes rich soil, so has long followed people. The nomadic tribes in the north—most of all, their shamans—used it as a drug when they went into a trance, and they probably once brought it west to central Asia and India, where it has long been used as a narcotic.

The character for *hemp* is included in words such as *anesthetic*, *numb*, and *apathetic* and in the names of several important medicinal plants such as *Gastrodia elata*, the 'heavenly hemp,' a well-known remedy for rheumatism, and *Ephedra sinica*, *ephedrine*, which is used all over the world for bronchitis and asthma. None of these plants belongs to the same family as hemp, but as hemp became generally used very early on as a medicinal plant, other plants with similar effects were gathered under that name.

the heavenly hemp

The character is also included in several composite words for diseases entailing severe skin changes, such as *measles*, *leprosy*, or *smallpox*.

pox-scarred person

Perhaps the character is being used in a transferred sense here—a person who looks as if someone had thrown a handful of hemp seeds at his face? Or a cruel but clear picture of the lacerated skin of a smallpox victim?

The low, bushy hemp produces a great deal of seed. Porridge was previously made from these, and hemp was actually classified as 'grain' in ancient China. But the seeds were used primarily to make oil. This might be the explanation for the character being included in the names of other important oil plants such as *sesame*, *castor*, and *flax*, brought into China during later periods. Botanically, they have nothing in common with hemp.

Excellent cloth can be woven from hemp, strong and light, cool in summer, and quickly absorbing body sweat.

I did not understand how this quality could be found in hemp cloth until I learned that hemp is one of the nettle plants, and nettles used to be woven into lovely, light materials in Europe. Nettles have been woven into cloth since very early times in China, and still are today. A nettle variety called 'China grass' (*Boehmeria nivea*), or ramie, is still grown widely in the southern parts of the country and is a truly practical plant. When the long stems are cut, new ones grow quickly, and three or four crops a year are usual if the weather and the soil are both good. The cloth woven with ramie fibers is almost as beautiful and pleasing as silk. The character for hemp is included in both *nettle* and *ramie*.

Cotton, now regarded as typical of China, was not grown there until during the Yuan dynasty and did not replace hemp as the main fiber for the manufacture of cloth in everyday use until the seventeenth century. For funerals, people still dress in cloth made from natural, undyed hemp.

There is nothing so dead as a discarded nylon shirt. But old rope, nets, and old clothes made of hemp can be made into paper. It is all cut up, boiled, and pounded into pulp in a huge mortar, then the pulp is spread very thinly over a reed mat or a fine-meshed net and dried into a sheet of paper. This invention may be China's most important contribution to mankind. Thrift, inventiveness, and concentration on what is useful are typical of the Chinese people. Nothing is to be wasted. Everything can be used, to emerge again in a new form.

All paper is still made on this basic principle, even in the advanced paper industry of today. The oldest paper still preserved comes from the first century B.C. It has yellowed, but after over two thousand years, it is not even brittle, despite the fact that it is only 0.01 millimeters thick. This paper was used

Papermaking during the Han dynasty. The wet paper pulp is spread over frames and dried into finished sheets. Modern drawing.

mainly for wrapping valuable objects. But two hundred years later, in 105, an official called Cai Lun and skillful paper workers at the Imperial Palace succeeded in making paper that was so fine-grained and strong that it could also be written on with brush and ink.

Hemp continued to be the main raw material for paper. Even during the Tang dynasty, 80 percent of all paper was made from hemp. Then bamboo, rice straw, and other materials took over.

For six hundred years, the Chinese were the only people who knew how to make paper. But in the summer of 751, the Arabs defeated the Chinese army at Talas in central Asia at one of the most important battles in the history of the world. From then on the Tang dynasty began to decline, the centuries-old contact with the West was broken, and China became isolated behind her natural barriers of deserts and mountains.

Among the Chinese prisoners of war taken by the Arabs were some paper workers. Under their direction, Samarkand developed into a center for papermaking in the Arab empire. After a thousand-year journey through Asia and North Africa, the technique of papermaking finally arrived in Spain in 1150, then spread all over Europe during the following centuries. At the end of the seventeenth century, paper arrived in North America. Now every child knows what paper is. What would our modern civilization be like without it?

Paper made from hemp is used in China today only as wrapping paper, just as it was in the beginning. For all other purposes there are special papers. The famous Xuan paper from Anhui is found in ninety variations and is used for many purposes, not only by artists and bookbinders. The Chinese are connoisseurs when it comes to paper. They choose paper for different purposes with the same care as the French choose their wine. What shall we have? 'Tiger Skin paper' or 'Cold Gold'?

Making paper is a fairly simple procedure—although some special papers take a year and almost a hundred different processes to complete. Weaving silk, on the other hand, is one of the most complicated processes of all. Yet the Chinese mastered this art as early as Neolithic days. The oldest known silk cloth found is considered to be 4,700 years old. But silk ribbon has been found that carbon 14 analysis shows as five hundred years older.

Silkworms come from China, as do the mulberry tree and the leaves the silkworm lives off. The silkworm has a short but intense life. From the moment the larva hatches out of the egg, to a month later when it spins itself into a cocoon of silk, it has increased thirty times in length and ten thousand times in weight. But then its time is running out. After a week to ten days inside the cocoon, its metamorphosis into a butterfly is complete, and it breaks out into freedom. It is gray and insignificant and has no mouth, so cannot eat. It has one more task in life—to reproduce itself—and that must happen quickly, for within a few days it is dead.

The breeding of these creatures is nothing to be done in one's leisure time. Just to pick the leaves the worms need is hard work, requiring a great many hands. A ton of leaves—leaves from thirty full-grown trees—are needed to produce five or six kilos of silk, and of that probably only half can be used to make thread.

Silkworms are very sensitive. The slightest change in the weather may mean disaster, and when they have pupated, they have to be watched carefully so that they do not break out of the cocoon, for then the valuable silk thread that is the purpose of the breeding is destroyed.

The thread is about a kilometer long. To get hold of it and wind it up, the cocoon is put into hot water, the butterfly killed, and the cocoon softened sufficiently to enable the extreme end of the thread to be found and reeled up. The threads from several cocoons are always reeled at the same time, as the individual thread is too thin to handle alone.

These are some oracle bone and bronze characters for **silk**. According to one explanation, they show a skein of spun silk; according to another, the cocoons and the thin silk threads.

silk

tie together,
bind together

The cocoon explanation is supported by the form of the character for *to tie together*, *bind together*, which shows cocoons and threads rather than a skein, as well as the actual process of reeling the thin threads out of the cocoons as they bob up and down in the hot water. In the modern character, the hand holding the cocoon has been reduced to a single stroke.

The character for *silk* was often doubled on the oracle bones and still appears that way in the character for *raw silk* or *silk cloth* in general, while in compound characters, only one character for *silk* is used.

In *Grammata Serica Recensa*, Bernhard Karlgren's dictionary of the Chinese language as spoken and written in Seres—Silk Country—in about 600 B.C., there are nearly two hundred characters containing silk.

About fifty of them are words for *tie*, *bind*, *braid* and *cord*, *rope*. There are special words for rope used for tethering domestic animals, ropes used at the well, the coarse ropes that hold fishing nets, and rope for the horse's reins, crupper, and stirrup straps. The strings of bows and musical instruments are also included. And two characters that mean *to strangle*—the *silken cord*. When the emperor lost confidence in one of his officials, he discreetly sent him a little parcel containing a silken cord, enough to hang himself with, and there was the end of that career.

The other characters are more directly concerned with silk, silk cloth, or elements in textile production in general: the quality of cloth and clothes, and ornaments.

Reeling up the thin threads of the cocoons. Spinning mill, Suzhou.

Scene with people weaving, spinning, and warping. A skein of yarn on the pole in the roof. Grave decor from Han dynasty.

The character for *silk* is included in one hundred or more characters that reflect all the time-consuming aspects of silk production. *Knots* and *tangles* develop easily when the thin *threads* of the cocoons are to be *reeled up*, for they are only a fraction of a millimeter thick. When they have been *spun together*, the *warp* can be set up. For a half-meter-wide cloth of good *quality*, three thousand warp threads are required, and for a first-class cloth, seven or eight thousand. Naturally, there are many opportunities for *confusion* and *putting in order* before everything is in place and the actual *weaving* can begin.

The quality of the silk determines what the *cloth* will become. During the Zhou period, there were already fifteen different kinds of cloth, all with names of their own. *Simple*, *undyed*, rather *coarse* cloths were mostly woven, but *patterned* cloths in variegated *colors* were also produced. Textile scholars say it is remarkable that there are characters for *patterned* and *multicolored*, evidence that the early Chinese used *looms* of a kind Europe did not have until toward the middle of the Middle Ages, two thousand years later.

When the cloth was ready, all that had to be done was to *cut down* the material and *roll up* the cloth, the result of so much labor. Then it could be *bleached* or *dyed* in one of the thirteen different colors in which the character for *silk* is included, for instance, in *red* and *green*.

Ribbons, *belts*, and *handkerchiefs* were also woven, and *sandals* and *bags* were sewn. *Embroidered borders* on *hems* or *cap edges* were made, and *tassels* of every kind. Some were put on the front of shoes, others hung on hats or as decoration on horses. For all this and quite a lot more there are special characters, and the character for *silk* is included in every one of them.

Funeral procession in Taiwan.

grandson

孙

simplified character
for grandson

When anyone died, white mourning clothes were worn, for in China mourning is *white*, not black.

Many years ago, I saw a funeral procession in Taiwan. The whole family behind the coffin wore white mourning clothes and walked with heads bowed. All of them were *holding on to* a thick white *rope*—children, the middle-aged, and the old. Then for the first time I understood the character for *closely attached*, *succession*, *continuation* and the little word *grandson*, the construction of which had been inexplicable to me until then.

Natural materials were not dyed until after weaving. Silk thread contains a natural glue that makes the threads strong and weaving easier. But color does not take easily on unwashed silk thread. If a multi-colored, patterned cloth is required, the thread must be washed and dyed first, but then the weaving becomes even more difficult.

Most colors were previously based on plants of various kinds. A few, such as yellow, probably came from minerals. A much-appreciated shade of red came from the sap of a tree. The blue color regarded as typical of China came from China's own indigo plant, *Polygonum tinctorium*, a plant native to northern China. With the exception of indigo, only artificial dyes are used today.

The silk left over—the cocoons from which the silkworms managed to escape, or in which the thread has become irretrievably tangled—was made into *wadding* and used to line winter clothes. For us, the word *wadding* has associations with damp, moist compresses and heavy, lumpy quilts of cotton wadding. But silk wadding, or 'silk floss' as it is also called, is light, thin, and supple, superior to goose down and all other lining materials. My most beloved winter coat is lined with silk wadding and is as warm as a fur coat. It weighs scarcely more than a kilo.

The technique for making silk wadding is simple. The cocoons are boiled and pounded together into a pulp, then washed and dried on thin bamboo matting. When the wadding is lifted off the matting, a paper-thin layer of silk is left behind. This was once used as protection around expensive objects, as we use tissue paper, and people also tried to write on it. Then, gradually, cheaper plant fibers came to be used, and that led to the arrival of what we now call paper.

But silk was also used for writing over a long period, so the character for *silk* is also included in the character for *paper*, for the material people used to write on.

Next to grain, silk and silk cloth were for many dynasties the most important raw materials delivered as taxes to the state. Skeins of silk and lengths of material at certain times were used as a means of payment. A bronze inscription from the early 900s B.C., says that a horse and a skein of silk were worth as much as five slaves.

On the lid of a bronze vessel from the Han dynasty, some women are sitting weaving. Each has one end of the warp fastened with a belt around her waist and the warp held stretched by putting her foot on the end bar. Backstrap looms of this kind have been

Women weaving. Lid of a bronze vessel from the Han dynasty.

found since Neolithic times and are still in use among ethnic minorities in China and the Indians of South America.

The first Chinese looms are thought to have been similar to these. They may seem primitive, but astonishingly beautiful and complicated cloth can be woven on them. Some of Japan's most exclusive kimono cloth has been woven on what is called the jibata loom, based on the same principle.

warp

Perhaps a backstrap loom or some other early form of loom can be seen in the character for *warp*. The character consists of two parts: on the left, silk; on the right, something the *Shuowen* dictionary maintains means *vein of water*, but no reference is given to any text or inscription in which it is used in that sense.

Bernhard Karlgren thinks that the right-hand part is the primary form of the character and says it may depict some kind of loom.

Anyone who has sat at a loom can understand the picture, because that is what it feels like. You see the warp stretching out in front of you like a keyboard as your hands search for the yarn or cloth rags that are to constitute the weft.

But there is a difference between the Chinese way of perceiving a loom and ours. In the West the weft is the most important. When a rag rug is being woven, the warp is coarse and sparse—on the whole, uninteresting. But then all the bright variegated rags are woven in. As in the making of tapestries, the weft gives the cloth its character and makes it come alive.

Not so with the Chinese. For them the warp is fundamental. Silk is tough and can be stretched a quarter of its length without breaking, and it is thin. So a very long cloth can be set up with a pattern that runs the length of the many meters being woven—and with a wealth of detail inconceivable in wool or flax. A warp is to the Chinese not just a plain underlayer needed by the weaver to show off his or her skill—it is the actual background of the design. It regulates the appearance of the long cloth—the geometrical figures, the clouds, flowers, and birds.

The only Western equivalent of this cloth is our linen damask—a historically recent attempt to recreate some of the beauty of the Chinese silks.

Bearing in mind the importance of the warp in the art of Chinese weaving, it is natural that the character for *warp* also stands for concepts such as *to pass through, go through, experience, regulate, continue*. Also like the warp in a cloth, *arteries* run through the body, *veins of water* run through the ground, and the vast network of *meridians* run around the earth.

Just as women had the warp tied around their waist as they wove, the whole life of human beings as social creatures is also dependent on rules, laws, and customs built up over the course of time. These can be seen as the moral 'warp' running through generations and periods of time and guiding our way of living and thinking. For this reason, certain most important classic books were also referred to with the character for *warp*. These thirteen leading books constituted the *canon* or *set of rules* on which people sought to model their lives for over two thousand years. In many respects, those books are still the 'warp' of Chinese life.

the simplified character
for warp

At the beginning of the Han period, when the women weavers of Yunnan were portrayed on that bronze lid, the simple loom they used had been abandoned for a thousand years in the more advanced parts of the country. As early as the Shang period, damask with intricate geometric patterns was woven in towns around the Yellow River, and in the early Zhou period, the weaving of brocade—the most complicated cloth of all—began.

Only a few pieces of cloth from the Shang period have been preserved, among them some plain damask from a grave in Anyang. Many objects were wrapped in silk when they were put into the graves. The cloth itself has now disappeared, but the dampness in the graves made the bronze axes and bronze vessels wrapped in it corrode, leaving behind imprints of the vanished cloth, imprints so clear that textile scholars can see the way the cloth was woven.

During the expansion of the Han period in central Asia, in the last couple of centuries B.C., silk played an important political role. To increase their influence among the nomadic peoples of the deserts and steppes, to establish diplomatic relations and draw them into their sphere of power, the Chinese showered these people with expensive gifts, especially silk. In 1 B.C. alone, thirty thousand rolls of silk were given away to the Xiongnu, the people then dominating the steppes in the northwest.

Chinese silk had already reached Europe in various ways a hundred years earlier, but regular trade was not established until the Roman Empire expanded so far east that it almost touched on the extreme outposts of the Han empire in the deserts north of Pamir. No direct contact was ever made between the two realms—trade was handled by central Asiatic and Arab merchants—but from the days of Emperor Augustine, silk was in general use and was an important status symbol among the upper classes of Rome. Roman imports consisted largely of silk thread, which, during the first centuries of the empire, was

Ancient form of loom for silk voile, a thin transparent cloth. Yuan.

dyed and woven in towns along the eastern Mediterranean, where the caravans ended their nearly five-thousand-mile journey. An extensive silk-weaving industry also arose in other parts of the Roman Empire, among other places in Constantinople, from 395 A.D. the capital of Byzantium, the Eastern Roman Empire.

The uneven supply of silk, however, remained a problem. Conflicts flaring between Rome and different central Asian peoples, as well as between China and the nomadic peoples, occasionally caused trade to cease. But in 552, the situation changed quite unexpectedly when silkworm eggs were brought to Constantinople. How this happened has never been clarified. The explanation that most fires the imagination is that some monks (or merchants) smuggled the eggs out of China in a hollow bamboo stave—although it is hard to fathom how production of silk could have begun from those few eggs. Who in Byzantium was sufficiently familiar with the life cycle of silkworms and the techniques of handling that thin thread? No one knows. But the experiment succeeded. At the beginning of the first century A.D., Italy and Spain had also learned to produce silk, but up to the fifteenth century, Europe was still dependent on imports from China to supplement their own silk production.

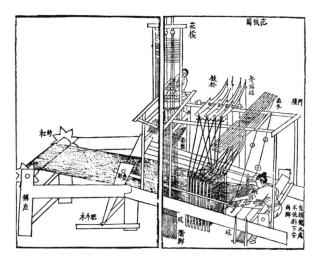

A draw loom out of the great work Tian gong kai wu (The Exploitation of the Works of Nature), *1637, in which the professional competence in agriculture and crafts of the day was summarized. A predecessor of Diderot's* Encyclopédie.

During the 1940s – years of war when everything was in short supply – soldiers in the Red Army wove their own straw sandals on a simple backstrap loom, not all that unlike the looms that were once the starting point for the character for loom. But they wove with straw and hemp, not with silk, as the character indicates. Photograph from Nanniwan in Shaanxi.

In China, cloth was woven during the Han period on a loom with two treadles and a firm, slanting frame, as can be seen in the weaving scene on page 217. Although the loom does not look particularly unusual today, in its time it was the most advanced in the world.

When brocade was being woven, a considerably more complicated loom was used, called a draw loom. Brocades preserved from the Zhou period indicate that it was already in use at that time, although little is known about how it looked. The most imposing portrayal of a draw loom in its classic form is this 1637 drawing which shows a loom that is worked on two levels by two people, one who slides in the weft and a 'draw boy' who regulates the warp by lifting groups of threads in a preordained pattern.

The draw loom came to Europe sometime during the late Middle Ages, bringing with it a sharp rise in silk production. In 1801 the Frenchman Joseph-Marie Jacquard demonstrated that, instead of the draw boy, punched cards regulating the warp could be used, on the same principle as a program fed into a computer. The weavers, afraid of becoming unemployed, attacked the loom and Jacquard himself, but both he and the loom survived, and it is on Jacquard looms that the Chinese weave their magnificent brocades today.

A great many old looms are still in use outside the large textile factories. In Yunnan and Tibet, backstrap looms are still used, and crude looms made by local carpenters can be found all over the country. In winter when the fields are empty and farm implements hang unused on the wall, many people spend their time weaving, although they no longer weave material for family clothing. They can't compete with the great variety found in the village stores, but instead weave coarse cotton cloth for sacks, bags, quilts, and so on.

Woman weaving in the village of Fengxian, outside Xi'an. 1982.

In 1971 a new hospital was to be built in Changsha, and a grave mound from the Han dynasty lay in the way; so it was decided to excavate it in order to get at the site. When the finds from the excavation were made known, they caused a sensation all over the world. Embedded in charcoal and white clay, the body of the Marquise of Tai, as well as all the objects buried with her in the grave, had lain as if in a vacuum-sealed space.

The marquise herself, after 2,100 years, was so well preserved that it was possible to perform an autopsy. She belonged to blood group A, and at her death in 165 B.C., she suffered slightly from arteriosclerosis, gallbladder trouble, schistosomiasis, and the after-effects of tuberculosis. Her skin and tissues were still elastic. When technicians injected preserving liquid, swellings arose and later subsided—just as they do after immunization injections into living flesh, such as those given before foreign travel.

Among all the art objects, necessities, and foodstuffs she had taken with her, the textiles are the most remarkable. It is extremely unusual for archaeologists to find such old and well-preserved objects, and of such fine quality. There were not only fifteen silk robes—eleven lined with silk wadding—but also hand-sewn stockings, shoes, and silk gloves, and forty-six rolls of silk cloth, woven in the most dexterous patterns and decorated with exquisite chain-stitch embroidery. They were no more spoiled than if they had lain in a chest in the attic for a few years. Some of the cloth had lost its colors, but most of it still glowed in reds, greens, yellows, blues, or black.

The robes are straight and have long sleeves and a broad band around the neck and front. They fasten to the right and are held together by the wearer's arm or with a soft belt. They most resemble an ordinary dressing gown, but are cut with much more sophistication.

There are two styles, one in which the two sides of the front part are straight, the other in which the right side is drawn out in a point at the hip.

These finds were considered unique until 1981 when some brick workers were digging for clay and found a grave that was about two hundred years older and filled with robes of all kinds—padded winter costumes in three-colored brocade and summer gowns in silk voile, a material as thin as a dragonfly wing. One of them weighs only forty-nine grams (about an ounce and a half).

They are made in the same style as those described above, and in fact, this is what the Chinese costume has looked like since the beginning of historical time. It can be seen on small sculptures from the Shang and Zhou periods.

Robes of this kind are reproduced in the character for **clothing**.

clothing, costume

One of the robes the Marquise of Tai took with her to her grave in 165 B.C. and two solemn court ladies in wood from the same grave. They are wearing similar robes. The pattern can be seen in the drawings.

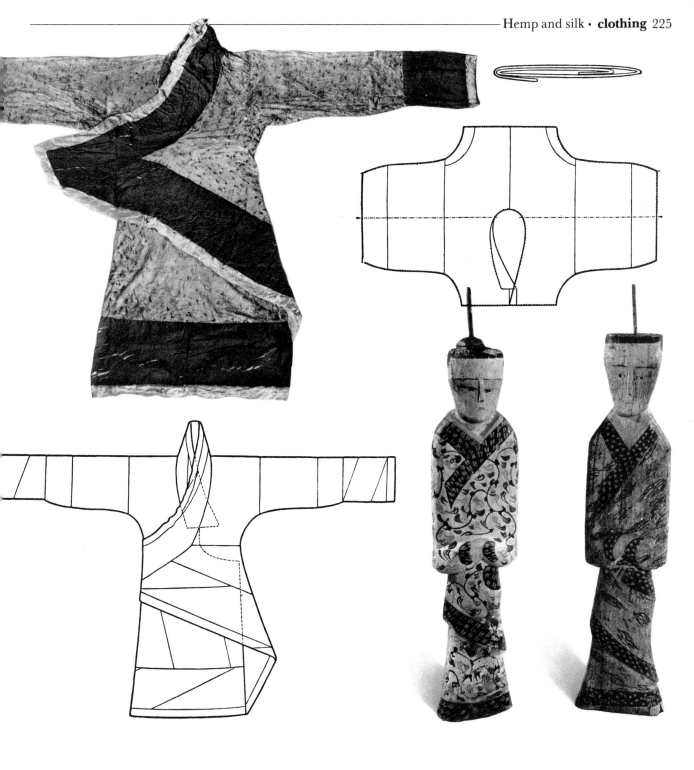

A Buddhist monk from the Huayan Temple in Datong in his winter attire. 1985.

The Chinese went on using this basic pattern for their clothes for three thousand years. Peasant coats reached halfway down the thigh and from the Han period on, were worn with a pair of wide trousers tied firmly in a knot around the waist with a soft cloth belt. Many older Chinese peasants still dress this way. Officials and others who did not have work in the fields wore theirs almost down to the ankles. As the years went by, their sleeves became longer and wider. During the Tang and Song dynasties they almost reached the floor.

When the Manchurians set up the Qing dynasty in 1644, they brought their national costume into the country. This was also a long, straight coat, but the sleeves were narrow and fastened with a number of small cloth buttons. The particularly lovely style worn by Chinese women is based on this model: a fitted tunic buttoned high up at the neck and slit high up the thigh.

Buddhist monks, however, were not to be influenced. They kept the ancient costume and still wear it today, as do the Japanese. The kimono is not a Japanese invention, but a close successor of upper-class Chinese clothing of the Tang period. It was introduced into Japan in the eighth century. A thousand years later, the kimono of Japanese ladies was complemented with a broad belt called an *obi*, but the gentlemen's kimono looks just as it always has.

Bamboo and Trees

No plant moves me as profoundly as bamboo—most of all the sound of its thin, dry leaves as they rustle in the wind.

In the summer breezes, they sough soothingly like the rippling of a spring, or rustle like silk, and the shade from bamboo foliage is light and shimmering.

On cold winter days, the leaves and stems act as a break for stubborn north winds. With a bamboo shield behind me, I can sit facing south, letting the pale sun pour around me. The wind cannot reach me, but I can hear from the high wail in the air and the whistling in the leaves how cold it would be if the bamboo were not there, protecting me.

From a purely botanical point of view, bamboo is one of the most remarkable plants in existence. It is a grass—but in a single year it can grow higher than many trees. It does not flower for a hundred years—then it dies. Tolerant, unassuming, continuously green, it puts up with whatever it gets in the way of soil, water, and care.

At the same time, it is stronger than most plants. Storms and rain bend it low to the ground, but as soon as they have passed, it once again rises and gracefully recaptures its living space.

It used to be said in China that this is how difficulties should be faced: Bend, adapt, of course, but never abandon ideals. Never be defeated. Other winds will blow, all in good time.

For over a thousand years, bamboo has fascinated Chinese artists. Using it as a metaphor for human life, they have given expression in abstract, but very clear form to feelings and thoughts otherwise difficult to represent visually.

There is also a great challenge to reproduce something as elusive as bamboo. It is constantly changing, the leaves hanging in heavy clumps in rain and mist,

floating lightly in the air in calm dry weather, and in the wind, suspended like pennants fluttering out from the bowed branches.

Bamboo is difficult to paint, the leaves most difficult of all, says the *Mustard Seed Garden Manual of Painting*. Wait until you are quite sure what you want to depict. In your mind's eye you must see every stalk, every individual leaf before you start.

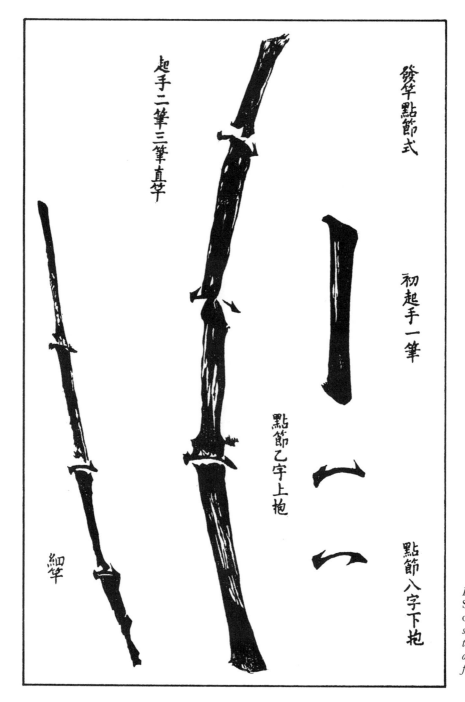

Page from the Mustard Seed Garden Manual of Painting, *showing how to shape the bamboo stalks — a series with the character for 'one' in vertical position.*

When you then put brush to paper or silk, your hand must move lightly, firmly, and effortlessly. The slightest hesitation makes the leaves thick and lifeless. Much can be learned from copying bamboo painted by great masters such as Wen Tong and Su Dongpo, the manual goes on to say. They devoted their whole lives to that motif. But if you lack talent, it is so difficult, you might as well give up immediately.

Calligraphy, the art of writing beautifully, has long been regarded as the most distinguished art in China, and the painting of bamboo can be seen as a variant of this. The same lines, the same brush strokes, the same ink are used to shape both the characters and the bamboo on the paintings. Leaves are reproduced with a complicated interplay between pressure and motion. The Chinese brush is outstandingly flexible, the tip capable of drawing the thinnest line, or, by increasing the pressure on the paper while making the stroke, widening into a leaf and, when slowly lifted again, forming the long, thin point of the leaf.

No single oracle bone character for **bamboo** is known and only a few individual bronze characters, but on the bronzes it is contained in a great many compound characters. What does it show? According to one common explanation, the character shows two branches with dangling leaves; according to another, two groups of leaves only. The latter explanation seems more convincing to me, not least because of the way bamboo actually grows. In the spring, when the trunks—or rather the stalks—race upward, they have no leaves at first. But after a month, when they have reached their full height, three lancet-shaped leaves break out at the very top and thin, fanlike ascending branches develop around the joints, also ending in a group of leaves. Weighed down by this foliage, the mature stem then bends over in a gentle curve and when the wind blows through the leaves, sways slowly back and forth in the breeze, a picture I seem to recognize in the character.

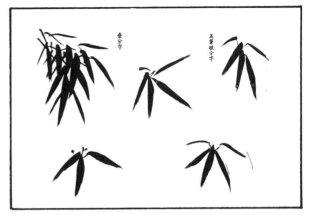

A spread in the painting manual showing groups of bamboo leaves in good weather. They form patterns in which we can see the characters for man, mankind, for share, divide, or the character for piece.

人 分 个

man   divide   piece

bamboo in compound characters

bamboo

Bamboo is not simply a concern of artists, calligraphers, and philosophers, but to a very great extent is also part of everyday life in China. Much of what we regard as typically Chinese is linked with the use of bamboo. What would the image of China be without peasants with bouncing bamboo carrying poles and bamboo baskets? And Chinese cooking without bamboo shoots?

Also, consider the high Chinese roofs with their upward-curving eaves. According to some scholars, these have acquired their curved shape because roofs were once made of springy, pliable bamboo.

No material has such multifold uses as bamboo or is both so cheap and so strong. Cables of braided bamboo strips were once widely used in shipping, for towing barges along the Yangzi and other rivers, and they also held up the suspension bridges across mountain ravines and valleys, their strength increasing the wetter they became.

Houses, bridges, and water pipes are still made today from thick bamboo stems, and paper is made from the pith inside. It would be hard to find a better building material. Thin branches are made into furniture and household goods such as buckets, graters, and steamers, as well as many other lovely and practical things such as bird cages, ladders, fans, hats, vases, pen holders, musical instruments, even whistles so small and light they can be fastened to the tail feathers of pigeons. As the flock swoops over the rooftops at dusk, the whistles sound, to the delight of people in the neighborhood. If you listen when cycling down to the Chaoyang quarter of Beijing, you can hear this harmonious sound almost any day.

The character for *bamboo* is found in many characters for everyday goods still made of bamboo—*basket, sieve, chopsticks, mat, pen, comb, hairpin, curtain, chest, folding ruler, tube, building,* and *flute.*

Umbrellas and **parasols** are also made of bamboo. Waxed paper or cloth is stretched across a framework of thin bamboo strips held together by a network of threads. This design appears clearly in both the traditional form of the character and in the simplified form.

The original construction was as simple as it was brilliant. A piece of bamboo was simply sliced into thin strips, leaving a short piece at the end whole. The strips were bent out like spokes of a wheel and covered with waxed paper or silk. A similar piece of bamboo, but only half as long, was sliced and bent out in the same way, upside down with the ends fixed to the top with thin threads. With the aid of a rod driven into the top and running through the 'hub' of the ribs, the umbrella could be opened and closed.

Bamboo umbrellas are still occasionally seen, but today umbrellas are more commonly made of metal and nylon. They are lighter, but the construction is the same.

umbrella

the simplified character for umbrella

tree

There are no leaves in the character for **tree**, only trunk and branches, which is how a tree looks for most of the year. Stripped of its finery, it stands dark under the winter sky. The picture is harsh but realistic.

To me, this picture is always associated with the first time I saw Chinese trees as a written character. In the early 1960s, I was a student at Beijing University. The Great Leap Forward had just failed, and that autumn, for the second year running, there was a desperate shortage of food—not even enough Chinese cabbage, the most important green winter vegetable. Every leaf was made use of and hung up to dry.

The trees outside our house had just lost their leaves and were now covered with cabbage leaves, at first brilliant greenish-white, then darkening each day like the remains birds drop when making their nests in the spring. As if decorated for a macabre sacrifice, the tree stood there with its outspread branches and the cabbage leaves rustled in the wind. Coming from a culture that had forgotten drying as a method of preserving, I found this an incomprehensible and frightening sight, and the smell was revolting.

Then spring came like pulling up a blind, and everything changed. The trees in the park were renewed, their foliage budding, trembling and gossamerlike as in a twelfth-century painting, the magnolias blooming. But there was something wrong with the picture. There were people all over the shrubberies, up in the trees, out on the branches, with cracking sounds everywhere as students, usually walking so primly along the paths, now ripped and tore like goats at the fresh leaves.

I can remember from my own childhood how good fresh beech leaves tasted in spring—green and sharp—but the Chinese students were not just nibbling. The trees trembled under them, and broken branches hung down like wings of shot birds.

"Vandalism," I complained to my teacher. "Can't they be stopped? They're destroying the trees."

"You must understand," she said quietly. "They haven't had any fresh greens all winter . . . none of us has . . ."

I remembered the scraps of Chinese cabbage hanging in the trees in the autumn and stopped complaining, as I had so often, about us foreigners having to eat in a separate dining room. With our pampered stomachs, we would never have survived on rice or millet porridge, maize buns, and the soaked Chinese cabbage.

Then it was that I saw the trees of the northern Chinese plain with different eyes. They were part of people's lives, not of the life of nature. They were exploited to the last leaf. They might well provide a little shade in the summer, and a little shelter from the wind in the winter, but most of all they provided wood for the stove and leaves for the animals—and for people, too—in bad times. The remaining green foliage had retreated into small clumps at the very tips of the branches, as if in an attempt not to be plucked. It would be hard to imagine anything more different from a tree growing and spreading in the open.

Though perhaps even more different would be the artificial miniature trees monks have cultivated for more than a thousand years as objects of meditation—pines, elms, and cherry trees in tiny pots. By keeping water and nourishment to a minimum, they have succeeded in producing dwarf trees with all the characteristic features of fully grown trees, but no more than a foot or so high. A stone is often placed next to the tree to symbolize Taishan, or some other holy mountain, along with a ceramic poet quietly contemplating the greatness of nature and the smallness of man. He helps the viewer to feel part of the picture. This is not just a curiosity of the past. Little trees of this kind are still tenderly cared for down through the generations in innumerable Chinese homes.

These old miniature trees do not lose their magic even when they die. A new tree can be planted in the hollow trunk. This is called 'the meeting of old age and youth.' Everything has a name in an ancient civilization.

Gardens of miniature trees are still found in the grounds of many old temples, hundreds of them standing in lovely pots. There is a three-hundred-year-old elm on the roof of the administration building in the Botanical Gardens in Xiamen, the old harbor town that used to be known as Amoy (from a southern pronunciation of the name).

"We sometimes take it down to the reception room at the New Year festival or when we have very important visitors. Otherwise it stays here in the peace and quiet. It is old now, and doesn't like change," the woman who was the head botanist explained to me when I was there a few years ago. The little tree is so old it has been immortalized on a postage stamp.

Miniature trees, Botanical Gardens, Xiamen. The three-hundred-year-old elm in the middle has been immortalized on a 1981 postage stamp.

On the 'central plain,' fully mature old trees with freely growing branches can be seen only in parks or temple grounds. They are there to remind people of the concept of the tree, an ancient image of free nature. They are often pine or cypress, which can grow to a great age. They are tough and tolerant. In some way incorruptible in their dark, evergreen foliage, they have also come to symbolize the honest official who is above all intrigues and pressures. After Zhou Enlai, the archetypal true official, had died, his memory was celebrated in a hall so full of pines and cypress that it resembled an eternal forest.

There are a great many really old trees in China, one of them in Shandong, outside Simenta, the oldest preserved Buddhist pagoda in the country, built in 611. The tree—a cypress—is said to have been planted at the same time.

"Oh, that old," I say, impressed, to my companion.

"Old? Fairly. But one day you must go to Qufu quite near here. Two trees there were planted by Confucius, and there is a three-thousand-year-old ginko tree which still bears a ton of fruit each year, sweet nuts used in various desserts."

I haven't yet seen those trees, but in the Songyang Mountains south of Zhengzhou, a town even before the Shang period, I saw a cypress that is as old as the oracle bones and bronzes. In its ancient starkness it has now almost been reduced to a character.

I said earlier that the character for *tree* shows a trunk and branches of a tree. But perhaps the bottom half of the character should be regarded not as hanging branches but as the roots of the tree. *Shuowen* maintained this, but for some reason that part of the explanation is usually left out. Several old characters reinforce this interpretation.

The three-thousand-year-old cypress at the Songyang Academy, one of the four famous academies of Chinese antiquity. 1984. Emperor Wu of the Han dynasty was so taken with the tree that he gave it the title of General of the First Grade.

But there is also a special character for *root* in which the lowest part of the tree is simply marked with a stroke. In its transferred meaning, the character stands for *origin, base, source*, just as the word *root* does in many Western languages. We speak of 'the root of all evil,' and we feel we 'have our roots' in a certain environment or period of time. So do the Chinese. But for them the concept of *root, origin* is even more charged than for us, a natural consequence of their long, continuous tradition and profound awareness of history.

The character also means *volume, book*, which may seem strange until the decisive importance of books as the foundation of Chinese culture is remembered—particularly the philosophical scripts in which the moral foundation for humans, as social beings, is formulated, and the calligraphy exercise books in which the foundations of this leading art were laid, the art of reproducing nature and the written characters with brush and ink. The oldest academy known, in the eighth century A.D., was called The Forest of Brushes.

Old trees growing among cliffs or close to a spring often have their roots exposed, says the commentary to the picture on the right from the *Mustard Seed Garden Manual of Painting*. They resemble hermits or legendary immortals in retreat from the world. Thin and smooth with age, their veins and bones shine from beneath the skin. When painting a group of trees, says the manual, one or two on which the gnarled roots are visible should be included. All the roots should not be shown, "or they will look like the teeth of a saw, not a pleasant sight."

The words in the painting manual come from observations anyone who has lived on the central plains of China would recognize. The fine-grained loess soil is easily washed away by summer rains, exposing the roots of trees, their long extremities wriggling several meters out from the trunk across the dry ground, searching for hidden pockets of moisture.

root

Tree roots above the dry soil in a village near Yan'an and a picture from the Mustard Seed Garden Manual of Painting, *showing the same reality.*

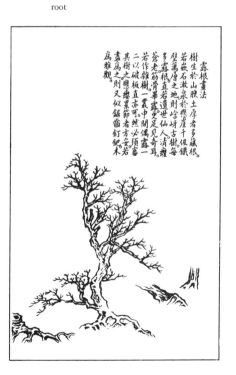

top, end

forest

burn

thick forest

to rest

assemble

Tree is included in a great many compound characters, for some unknown reason occasionally in another form, though nevertheless *tree*.

A tree in which the upper part is marked with a stroke means *top, extreme end of a branch*. In a transferred meaning, it also stands for *last* and *dust*—the only thing left at the end.

'A lone tree does not make a forest,' runs a Chinese saying—an excellent comment on this character, which means *forest*.

Forest and fire together form the character for *burn, set fire to*—a forest fire or perhaps a memory of the days of clearing land by burning? Maybe so. But the character is also used in several oracle bone texts concerned with hunting. They show that men set fire to the forest to flush the deer, wild pigs, and other game out of their hiding places—an ancient method of hunting used in many parts of the world.

Three trees together: *thick forest, many trees* and *dark*—dark as a thick forest—also *severe*.

A man by a tree, perhaps seeking shade? The character means *to rest*.

A bird in a tree means *to assemble, gather together*. This may at first seem rather peculiar—how can one assemble with oneself? But according to some scholars, the original meaning of the character was *sit down, spend the night*, and then the picture is at once clearer, especially considering the region where the character was created. Many of the birds in the old core area around the Yellow River were gallinaceous birds which roost in branches, preferably grouped together. So the character for *to sit down* gradually also acquired the meaning *to assemble, come together*. To clarify the character, another pair of birds was added, and in that form the character appeared for a long time. But now the extra birds have vanished, and the original bird is roosting alone in the tree. The character is also used for *to compile, edit, collection of writings*.

Sounds from the beaks of small birds are heard up in trees: *bird twitter*. During some periods, though, it must have been rather quiet in the treetops, for instance, in the 1950s when regular eradication campaigns were carried out against sparrows and other birds. They were thought to eat too much of the seed that people needed for themselves. But then when insect attacks on crops increased, the campaigns ceased.

bird twitter

An open mouth under a tree. What fruit does it crave? The mouth is waiting for an *apricot*.

apricot

Tree and child. A tree with many 'children' = much fruit? *Plum*.

plum

An irritatingly multistroke character meaning *foliage, leaf*. When one goes back to the oldest characters, it turns out to be a fairly clear picture of the crown of a tree. The addition of the character for *grass* on top is only confusing.

foliage, leaf

One of the many words for *red* in the Chinese language shows a tree on which the trunk is marked with a stroke or a dot—the tree from which red coloring was extracted from the trunk.

Other red colors were extracted from cinnabar and the shrub *Rubia cordifolia*—several of the silk gowns of the Marquise of Tai are colored with one or the other of them.

red

During the Zhou period, perhaps even during the late Shang period, red was the imperial color and used for everything—clothes, chariots, palaces, banners, household goods, and so on. For the brief Qin dynasty white was its color, for the Han dynasty black, but red continued throughout history to be the color bringing fortune before all others. Temples and palaces are still red—the Forbidden City in Beijing is a good example, as are the round silk or paper lanterns the Chinese love to hang up on festive and ceremonial occasions.

A bride was carried in a red sedan to her new home, and the quilt she and her husband crept under was also red, as was the gown she wore during the day. Brides are no longer carried in sedans, but quilts are still red, as are the invitation cards to the child's naming ceremony, and often the clothes the child later toddles around in, the drums to which schoolchildren march and dance, and the rosettes pensioners are given on their last day at work. It is no coincidence that Mao's little book was red. The color red runs all through the lives of the Chinese. Red is festive and joyous, but also ceremonial. The red banners swaying over China perhaps have less to do with Communism than we are inclined to think—in any case they are the continuation of a long indigenous tradition.

fruit

This is the character for *fruit*. In its modern form, it is not particularly clear—apparently consisting of *field* and *tree*. But in the old forms, the picture at once becomes clearer.

The oracle bone character shows a tree with round fruit at the tips of the branches, and the upper part of the bronze character can be seen, with a little stretch of the imagination, as the crown of a tree, the dots marking the fruit.

A similar concept and rendering of a fruit tree can be found in this papercut from Yan'an.

The character for *fruit* also means *result, consequence*—just as we often speak of the 'fruits of . . . this or that.' To distinguish between the two concepts, fruit in the concrete sense of the word is called water fruit, a refreshing image—fresh fruit juice against the palate.

In the oracle bone character for *picking, gathering,* the same tree is apparent. There is also a hand grasping for the fruit, reminding us that oranges, mandarins, apricots, peaches, and kiwifruit originate from China, as do kumquat, lichee, pomegranates, and many other delicious fruits often sold by Western grocers today.

Unfortunately, the fruit vanished from the character as early as in the bronze characters, and did not reappear, even in the final form given to the character.

to pick, gather

The gatherers and early farmers of ancient times must have found the great quantity of different fruit an invaluable resource, and throughout the history of China, fruit has played an important part in the diet. Today one of the most favored delicacies in China is still preserved or candied fruit, especially the kind from Beijing—glistening, sweet, and rather chewy.

What the hand in the character for *picking, gathering* is grasping for, is not made clear, nor is that really necessary—all sorts of useful things grow on trees.

The character for *mulberry tree* is usually described as a picture of a tree and many picking hands, an explanation easy to accept—the three hands up in the treetop are clearly visible. Nor has any tree in China been more intensively subjected to human hands than the mulberry. The silkworms have to be fed around the clock with fresh leaves, and basket after basket has to be filled and carried to them, work that tries the patience and demands the constant participation of many hands.

But going back to the oracle bone character, the accepted explanation for the character for *mulberry tree* appears less convincing. Are those really hands that stick out from the trunk? Aren't they leaves, foliage? Some scholars have recently maintained that they are, which certainly seems more reasonable. Leaves

mulberry tree

are the most valuable part of the mulberry tree, so it seems perfectly natural that they should be included in the character for mulberry tree.

On a bronze vessel from the Zhou period, work on mulberry trees can be seen in full swing; the leaves, not the hands, are clearly the most important.

Earlier in the book, in association with the character for *arrow* and *bow*, we saw a handsome bronze wine jar decorated with hunting and battle scenes. Several similar vessels have been preserved, and although their shapes vary somewhat, the motifs on them are the same. At the top of the vessel, women are curled up in the treetops, picking leaves. The leaves are large and the pattern of the branches as elegant as on a silk brocade. The woman on the left is alone, but an assistant is on the way up to her. The two on the right are collaborating on the picking, one holding the branch while the other picks, a basket dangling below them.

Picking mulberry leaves. Detail of decoration on a bronze vessel from the Zhou period. The whole vessel is shown on page 80.

Until a few years ago, everyone agreed that the women were picking mulberry leaves, but according to a new interpretation, they are collecting branches for bows—not a very convincing suggestion. Bows do indeed appear in many of the scenes, and the whole portrays the preparation for war, either with ritual ceremonies such as music and dancing, or with practical exercises, target shooting, and hunting. But it is quite clear from this picture that the leaves are being picked, not branches. Look at the gestures of the women picking.

Bow strings were made of silk—there is no stronger and lighter material—and to produce the silk needed, the larvae have to have mulberry leaves. By tradition, the women's task was to pick the leaves, weave the cloth, and make the strings. On the top band of the vessel, one woman can be seen stringing a bow, while the others try theirs out.

The mulberry tree was and is still today the fundamental basis of silk production, and the picking of the leaves in particular is often the *pars pro toto* of the whole process. With no leaves, no silk; with no silk, no bow strings—and no thin silk cords for the arrows, either, enabling the archers to haul in their prey or retrieve the arrow, should the bird manage to get away.

At one time, 50 percent of China was covered with forests, but now forests cover no more than 8 percent. Climatic changes at the beginning of historical time were partly responsible for the loss, but most is due to the activities of man.

As the population increased, forests were burned down to clear land for cultivation. The result was erosion of the mountainsides and new layers of soil down in the valleys. Elsewhere, the soil was impoverished by overgrazing, the firm pastureland vanishing and surface soil washed away by summer rains.

The wind stripped the rest. When the spring storms from Siberia roared down over northern China and the plains around the Yellow River, they took with them the thin, dusty soil, and in thick yellow clouds, the soil disappeared out over the sea.

Before 1949, no government was strong enough to do anything about this, but a few years after the revolution, tree planting began, on a vast scale. 'May the fatherland be green' was the slogan. Along the Great Wall, built to stop the ravages of the Mongols on the plains, a new living wall of trees has been created—kilometer-wide belts of trees, largely poplars, willows, and acacias, all swift-growing and tolerant species, on guard to capture the north wind and stop it from racing at full force over the land and tearing away the soil.

Hundreds of millions of trees have also been planted around villages and towns, along roads and rivers—a million a year since 1949 in Beijing alone. The bare, treeless mountains in Shanxi and Shaanxi have been terraced in many places, and the deep ravines flourish with orchards, largely of apples and apricots. Spring storms have actually been considerably subdued in what is called the Three Norths area (northern, northwestern, and northeastern China). The humidity of the air is raised, hailstorms are now less frequent, and the frost-free period is longer.

But there have been many reversals. Over some periods, people ravaged the forests to supply the need for timber in industry and agriculture. In the eagerness to produce grain, the important aim of increasing the forested acreage of the country has been forgotten.

In 1980, a new tree-planting campaign began, followed by yet another. All Chinese over the age of eleven are obliged to plant five trees per person over a period of five years, with only the old, the sick, and the handicapped exempt. Five times five is twenty-five, times a billion comes to twenty-five billion trees—the world's greatest attempt at tree planting ever. Let's hope the trees thrive.

If there are no seedlings, seed is sown directly onto the mountainside, and in some distant places the seed is sown from the air by plane. This has actually worked. Every mountain is a tree nursery, the aim being that China shall live up to her name, the Flourishing Central Kingdoms.

It is about time. As long ago as in the year 300 B.C., the philosopher Mencius complained of the ruthless exploitation of nature. He suggested that mulberry trees should be planted around fields and ponds. It has taken time, but now it looks as if he is at last to have his way. Mulberry trees, with their leaves to feed the silkworms, are being planted around the fish ponds. The excrement from the silkworms is fed to the fish in the ponds, and the droppings from the fish, in turn, are hauled up from the bottom and used as manure for the mulberry trees—a more or less perfect ecological cycle and profitable enterprise, for half a ton of fish are produced for every 2.5 tons of mulberry leaves.

A Shanghai youth cooking lunch for the family. The hot oil is already in the pan and a large piece of pork on the cutting board. On the wall above is a poster about the importance of saving energy, as well as some of the baskets used for shopping. They are also used for holding such food as onions and eggs.

The scene we saw earlier with women picking mulberry leaves is clear as a picture and would require little stylization to function as a character.

Compare this detail from the decoration on the vessel of a woman walking along with a basket in her hand, with these bronze characters for *man, person*, which is contemporary.

Compare her basket with these bronze characters for **basket**, which are also contemporary.

Over the years, the character was complemented with the character for *bamboo*, which is appropriate—most Chinese baskets are braided of bamboo cut into long thin strips. In that form, the character now means *winnower*, the basket used to separate the chaff from the seed.

The original form for *basket*, on the other hand, was borrowed at an early stage for use in demonstrative and possessive pronouns, a sad fate for such a clear old character.

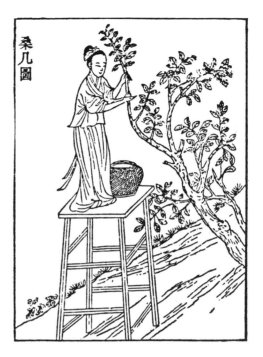

The women were later given a stool to stand on when picking mulberry leaves, as can be seen on this old illustration from a Ming dynasty manual on silk production.

The character for **stool**, **small table** appears neither in the oracle bones nor the bronzes, but it is known that furniture of this kind existed at the beginning of the Han dynasty. A delicate lacquered stool with slightly curved legs was found in the grave of the Marquise of Tai, its shape not unlike that of the character.

basket, winnower

basket
his, hers, this, that

stool

Tools and Weapons

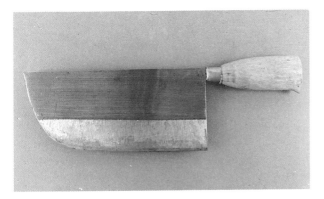

The first time I saw a Chinese kitchen knife, I was frightened. This wasn't a knife; it was an executioner's axe. The huge blade and the stubby handle seemed to me both dangerous and clumsy.

Dangerous they may be, but clumsy they are not. Once one has learned to handle them, there are no better knives, at least for Chinese cooking, based as it is on everything being shredded, sliced, or chopped beforehand, so that it can then be eaten with chopsticks.

The broad and sharp steel blade is just right when it comes to shredding. The knife stands on its cutting edge and rocks gently over meat and vegetables, never actually losing contact with the cutting board. One's hand can move freely in large, efficient motions, and one never cuts one's knuckles.

When chopping, it is the weight that is appreciated. With a chopper in each hand, meat can be rapidly minced as finely as through a meat grinder. The result is even better, for the meat keeps its structure and is not mashed as it is in a grinder. There is nothing more impressive than a Chinese cook chopping, the hands light as lark's wings and the heavy knives producing a dull resonance from the chopping block in long rhythmical sequences as though on a drum. This most characteristic sound from a Chinese kitchen is music to the hungry.

The form of the knife is unique, found, apart from in China, only among some north Asian peoples, American Indians, and the Inuit. During the Stone Age it consisted of a thin blade of sandstone, quartz, flint, or shell, with no handle. The knife was held inside the hand as reinforcement to the fingers and allowed to protrude just so far that fingertips and nails were protected, but the cutting edge was free. Many knives had holes in them, through which a noose of rope or leather was fastened. By threading a couple of fingers through this, one gained a more secure grip.

Knives of this kind were also used when harvesting millet. The spadix and panicles of the more primitive species of millet ripen unevenly, so the whole plant cannot be harvested at once with a sickle, as wheat can. The spadices have to be taken one by one as they ripen to ensure that they do not scatter their seed.

As species of millet that kept their seed better and ripened more evenly were developed, the old harvesting knives lost their importance, but even in the 1930s they were in general use in northern China, most of all when harvesting gaoliang, a common form of grain used in that area for brewing spirits. The knife was then no longer made of stone, but of iron, though still without a handle.

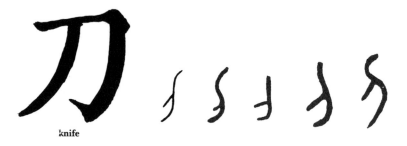

knife

Is an ordinary everyday knife depicted in the character for **knife**? I thought so for a long time, and it is certainly tempting to see the stubby handle and the strong curve of the blade in the lines of the character.

Yet the character does not seem to originate from this sort of knife, but rather from the expensive bronze knives used at sacrificial ceremonies in the Shang period, which were thick across the back with a curved blade and the point drawn upward. This type of knife, like the old stone harvesting knife, is unique to China.

Pottery fragments with inscriptions on them have been found in the old trading town of Gaocheng, north of Anyang. The characters on them are predecessors of those on oracle bones and bronzes. Depictions of a knife are on two of the twelve fragments found so far. One has a broad blade rather like the old stone knives, but with a more marked point and a short handle, strikingly like the kitchen knives of today—especially the kind used for cutting up vegetables.

The other image has a considerably narrower blade and is very like the bronze knives used in sacrificial ceremonies. This kind of knife, full of vitality, gradually spread over Mongolia and central Asia, then, through the mediation of the Arabs, seems even to have reached Spain. Just how that happened has not yet been investigated.

As far as I know, the relation between the two forms of knife has not yet been properly studied, either. Because of its exclusively sacrificial use, the narrow knife seems to have had a higher status than others, and so this kind is often depicted on the oracle bones on which questions to the dead and to Heaven were written, in connection with the ceremonies.

Sacrificial ceremonies can be seen on several Shang and Zhou bronze vessels, which is hardly surprising, since the vessels were used on those occasions. The animals are already lying on their backs, their legs in the air, mouths gaping, as a hand with a long, curved knife approaches the soft skin of their bellies.

Pottery fragments with pictures of knives. Gaocheng. Shang period.

Many similar bronze and jade knives have been found in graves from the Shang dynasty, the older examples simple and austere, while more recent ones often have protruding flanges and ornamented strips along the back.

The character for *knife* caused me trouble for a long time. Not only is there no independent bronze character for *knife*—those at the top of the previous page are taken from various compound characters—but I did not understand the form of the character. Is it a picture? In that case, which part is the handle, and which the blade and cutting edge? After going through all the characters containing *knife* in the basic dictionaries of inscriptions on oracle bones and bronzes, I now know that in nearly 90 percent of all cases, the knife is on the right-hand side in compound characters. Interestingly enough, it always faces the same way, in toward the other parts of the character, that is, the small 'point' protruding from the main line of the character faces in. In the few cases where the knife is on the left, it is reversed, with the point also directed toward the rest of the character.

Could this be of any significance to its interpretation? I am convinced it is. Together with a limited group of abstract characters, the oldest characters are simple, straightforward descriptions of objects or phenomena seen from the front, from above, or in profile. The characters for various kinds of motions often start out from the way the person involved must have seen and perceived the occurrence, such as the characters for *grasp*, *strike*, *shoot*, and many others in which the hand can be seen acting from the right. Although a small percentage of the population of the world is left-handed, the right hand is the one most people naturally choose when using a knife. So I think the character for *knife* in stylized form shows a knife with the point upward and the cutting edge turned to the left, much as can be found on the knives in what are called the clan characters in the bronzes.

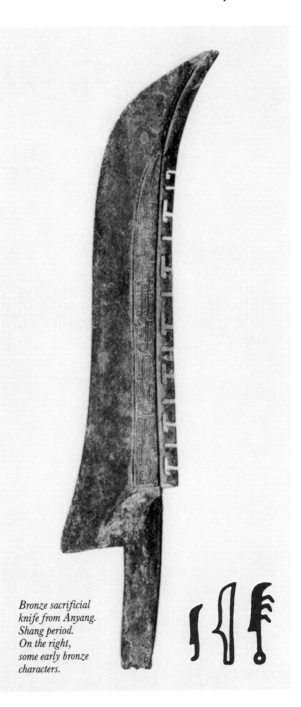

Bronze sacrificial knife from Anyang. Shang period. On the right, some early bronze characters.

knife edge · knife edge

to divide, separate

beginning, first

sharp, cutting, harvest

Further support for this interpretation can be found in the character for *knife edge*, in which the cutting edge is marked with a stroke, just as the root or the top of the tree is marked to show the appropriate part in the character for *root* and *top*. The stroke is placed either slanting over the cutting edge or—like a drop of blood—beside it.

The character for *divide, separate* shows a knife cutting through or dividing something. It is often used to indicate smaller units into which a larger unit is divided, for instance, *minute, penny, department, branch*.

Beginning, first. On the left, the simplified form of the character for *clothes*; on the right, *knife*. The construction of the character indicates it may originally have been concerned with the cutting out of clothes—in that case, the association must have disappeared early on. The character is included in expressions dealing with the beginning of various periods of time such as *first day of the month, at the beginning of summer* or indicating that something happens or manifests itself for the *first time—the first snow, first love, first edition* of a book, for instance. The character is also used in the sense of *fundamental*.

The knife often appears in a form that may seem quite distinct from those seen so far, but it has the same origin. It is seen as early as in the bronze characters and was in general use in 300 B.C., in time becoming the most common. The main line in it has been rotated into a perpendicular position, and the cutting edge is quite free.

In the character for *sharp, cutting, harvest*, the character for *knife* in its simplified form is on the right, the grain on the left—a millet plant with its heavy spadix. Harvest is equivalent to gain, gain equivalent to profit, profit equivalent to advantage. So the character also means *gain, profit, advantage* and is included in many composite words concerned with the tough world of business, from *to make use of, egoism, opportunism, exploit* and *blinded by lust for gain* to *efficient, success* and *economic power*.

The character on the right is usually translated as **axe**.

Its definitive form was, in principle, already evident on the bronzes, and stylization had already gone so far that it is hard to see what is what.

The oracle bone character is clearer, the shaft of the axe almost visible, as is the blade protruding with its sharp cutting edge.

Axes, mattocks, and hoes of various kinds are common among archaeological finds. All of them have special Chinese names, but unfortunately there is no real order in the terminology. Some are called axe but look like a mattock or vice versa. Of course, axes and mattocks must have been very close to each other in both form and use for a long time, and the tool we usually call an axe did not appear until well into historic time, when ordinary farm implements began to be made from metal.

A hint of what that tool depicted in the character for *axe* actually looked like can be seen on a clay vessel from the Dawenkou culture, which flourished on the Shandong Peninsula between 4500 B.C. and 2500 B.C. It shows something resembling a heavy, pointed mattock or pickax, or an adze, a heavy hoe.

Apparently common all over northern China in Neolithic times, tools of this kind were made of deer horn or forked wood and later made more effective with a stone, bronze, or iron blade. They still existed during the first dynasties alongside more sophisticated bronze axes used in sacrificial ceremonies.

An 'axe' of this kind, made from the horn of a deer, was found in Dawenkou and can be seen in the Shandong Provincial Museum in Jinan.

axe

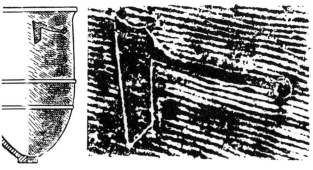

Adze on a clay vessel from Dawenkou. Neolithic period.

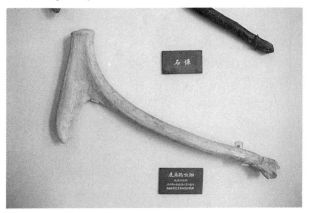

Deer horn adze from Dawenkou.

Children of Dayudao village in eastern Shandong working in their school sweet potato field.

In some ways, the old axes still live on in the China of today—at least to the eye. The implements the peasants use when working in the fields or leveling land to build terraces resemble them, more or less. Or do the present mattocks stem from the old stone axes with a hole in the middle for driving in a handle? No one seems to know the origins.

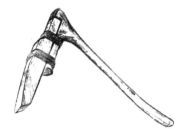

Reconstruction of an adze.

"The libraries are full of books on exquisite bronze, porcelain, and ivory objects of Chinese art," I said to some archaeologist friends in Beijing. "But the history of everyday tools has not yet been written. Why is that?"

"That's not at all odd," they said. "Ordinary old working implements everyone has used since childhood are nothing to do research into. Mattocks and axes have always looked like that."

But when we went further into the subject, they remembered a colleague who had studied minorities in southwestern China, primarily the Miao, the Naxi, and the Hani, and through him I found a number of papers showing that mattocks and axes of the same primitive kind as the adze from Dawenkou are still in use there today, when barking a tree for instance, or breaking up the soil of a field. These two operations must have been most important to the communities where the character was created.

Tree and axe form the character for *to split wood, divide*. In its oldest forms, the character clearly shows the situation involved—on the left, the tree with its outspread branches; on the right, the axe threateningly directed at the trunk, a sight that must have been common in ancient villages when land was being continuously cleared to create new fields for the rising population. Clearing also provided timber for the new roofs and fencing needed, new agricultural implements, plows and mattocks, and boats and carts.

A rather similar character means *to break off, bend*. In the older forms of the character, an axe can also be seen attacking something—according to current explanations, two characters for *grass*. The bronze characters do seem to indicate this, but is it really 'grass' (turned in various directions) on the oracle bones? To 'hack off' grass with the aid of an axe would seem to be using rather more force than required. Could the character be a tree already stripped or cut up? The scribes of the first emperor solved this problem by replacing the two characters for *grass* with the character for *hand*, and the character has appeared in that form ever since.

An axe on which the cutting edge of the blade is marked: *upbraid* (or *reproach*), *scold*, *expel*.

Axe and box: 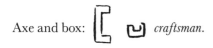 *craftsman*.

The borderline between tool and weapon was fluid in ancient China. The same axe used for felling trees, building stables, and making carts could be used for defending house and home and striking enemies. The character for *soldier* shows two hands grasping an axe.

to split wood,
divide

to break off . . .

斥

to upbraid . . .

匠

craftsman

兵

soldier

been found. As far as can be judged, they were mounted on a shaft, perhaps in the same way as the dagger-axe characters that can be seen depicted in the bronze characters above. These fittings would certainly make very effective weapons—an equivalent of the pitchforks that the European peasant armies fought with. This part of the weapon also seems to have a long history. The oracle bone characters are indeed straggly and thin and show none of the primitive strength found in the bronze characters, but the construction of the weapon nevertheless appears fairly clearly.

The next most common weapon in ancient China was what is called the dagger-axe. During the Shang period, it consisted of a short, broad dagger, often inserted into a meter-long shaft and fastened with a plug through the shaft and handle; or the dagger was bound to the shaft with leather straps—much like the Western halberd, but the Chinese form is distinctive and lacks any equivalent in contemporary Bronze Age cultures.

Although no shafts have been preserved—the wood they were made of soon decayed—the bronze characters can still give some idea of what the weapon looked like. Many of the characters have a lower part that looks like a trident, but little is known about how that part was used, although just over decimeter-long bronze fittings with unpleasantly sharp points have

Parallel to these clear pictures of the dagger-axe, among the oracle bone characters are more stylized versions, and from them stems the character for **dagger-axe**, **battle-axe**.

dagger-axe, battle-axe

Over its long history, the dagger-axe underwent many changes. Scholars have spent a great deal of time recording these. The blade became longer and acquired a long, curved edge like a sickle. The part of the blade that goes through the shaft was drawn out at the other side into a sharp hook, with a knife or a spearhead often mounted on top. Whichever way the warrior struck, there was always a sharp point with which to confront his enemy.

Dagger-axes were even fastened to war chariots, two and two together, with saw-edged blades like a huge bread knife between them. These must have been terrifying weapons as the chariots came charging at full speed through a crowd.

Dagger-axes of the time can be seen in full action on a bronze vessel from the period of the Warring States, both a meter-long for foot soldiers and three meters long for use against enemies in chariots or boats.

Dagger-axe and foot together form the character for *military, warlike, violent.* No one knows what the small top left-hand stroke means, but as it is a late addition, perhaps no great importance need be attached to it.

military ...

Two hands and a dagger-axe: *to guard against, to warn.*

to guard against ...

Man and dagger-axe: *to attack, cut down, punitive expedition.* The character appears very often in oracle bone inscriptions, usually just the two components *man* and *dagger-axe,* quite sufficient to understand the content.

But there are some bronze characters that are considered today to be variants of the character *to attack, cut down,* and in these the brutal situation is all too clear: a strong hand holding a dagger-axe and strik-

attack, cut down

ing a person from behind—an execution. In one of the characters, the victim is kneeling. This made me remember a photograph from China in the 1860s in which a man with his torso bare and hands tied behind his back is bending over, surrounded by curious spectators. With a firm grip on his pigtail—a symbol of submission during the Manchurian dynasty—the executioner's assistant is holding the condemned man's head in position for the fatal blow.

The dagger-axe is also included in the character for *I*. According to the traditional explanation in *Shuowen*, the character shows a hand holding a weapon. With reference to the form the character has on the oracle bones, more recent scholars have suggested that it depicts a weapon with three points. Others, referring to the bronze characters, seem to see two weapons clashing.

Whichever it is, the character for *I* undoubtedly includes a weapon—a depressing thought, but considering man's history on Earth, not really very surprising. The character had its origins in sacrificial rituals and in the ceremonies the king carried out with his diviners to ascertain and influence the future. A very large proportion of the oracle bone inscriptions are about wars fought against surrounding states and tribes, and it was with a weapon in his hand that the king—the dominant I—exercised his power.

Wars during the Shang period had a dual purpose—to defend territory, of course, but also an excuse for taking prisoners of war. A minor misdemeanor by one of the neighboring peoples could lead to widespread punitive expeditions. According to one oracle bone inscription, thirty thousand prisoners of war were taken in a single campaign. These were used not only as slaves in farming and building activities, for which many hands were required, but also as sacrifices together with oxen, dogs, and sheep on major ceremonial occasions.

Men with battle-axes, probably names or characters denoting occupation.

A huge bronze axe used for human sacrifices appeared earlier in connection with the character for *tooth*. Similar axes are found in the more violent bronze characters, in which heads already seem to have rolled. The page on the right from the *Jinwenbian* dictionary—the most comprehensive presentation now available of the early bronze characters—shows some of these. They have no modern equivalent, so are considered to be names and occupations that, fortunately, have disappeared.

Reality in ancient times could be very harsh and, at major ceremonies, a great many people were sacrificed. When a large building was inaugurated in the village of Xiaotun, outside Anyang, 600 people were simultaneously killed. In a grave not far away, 164 sacrificed people have been found, and in Zhengzhou 100 people were decapitated at eyebrow and ear level. And so it has gone.

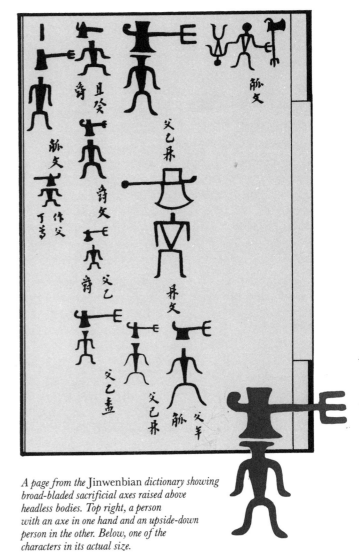

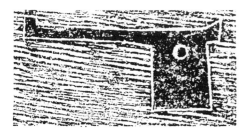

The same type of axe is reproduced on a pottery fragment from the Dawenkou culture on the Shandong Peninsula, which is at least a thousand years older than the character on the bronzes.

A page from the Jinwenbian *dictionary showing broad-bladed sacrificial axes raised above headless bodies. Top right, a person with an axe in one hand and an upside-down person in the other. Below, one of the characters in its actual size.*

ruler

As far as can be judged, since the earliest times, the character for **ruler**, **king** was also the picture of a weapon. The character has been discussed a great deal over the centuries, and because of its apparently simple form and the great importance of the king or ruler in society, it has given rise to some rather sophisticated philosophical interpretations.

According to one of them, the character showed a huge flaring fire symbolizing the power of the king. According to another, the vertical stroke represented the king, in his person combining Heaven, Man, and Earth—the three horizontal strokes. According to yet another interpretation, the king (the vertical stroke) was the link between Heaven (the upper stroke) and the dualistic world in which the great forces of nature, Yin and Yang (the short and long stroke), alternate with each other in eternal succession.

These are beautiful thoughts, but more recent archaeological findings seem to indicate that the character simply depicts a broad axe of the kind used at executions and sacrifices. Axes of that kind already existed as early as in the Shang period, and functioned just as other purely ceremonial jade axes did, as symbols of the power and authority of the king. Many of them have probably never been used for their original deadly purposes.

Bronze sacrificial axe, Fu Hao grave in Anyang. Shang period.

A great many axes with characteristic forms have been found during the excavations of recent decades, some of them with a cutting edge only slightly narrower than the upper part of the axe, others with a powerfully curved edge. Both types have their equivalents among the characters.

For the ruler or king to be represented by his principle means of power—the ceremonial axe, the executioner's axe—should be quite understandable to Europeans, where the *fasces* of the Roman Empire, the bundle of rods containing an axe, to this day still functions as a symbol of power.

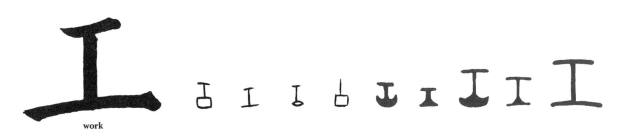

work

To return to more peaceful activities, this character means **work**, **labor**, **worker**. According to traditional explanations, it shows a carpenter's try square—the picture of the tool stands for the whole activity.

As evidence of the correctness of that interpretation, scholars have referred to the character for *try square*, in which a person is seen with an object in his hand resembling the character for *labor*. This is the bronze character; no oracle bone character is known.

This evidence is hardly sufficient. On oracle bones the character for *labor* has a strange form that does not fit well with the meaning *try square*, at least not as usually seen, but gives the impression of describing a tool or implement used to thump or pound something.

What it is, no one knows, but even before the Shang period, there were tools that could be excellent prototypes for this character for *work*, at least as likely as a try square. One of them was a small pounder that potters used for making clay vessels before the potter's wheel came into use. They built up the vessel with long coils of clay placed in rings on top of each other, then pounded them together into a smooth wall. When finished, patterns were then imprinted as decoration. These pounders ceased to be used once the potter's wheel took over but can be seen occasionally in museums, where they are labeled 'beaters' or 'patters.' What they were called during their lifetime is not known.

Small Neolithic 'pounders' used when making clay vessels. 10–12 cm. Henan Provincial Museum, Zhengzhou.

A lump of stone with a handle driven into it, an ancient but very effective tool used for making foundations for houses, walls, and embankments. Layers of earth are pounded into a timber framework. The various layers can clearly be seen on the finished part of the wall. Shaanxi. 1987.

Another kind of pounder is used when building houses or walls of earth. Probably one of the oldest, most important, and most used tools in the whole history of China, this is still in full use today. In the spring when the ground is dry and agriculture not yet started, the opportunity to mend or add to houses and walls in the compound is taken. A layer of earth ten centimeters or so thick fetched from nearby is pounded into an oblong H-shaped timber framework of roped planks or logs. When that layer is hard, the frame is lifted off the finished piece of wall, filled again with earth, then again thoroughly pounded. The wall is built in this way until it has reached the required height.

The most usual pounder is made of stone and rounded at the bottom, about twenty-five centimeters high, twenty-five centimeters wide, and equipped with a wooden handle. In the loess soil areas and on the plains, there is a pounder of this kind on every farm, as common as a hammer or saw in Europe.

There are also larger pounders that can be up to half a meter wide and can weigh between fifty and sixty kilos, used for foundations of houses, marketplaces, or large embankments. Five people usually handle them, but some require eight—one person holding the handle and directing the pounder toward the earth, the others lifting the stone with the aid of long ropes fixed into holes in the side of the stone.

This technique has been familiar since Neolithic times, and although apparently primitive, walls built in this way are astonishingly durable. The town walls around Zhengzhou, built in about 1400 B.C. in the great days of the Shang dynasty, were on average ten meters high and twenty meters wide; and today, over three thousand years later, they are still four meters high, despite the passage of years and the ravages of man. A section of the wall lies in the middle of the town. People treat it rather disrespectfully, growing vegetables on the top and pumpkins and tomatoes at the base. As long as no one sets upon it with mattocks

Two men building an earth wall.

or earth movers, it will certainly stand for another thousand years. The different layers of earth making up the wall are still quite visible, and even more remarkable, so are the deep marks from the tools used as the earth was pounded.

Until quite recently, nothing much has been known about what the implement originally looked like, but during excavations recently made in the central area, stones thought to be old pounders have been found in many places, the oldest resembling an ordinary pestle of the kind used for separating husk from seed, others stronger and wider. They all have a thick, rounded base. They are between twenty and forty centimeters high, some narrow at the top and broad below, others of more even thickness with a hole at

the top where there was probably once a wooden handle.

A similar implement was used when making bricks. There were several different methods, but the one producing the best bricks is very similar to that used for building walls. A wooden frame was filled with earth, then the earth pounded in; when it had dried, the result was a brick considerably more durable than ordinary clay bricks, one which also tolerated much greater loads. The pounding implement was usually a stone into which a wooden handle had been inserted.

From an archaeological viewpoint, the implements used for building walls or making bricks are not particularly remarkable, actually just lumps of stone of a fairly simple kind. But from a *language* point of view, they are extremely interesting. I am more and more convinced that they are prototypes for the character for *work*. As far as I know, nothing has yet been written on the subject, and this is not the place for a more detailed account. But going back to the older forms of the character, it is obvious that many have a heavy lower part that could be interpreted as the stone used to pound the earth; the upper part in that case would be the shaft or handle.

The use of earth as the basic material for building in early Chinese architecture is well documented. The supply of accessible earth was excellently suited to the purpose, and as long as it was pounded sufficiently well, the earth became as resistant as the rocks up in the loess areas. City and town walls are good examples of this. Huge terraces or platforms on which palaces, ancestral temples, and other important buildings were placed are another. Many of them still stand twenty or so meters above the ground.

Immense labor was required for all this building. The perimeter of the walls of Zhengzhou is about seven kilometers long. Archaeologists at the Henan Provincial Museum have reckoned that a wall of such dimensions would have taken twelve and a half years to build, assuming ten thousand men were available to work for 330 days a year.

Practically all towns in northern and northwestern China have been surrounded, well into our time, by walls of this kind. Many sections of the Great Wall built to hold off against deserts and barbarians on the extreme boundaries of the country were also built in

this way, and over the years the walls have also had to be maintained. Together with the canals and embankments, the construction of walls constitutes one of the greatest examples of collective labor carried out in the history of mankind. This could be yet another reason for considering whether the tool used for building was not the prototype of the character for *work*.

The thumping of pounders may well have been as characteristic for Chinese towns as the sound of cars in our towns today. Not only the sound of pounders: to find the rhythm to coordinate and ease the labor, people sang, as people all over the world have done when carrying out heavy toil together, hauling sails, drawing up boats and nets, harvesting, loading and unloading.

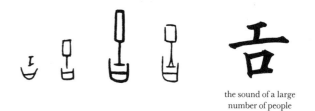

the sound of a large
number of people

Work and mouth together form a character meaning *the sound of a large number of people singing*, which appears in a surprising number of oracle bone inscriptions. It is also said to be the name for one of the hostile tribes in the west with whom the Shang realm was constantly in conflict. In a variant of the character, *work* is replaced with the similarly sounding *joint, all together*, which shows a picture of two hands jointly lifting something. I can't imagine a picture that better describes the collective slave labor on walls than this character, but there are so many other interpretations that perhaps it would be best to return quickly to firmer ground.

Roofs and Houses

roof

The first time I learned that this character meant **roof**, I thought I saw the roof clearly in front of me, flat and with a chimney. But I was wrong. A great many roofs in China do look like this today, but when the character was created, most roofs were pointed and conical. The character for *roof* also appears in that form in the oracle bones.

Roofs were held up on wooden posts supporting a light trellis of ribs that converged toward the opening for smoke. The oldest known forms were thatched with reeds. The drawings on the right are reconstructions of what they may have looked like.

This type of house was already used in Neolithic times, the roof then resting directly on the ground, while people lived below in a hollow about three meters deep and four or five meters in diameter.

Houses gradually moved up to ground level so the roof was free of the ground, raised on posts, not held up by walls. The roof was the basic unit, and the main purpose of the walls was protection against weather and wind, not to carry the roof. Both walls and roof were plastered with earth.

Roundhouses of this kind were common in Banpo around 4000 B.C. and continued to be so during the first dynasties, the door usually facing south.

The shape of these houses resembles the tents still found on the Mongolian grasslands, but with the important difference that walls and roof there are covered with felt. Scholars maintain that there is no connection between the two kinds of houses—which is difficult to understand, because the Mongolian roof is also the primary structure and is held up by a similar construction.

Neolithic cave dwelling and roundhouse in Banpo.

Reconstruction of a roundhouse. Banpo Museum.

Model of Banpo village.

Two square houses were also found in Banpo. According to the reconstruction, one resembles a pyramid-shaped tent with a wind and rain shelter above the entrance. This one stood in the middle of the village and appears to have been used for the clan's communal activities. Although apparently so dissimilar, the construction is largely the same as that of the roundhouses. The floor surface is about 160 square meters.

In its time, Banpo was a large, well-organized village. Remains of forty-six houses have been found, as well as over two hundred storage caves for grain and other important goods, as well as a burial place to the north and a pottery works to the east. The village was probably inhabited for a very long time, but not continuously. Crop rotation was practiced, and when the soil did not produce enough, villagers moved to a new place and did not return until a generation or two later, when the soil had recovered. Then new houses were built—of earth and timber, as usual.

The foundations and holes for the posts can still be seen in the dusty yellowish-gray soil inside the museum, the houses having once stood on exactly that spot. After the excavations were completed in 1957, a roof was erected over them, and it is now possible to go around the wooden walkways, separated from the village only by a light fence, and to imagine what life was like for people who lived there six thousand years ago.

In one of the exhibition halls containing a number of vessels, implements, and other objects found during the excavations, there is a model of what the village may have looked like on its terrace by the river, surrounded by a deep 'moat' five or six meters wide.

Foundations of a house, Banpo Museum. Approx. 4000 B.C.

Over the years, square and rectangular houses became increasingly common. In the village of Dahe near Zhengzhou are the remains of a four-room house about a thousand years more recent than the houses in Banpo. Excavations have been completed, but work on the archaeological finds is still in progress. One Sunday afternoon in 1984, when I had nothing else to do, I went there and was allowed in by a friendly archaeologist.

The village is by the river in the middle of a fertile agricultural area where people were just planting out the rice in the steaming fields. Just as in Banpo, a simple building has been constructed to protect what is left of the foundations, storage pits, and fireplaces, and everything is just as the archaeologists left it. A thin layer of moss has begun to grow over the damp earth, contrasting with the reddish-colored remains of what were once walls. Drifts of newly harvested garlic were draped over the railings, and the earthy smell of moss and garlic, of the thousands of musty pottery fragments in bags around the walls waiting to be reassembled, filled the air and swiftly took me back thousands of years—five thousand, to be precise.

Foundations of a Neolithic house in the village of Dahe near the Yellow River. Left: The plan of the house and a drawing of what it might once have looked like.

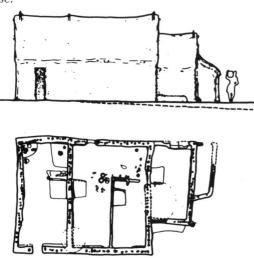

The palace in Erlitou, in use from 1600 B.C. to 1300 B.C., is one of the oldest yet found in China. From the archaeologists' reconstruction, it appears that the main building had eight beams along its length, three beams across its width, and was placed on a terrace of tamped earth. The main entrance faced south, and a gallery ran around the courtyard, held up by rows of pillars. Excavations in the 1970s have shown that the palace was already inhabited before 2000 B.C., during the days of the legendary Xia dynasty, in the area where, according to many old scripts, Xia centered its activities.

How far back this building tradition goes is still not clear, but in the 1970s in Hemudu near Hangzhou, where the Great Canal starts on its way north, house beams carbon 14 dated to over seven thousand years of age were found. Apart from the amazing fact that old timbers of that kind could survive such a warm, humid climate, they are also evidence of astonishingly sophisticated building techniques in which beams were joined together with great meticulousness—this when only stone tools were available.

No such clear evidence has been preserved from Anyang. Foundations of houses and walls are covered over again when excavations are completed. After a brief guest appearance in daylight, they are once again preserved under the yellow earth and corn is again being grown there.

It is known from excavations that most homes were cave dwellings of the kind previously mentioned, but broader, shallower, and—most conveniently—nearly always with steps. There were also buildings of a quite different kind, huge longhouses on high plinths of tamped earth, one twenty-eight meters long, eight meters wide, on a meter-high platform reached by steps. The roof, probably thatched with reeds, was held up by thirty-one wooden pillars, each in a base like a candle in a candlestick. The nonbearing walls were made of earth mixed with straw and plastered with clay.

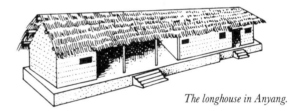

The longhouse in Anyang.

Similar longhouses have been found in the capitals of the Shang kingdom before Anyang—the oldest in Erlitou near Zhengzhou and the Yellow River, the largest in Panlongcheng, further south.

Roof seldom appears alone on the oracle bones, and not at all on the bronzes, but is included in a great many compound characters concerning houses, homes, and construction work.

Peace, quiet: a woman under a roof. Does the character reproduce the calm a man feels when he has a woman under his roof, or is it perhaps her own calm inside by the hearth? That is impossible to know, but she can be seen squatting on her heels with her arms held out as if working on something.

Home, family: a pig under the roof. The place where people live has domestic animals. The oracle bone character is, as usual, rather straggly and insipid, but there is plenty of force in the bronze character.

peace, quiet

home, family

Overnight, spend the night: a person on a mat under the roof.

overnight,
spend the night

Pen, firmly, prison: ox under a roof. The oracle bone character shows that what is now written as *roof* perhaps once portrayed a kind of enclosure. In some characters, the ox is replaced by a sheep or a horse.

Although no remains of pens or other enclosures have as yet been found, it is known from other sources that raising oxen, sheep, and horses must have been widespread during the Shang dynasty. These animals were used in the perpetually recurring sacrificial ceremonies when large quantities of meat were offered to ancestors and consumed by the king and his men.

pen, firmly, prison

The character also has a more special meaning associated with *offering, sacrificial animal*. It is included in the names of two of the leading ceremonies, the Great Offering, at which an ox was sacrificed, and the Small Offering, when a sheep was sacrificed. Both ceremonies still existed into the 1900s.

Peaceful, rest: a heart and a bowl under the roof. Is this the peace that spreads through body and soul when settling down under one's own roof after the day's labors and having something to eat? When the character was simplified in 1958, both heart and bowl disappeared, unfortunately.

To guard, protect. The bronze character shows that the lower part of the character was originally a picture of a hand, sometimes complemented with a small stroke said to be the thumb. Does the hand here stand for defense and protection? Or is it a threatening or thieving hand in action?

Dwelling house, palace, temple. According to one explanation, this character shows a plan of two rooms, complemented with the character for *roof*. That interpretation is supported by the fact that the characters on the oracle bones as well as on the bronzes often appear without a roof, and what can be seen certainly gives an impression of just two rooms alongside each other. From the first standardization in the second century B.C., the character has appeared in the version containing the character for *roof*. The reason could quite simply be that, at the time, all the characters of a certain meaning—for instance, those concerning the concept of 'house'—were being collected under one common heading, in this case, *roof*.

According to another explanation, the character is a picture of a house with a door and window. Two small clay sculptures from Neolithic times in the shape of houses have been put forward as evidence for this theory. Both were found in the Wei Valley not far from Banpo and have obvious similarities with the archaeologists' reconstructions of dwelling houses there. Houses of this kind were common also during the Shang dynasty, when the character acquired its form.

窨

peaceful, rest

宁

the simplified character
for peaceful, rest

守

to guard, protect

宫

dwelling house . . .

ancestral temple...

According to *Grammata Serica Recensa*, this character means *ancestral temple, ancestor, clan, to honor, dignitary* and *the summer audience of the king with the feudal princes.* What could explain these various meanings better than the function of the great house in Anyang as the center of the most important events in the community?

In its oldest form, the character appears to be a surprisingly clear picture of the gable end of the longhouse as the archaeologists imagine it, with pillars and cross-beams holding up the roof. But according to current explanations, it consists of the characters for *roof* and *omen, to show, inform.*

omen, to show

Bernhard Karlgren always used to say that *omen, to show, inform* was a picture of 'stalks used in divination,' but unfortunately, what the character shows is very uncertain. According to the traditional explanation, the upper stroke stood for Heaven, the three below for the sun, moon, and stars, through which Heaven made its will known to people, and the message of which they tried to interpret. Other commentaries say the character shows an altar with a stone on which sacrifices were made, or a commemorative tablet on which the names of ancestors were written.

None of these explanations is really convincing, particularly not when going back to the oracle bone forms. The only certainty is that the character has something to do with observations of various natural phenomena and predictions of fortune or misfortune—activities that all took place in or near the great ancestral temple. The character is included in several compound characters concerning beholding, watching, and rituals.

The character for *roof* appears in many different forms and intrigued me for a long time. Throughout the oracle bones the character with few exceptions has a form close to the round, beehivelike roof of cave

dwellings, while in the bronzes the character seems more often to be a house with a clear relation between roof and walls—the house is more like a real house as we know it and is reminiscent of archaeologists' reconstructions of great ceremonial halls. Was the difference between the two ways of writing the character due to depicting two different kinds of roof?

Chinese linguists I spoke to definitely rejected the idea and said the difference was chance, due only to the individual handwritings of the various scribes: "The knife slipped," they said. But in the summer of 1984, I met a group of scholars in Beijing who had jointly written the history of Chinese architecture, and they at once understood what I meant.

They said that two different forms of house existed side by side for a long time. Ordinary people went on living in caves and houses that often were below ground, while more important houses were built along the same lines as the longhouse in Anyang. In time, houses of that kind became more and more common. Naturally, this development is reflected in the characters, they said, but unfortunately no systematic study of material that would establish this has yet been made. I gladly leave this question for the reader to ponder.

Whatever the circumstances of the character for *roof*, the Shang period longhouse introduces a building tradition that lasted for over three thousand years.

The houses stand on a platform of tamped earth, later often tiled.

The roof is held up by wooden pillars standing freely in holes in the platform, or in special stone 'candlesticks.'

The walls are not bearing, the space between them open or filled with doors, windows, or fine wooden latticework.

The door is placed in the middle of the long wall, facing south.

The Chinese have adhered to this way of building with extraordinary tenacity up to the present day. Naturally, the houses vary in size and splendor, but the basic principles of construction both for private dwellings and ceremonial halls such as pagodas and pavilions remain the same. During the Han dynasty (206 B.C.–220 A.D.), both house and roof forms were given their definitive design; and since then, they have survived to a great extent unchanged until recent decades, when new ideals brought from the West have gained a footing.

Neolithic roundhouses lasted as a type long into historic time, but during the Han dynasty, Chinese houses were given a design that lasted for two thousand years. Dwelling houses, pavilions, temples—are all built along the same principles.

The oldest house in China, an ancestral hall in Feicheng.

The oldest Chinese house still standing is in Feicheng on the Shandong Peninsula, a few miles from the place where the laborious climb up to the peak of Taishan begins. Built of stone, the house stems from the Han dynasty and was consecrated in the year 129, since when it has perched on its mound in the Village of Filial Piety. Then in 1978, a protective building was at last erected over it, and the roof was propped up with some wooden beams.

This ancestral hall is dedicated to the memory of a man called Guo Ju. He was poor and had a hard time supporting his family. His old mother used to share her portion of food with her little grandson, and the boy grew and flourished, while she herself grew weaker and weaker. To save his mother's life, Guo decided to do away with his son—one can always have another son, but never another mother—so he set about digging a pit in which he was to bury the boy alive. His faithfulness to his mother in the end had its reward. After a few spadefuls, he came upon a pot of gold on which was written: 'Gift from Heaven to Guo Ju. No one may rob him of it.' Now rich, Guo Ju was able to let his son live, and in the future everyone had enough to eat.

The story of Guo Ju's praiseworthy respect for his mother can be read on the west wall of the memorial hall and is one of the best known in a collection of moral tales. Under the title of 'Twenty-four Examples of Filial Piety,' it has been part of the upbringing of Chinese children until today. Other stories tell of the boy lying naked at night to attract the mosquitoes, thus helping his parents have a good night's sleep, and another who lay on the ice on the river in the middle of a freezing-cold winter to thaw it out and get the fresh fish for which his stepmother yearned. Piety, for sure.

The development of Chinese architecture after the Han period focused primarily on the roof. A complicated system emerged in which the bearing beams were joined and held in place with brackets or consoles hooking into each other, locking the various parts together without a single nail being required. Beam upon beam of similar construction but of decreasing size are borne aloft by their brackets, free and mobile in relation to each other, joined together in a dynamic equilibrium, neutralizing the movements of the earth—important in an earthquake area—and balancing the weight of the great, curved roof.

Seven-thousand-year-old beams from Hemudu and a construction plan in the Yingzao fashi *manual from the year 1100—one of the many examples of continuity in the tradition of Chinese house building.*

The system is very similar to the Chinese and Japanese puzzle consisting of a number of wooden pieces that fit together in only one way, to form a cube or a ball.

Yingzao fashi (Treatise on Architectural Methods), from which the illustrations on this and the following page are taken, is a manual on the art of building. It was presented to the emperor in the year 1100 by his state architect, Li Jie, an experienced builder himself. His specific and detailed account of the various parts in a building and their internal relationship—a summary of hundreds of years of building experience—became a canon for the Chinese art of building until the present day.

Once the site of the house had been decided on and how many beams long and wide it was to be, there was nothing else to do but start building. The manual contained all the necessary information on dimensions, sections, and quantities of materials, described in extraordinarily instructive illustrations.

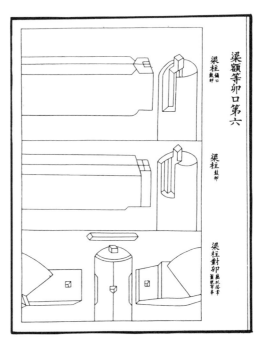

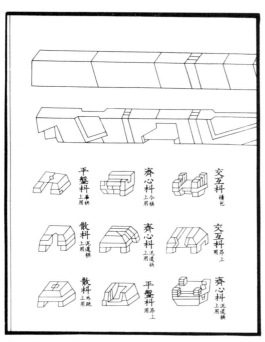

From the 1100 Yingzao fashi *manual.*

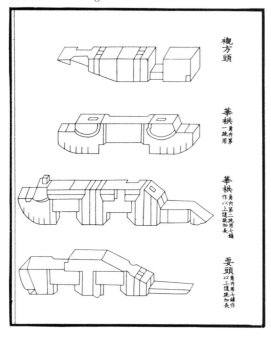

If a small private house is required, the width of the house is limited to the length of one single beam. The manual shows what the house would look like from the gable end.

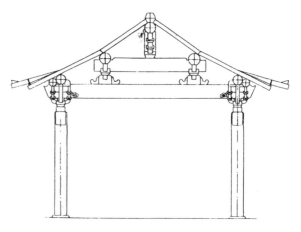

If a large temple was to be built, the width and length were simply increased. The Foguang Temple in Wutai in the Taihang Mountains in Shanxi is three beams wide and seven beams long. It was built in 857, but is still intact after more than eleven hundred years, despite the many earthquakes that have afflicted China. One explanation for why this temple and many other wooden buildings have survived so well is that the various parts are mobile in relation to each other—not anchored in the ground, but standing freely on a platform. They 'float,' to use a modern building term. Even the tall pagodas stand free without a single nail. When the ground shakes, a tremor runs through them but they do not fall. Fire is the only thing to affect them. The pagoda in Yingxian, sixty miles north of the Foguang temple is the oldest wooden pagoda in China. It is sixty-seven meters high: the world's tallest wooden building. It has stood in its place since 1056.

The Great Hall of Harmony in the Forbidden City, Beijing.

Every part of such roofs has a function, bearing and sharing the pressure. Later, roofs became much more purely decorative and many details are meant merely to delight the eye. Yet it is the continuity in Chinese architecture that is most striking. Taihedian, the Great Hall of Harmony in the Forbidden City in Beijing, where the emperor celebrated the New Year and the winter solstice, where he appointed generals and read out the names of the fortunate who had passed the civil service exams—this hall is built along the same principles as the simple dwellings along nearby small streets in central Beijing and in the villages out on the plain, as well as those of the houses where the first kings in the history of China made offerings to their ancestors.

The pagoda in Yingxian in Shanxi province, built in 1056, the tallest wooden building in the world.

The Forbidden City in Beijing, from the north.

Chinese houses are their roofs. Nowhere else can this be seen so clearly as around the Forbidden City in Beijing. Here, too, one can understand more clearly than anywhere else how it came about that *city* and *wall* are written with the same character, for all buildings there are still surrounded by walls, as in the past.

The palace lies right in the center of Beijing inside a high red wall, a city within a city. Its 9,999 rooms are symmetrically arranged along a north–south axis. Despite the immense scale—960 meters from north to south, 750 from east to west—this palace has nothing of the grandiose, almost crushing perspective of the European Renaissance and baroque. One cannot see from the entrance straight ahead to the main building, nor can one in any other Chinese monumental building. Instead, courtyard after courtyard opens up, with halls and terraces adorned with marble, just as one 'roams' through a Chinese painting, letting the images merge one by one before the eyes.

The impression is much like that of the sea when it rolls in to the coast on a windy summer's day. First come some small, good-natured waves; then they grow, and slowly the sea piles up into a huge wave— its accumulated strength pausing for a moment, then in supreme freedom breaking and scattering in cascades of drops, sinking back into the sea again, glistening and calmly reflective, drawing breath before gathering into new waves.

So, too, in the architecture of the Forbidden City all movement culminates around the Great Hall of Harmony. Then the palace sinks slowly to the north, sloping into a peaceful garden—the private garden of the emperor—with cypress and flowerbeds among tall bamboo thickets and paved areas.

Spacious residential areas of gray single-story houses spread out beyond the palace, surrounded by gray walls. They face south and, like the palace, consist of a series of buildings like boxes inside a box, surrounding paved courtyards, where melons are grown, trousers mended, and the dumplings known as *jiaozi* 'tied.'

Only a few decades ago, the great wall of the city towered above all these houses and walls with its watchtowers and gatehouses. It has gone now—to many people's great sorrow—and has made way for highways and new residential areas. But in the 1960s when I first lived in Beijing, it was still largely intact, and we always thought in terms of 'inside' or 'outside' the wall, as the Chinese people have done since time immemorial.

'Inside,' the world was well arranged and orderly despite the throngs of people and houses, and it felt safe to be there. 'Outside' lay the northern Chinese plain, the flattest of all things flat, stretching out endlessly, giving the feeling that there was nowhere to go. The wall was not only the visible boundary between city and countryside, but also gave the city a definite form and the people a sense of being looked after. One knew one's place in the world.

The reason why the city felt well arranged had much to do with the actual plan of the city, which goes back to the beginning of historical time. In *Zhou li*, the *Book of Ceremonies*, like so many texts from Zhou, drawn up during the Han period, there is a section on town planning. The city was to be a rectangle of nine square *li*, with three gates on each side of the wall. Nine east–west thoroughfares and nine north–south thoroughfares divided the city like the warp and weft of a cloth. This was the ideal, and although not always carried out like that in reality, the ideal survived with the same tenacity as the style of building houses. The quarters formed between the thoroughfares were often administrative units of their own, surrounded by their own walls—an equivalent of the street committees into which today's towns are divided.

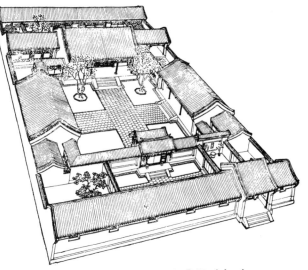

Protected by the city walls, over many centuries Beijing's low houses spread around their courtyards. An outwardly austere façade—a blank wall and an entrance—opened into a peaceful courtyard with trees and flowers. The Imperial Palace was in the middle—no one was allowed to build higher than the emperor.

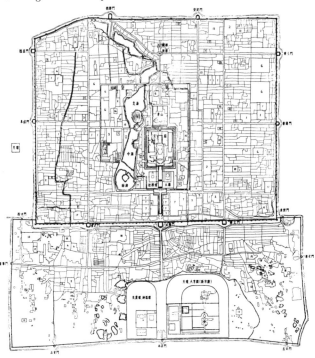

West Beijing residential area. 1987.

Inside the wall, individual houses were protected, and in the same way, villages and towns in the countryside lay in the shelter of their walls; and along the farthest boundaries of the country was the Great Wall of China, guarding civilization against barbarians and the dangers of the outlying areas.

That Chinese towns have been surrounded by walls since the beginning of historical time is well documented, both in archaeological material and literature. Recently, not far from Zhengzhou, the remains have been found of what is considered to be the town of Bo, the first of the capitals of the Shang dynasty, said to have been founded in about 1700 B.C.

The town lies on a hill just where the Yi and Luo rivers meet, immediately south of the Yellow River and within sight of the place where the Great Yu is traditionally said to have lived. In the early 1930s, the Chinese Academy of Science made a preliminary investigation of the site, but then Japan attacked China and all archaeological investigations were postponed. In 1938, when General Jiang Jieshi (Chiang Kai-shek) tried to stop the Japanese advance, he broke the Yellow River embankments. The attempt was unsuccessful, and the whole region was overrun by huge masses of rushing water. When it had finally drained away, the topography of the area was so changed that the site could no longer be found. But after a great deal of assiduous labor, by the end of the 1970s the ancient town of Bo was finally located again, and the excavations have provided a wealth of finds.

Among other things, they show that the town was surrounded by an eighteen-meter-thick wall. The streets were laid out in the squared pattern that was later to become the norm. The southern part of the wall has been partially destroyed by the Luo River, but seven gates are still there. Perhaps they once matched the classic ideal of twelve.

high

The character for **high** reproduces the picture of a tall building, perhaps one of the many watchtowers, or the huge gatehouses over the walls. Few buildings are as imposing as Chinese town gatehouses, terrifying but at the same time promising shelter and safety. People who lived near them must have regarded them as the incarnation of the notion of 'high.'

In the late-seventeenth-century *Mustard Seed Garden Manual of Painting*, there are several gatehouses resembling the character for *high*. Although they stem from a later period in China's history, they nevertheless provide some idea of what the wall and the watchtowers looked like.

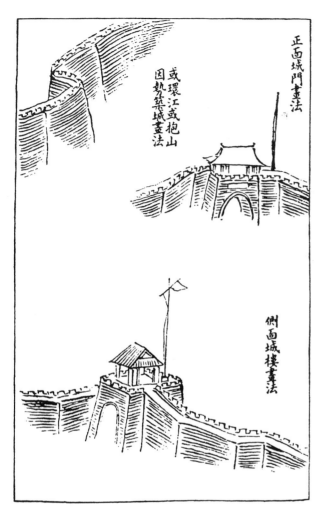

Example of how to paint a city wall with gatehouses and watchtowers. From the Mustard Seed Garden Manual of Painting.

The character for *outer city wall* in its oldest form is a clear picture of a wall with watchtowers, although in detail it does not come up to the ideal in the *Book of Ceremonies*.

In the standardized form of the character, the clear picture has vanished, but the part that apparently shows the watchtower or the gatehouses appears again in several other characters also concerned with high buildings. The right-hand part meaning *town* is a late addition.

outer town wall   Bo

The upper part of the watchtower also appears in the character for *Bo*, the first capital of the Shang dynasty, which is written like this on the oracle bones:

The same upper part occurs in the character for **capital**, which in some older texts such as the *Book of Songs* also means *large granary*. This is not necessarily as confusing as it at first seems. A high proportion of taxes was paid in grain, and with these stores the ruler maintained his administration and his army. The grain was also needed for the important ancestral rites. In addition, it was the ruler's duty as leader of the country to ensure stores of grain for the people in the event of bad years. Great quantities of grain had to be stored, and this happened in the capitals, inside the protection of the walls.

The character for *capital* could simply be a picture of a stilted granary raised off the ground to protect the grain from damp and rats. This type of building is still common among the ethnic minorities in southern China, who live in a warm and humid climate rather like that of central China during the first dynasties. It was also found in Japan from the Han period onward, imported from China, just as the techniques for building temples were later imported. Some bronzes from the Shang and early Zhou periods used for offerings of grain are considered to be models of granaries. Several bronze characters show a similar construction.

There are also several ceramic grave sculptures from the Han period showing granaries on stilts or high platforms with the same function as the stilts.

capital

In front of the granary on its high stilts, the two men on the left are hulling rice with 'tilt-hammers,' the two on the right winnowing the grain.

Outer door of the Wei family's house in the Village of the Flowering Mountain outside Wuhan.
The door is locked with the two transverse bolts.

This is a **door**, a door that everyone who has been to a cowboy film will have seen. 'Saloon doors' are also found in China, particularly in the southern part of the country. They have the advantage of demarcating the room from the outside world, without stopping the circulation of air—practical on hot summer days as well as in winter when the sun-warmed air outside is really needed in the unheated rooms.

But most doors cover the whole doorway and consist of a strong frame with vertical planks inserted into it. They do not hang on hinges, but are upright and held in place on each side by two pegs that extend above and below the outer frame. These pegs, in turn, fit into holes in the base and the beam above the door.

This is a simple, practical, and cheap construction requiring no metal and is used for doors of many kinds, from the outer doors of houses to the elegant cabinet cupboards of rosewood and lacquer.

In principle, the doors are easy to lift off and as easy to put back again, with the longer upper peg fitted first up into its hole, then the door allowed to sink down into the hole in the base, where it stays free, mobile, and stable.

In the past, when a country family had an unexpected guest for the night and all beds were occupied, they simply lifted off a door and the guest slept on it, out of the floor draft. A great many unexpected visits were necessary during the long years of war before the 1949 revolution. In the basic regulations for how a good soldier should behave, Mao included the following instruction: Always hang the door back when you leave!

door

Handsome door from the 1100 Yingzao fashi *architectural manual.*

门

the simplified character for door used since 1958

The oldest character provides a good picture of the construction of the door. So do the three gates at the bottom of a famous 1229 map of the town of Suzhou carved on a two-meter-high gravestone from the same period. The gates show the entrance to a residential area surrounded by walls in the center of the town. The whole stone can be seen in the old Confucian temple next to Middle School Number One in southwestern Suzhou.

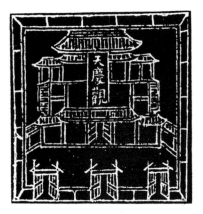

Older Chinese houses seldom have locks inside, but the entrance in the wall onto the street is always barred at night, just as the gatehouses were in the past. One of the most common types of lock can be seen on the Wei family's house in the Village of the Flowering Mountain, outside Wuhan. Two bolts from opposite directions are shot across the door. In the picture a simple lamp casts a dim light over the rough planks, the earthen wall, and the mattocks, carrying poles, and other tools left in the corner.

Heavier doors are often locked with a long bar right across the two halves of the door. The character for *lock, bolt, close* clearly shows that this way of locking has a long tradition.

lock, bolt, close

When the bar is to be withdrawn in the morning, considerable strength and two hands are needed. This can be seen in the character for *open, begin, to start.*

開

open, begin, to start

In today's simplified form, the door has vanished, but the essentials are still there, and the character has become much easier to write.

开

Someone disappears rapidly out of the door, only his legs visible, then he has gone: *to run away, dodge, to flash like lightning.*

to run away, dodge . . .

戶

The character for **household**, **family**, used when speaking of how many households in a town or village, was from the beginning a picture of a door—not a double door like the street gate but an ordinary single door of the kind normally used for individual rooms inside a house. In some compound words the character still means *door*.

One family, one household per room is still common in China, just as it was in many European countries not long ago. In 1985 in Shanghai, it was considered a major triumph to have at last achieved 4.7 square meters per person. In the countryside there is generally more space, but it is still logical for the picture of a single door to mean *household, family*, for a great many families have no more than one room.

Single door and wings: the *door* that flaps like a wing when people keep going in and out of the house during the day. The character also means *to fan*, like wafting a hand or a stiff leaf back and forth to revive the fire or to cool off on hot summer days. In a transferred sense, the character also means a *fan*.

Half-door leading into a dwelling in central Shanghai. Outside is a portable charcoal stove with a kettle and washbowl. Household chores are often done on the pavement.

leaf of door, fan

Single door and axe: *site, place*. Bernhard Karlgren says 'to axe out a living place.' Others think the axe stands for the sound of wood being chopped, common near the places where people lived. Six of one, half dozen of the other?

site, place

The character for **cave** in its early forms is almost identical with the character for *roof*, which makes sense, considering what houses and roofs looked like in ancient times. What the two strokes inside under the actual roof mean is not clear. A possible explanation would be that they indicate the inside of the roof and the space below, while the character for *roof* stands for roof in general. We saw this type stroke earlier in the character for *top, root* and *cutting edge of a knife*, indicating which part of the object is meant.

Together with *dog*, this character forms another for *suddenly, abrupt, come rushing*. A jolly character!

suddenly . . .

Peking man and his (her) successors of the Paleolithic period lived in deep natural caves. In later periods caves were dug out of the mountainsides and the loess soil of the plains. Even today, about 40 million Chinese in Henan, Shanxi, Shaanxi, and Gansu live in caves. Primitive, perhaps, but also practical, pleasant, cheap, and perfectly in accordance with ten thousand years of tradition. In an area where the shortage of cultivable land is catastrophic, where since very ancient times and until only recently there has been hardly a tree to use for timber, and where money for timber from elsewhere was lacking and stone of suitable quality hard to find, caves were a simple and ingenious solution.

Well-designed caves make surprisingly good and attractive dwellings and are superior in several ways to more conventional housing. If I lived in the loess soil area, I would prefer to live in a cave rather than an ordinary house. This has nothing to do with nostalgia or exoticism; the caves quite simply have qualities with no equivalent in modern houses. The rooms are quiet and calm and retain a certain humidity in the dry winters, making it easier to breathe. They are warmer in winter and cooler in summer, with less fluctuation in temperature—a great advantage in a climate of extreme fluctuations between day and night and between seasons. Winters are very cold in the area, and although the north wind blows persistently, it does not get into the caves. Even when there are frosts and high winds, caves maintain a natural temperature of $11°$–$12°$ ($51°$–$54°$F), and if it is too cold, fuel can be added to the stove. In summer when the temperature outside is far above $30°$ (over $85°$F), it is $21°$–$22°$ ($70°$–$73°$F) inside the caves, equipped as they are, so to speak, with silent, built-in air-conditioning that costs nothing to run.

The caves are usually built on a ledge in the side of the mountain, for it is important to be up out of the humidity of the valley and not use valuable cultivable land. They are not particularly big—three or four meters wide and five to six meters in depth and height—but the roof is vaulted and that, together with the whitewashed walls, gives the room a quiet, dignified atmosphere. Several caves are often made in a row, connected with a door or an open porch. Most beautiful of all is the light trickling through the latticework of the windows, thin wooden slats covered with rice paper. The windows around

Cave dwellings in the village of LiuLin, outside Yan'an. 1976.

Cave dwellings under construction. LiuLin, outside Yan'an.

Yan'an are famous. From the highest point of the arch, they extend down to about a meter from the ground and constitute a secular Chinese equivalent of our medieval church windows of artificially welded pieces of glass.

Under the window, or along the long side, is what is called the *kang*, a fixed brick bed heated from below and best described as a horizontal tiled stove. That is the focal point of the room, where the whole family sleeps at night, tucked into the cozy red cotton quilts on the warm stones of the *kang*, or on a cool reed mat, and sits in the daytime to mend clothes, make shoes, do homework, cut out papercuts, and so on.

If possible, caves are placed facing south or southwest. That protects them from the north wind but allows the low winter sun in to warm up the room, extending the day indoors—an essential detail in an area which until quite recently lacked electricity. In summer, when the sun is high, it does not enter the cave until the late afternoon, when it has already lost its sting, and then the cave is still cool and pleasant, so it doesn't matter.

Most everyday tasks are carried out year-round along the courtyard that runs past the caves. There is a small vegetable plot of onions and garlic, a few flowers in a pot, an outdoor stove, and a shed for the black pigs when they are not running free. In many places there is a wall of tamped earth 'fencing in' the plot.

At a distance, the caves, yards, and walls merge into the side of the mountain, and all that can be seen is a yellowish-gray hillside, with windows set in the high arches. Their form seems familiar—reminiscent of the cave dwellings in Banpo and other Neolithic dwelling places.

Up on the high plateau, as well as down on the plain around the Yellow River where there are no mountainsides to dig into, mountainsides are created by digging straight down about eight meters and removing all the soil within a square of about ten-by-ten meters. This produces a gigantic sunken cube, its floor about a hundred square meters, and from the walls of the cube, caves are then dug in the ordinary way, generally three caves per cube. There is usually no cave, at least for living purposes, on the south side where the sun never reaches. One family per cube is usual, a small walled yard in the shelter of the earth. Most families have trees and a well of their own, and it would be hard to find a safer place for chickens, pigs, and small children. The peasants live in these caves, deep down under the very soil they till. Up on the plain, the winds and clouds blow over the crops, and travelers see nothing but fields and soil until they are standing in the middle of the village and yard after yard suddenly appears in the ground like dark squares on a modernistic piece of cloth.

The caves are based on many thousands of years of tradition, and every detail over the generations has been adjusted to people's needs and the demands of building materials. For a large part of the 1900s, the caves were regarded as contemptible remnants of a poverty-stricken, underdeveloped life that must be eradicated, the sooner the better. Now their advantages are beginning to be recognized. Ways of preserving the building experience hidden in these caves have recently been discussed at several major conferences, as well as ways of modernizing without destroying their original qualities.

Cave is also included in the character for *window*, but that is a fairly recent addition. The lower part, considered to be the original, shows a window opening of some kind, perhaps a simple wicker panel to let air, light, and smoke through, but to keep out unwelcome visitors.

window

A window opening of this kind can be seen in the roof above the door in the small clay sculptures of houses from Neolithic times, as well as in the archaeologists' reconstructions of the Banpo houses, a necessity for the circulation of air in the house. A door with an opening above it created a sufficiently strong draft to draw out stale air and smoke from the hearth.

There was no difficulty about putting a window into the roof. When the woven lathes of which the house consisted were to be covered with clay as protection against the rain, a section was quite simply left open, and wicker of osiers or bamboo could easily be woven in so that there would not be a yawning gap. It was also easy to build the roof protruding slightly above the window to keep the rain out. Similar ventilation openings were found in the roundhouses and cave dwellings of the Shang and Zhou periods, and they still exist high up under the vaulting in the tall cave windows of the loess area.

The small openings of ancient times were probably not particularly remarkable, but a few hundred years later the Chinese window had developed a style all its own, a style that in time became the most expressive and aesthetically appealing element in Chinese architecture. On Han period grave tiles and grave sculptures in the form of houses there are windows consisting of crude wooden grids of upright, horizontal, slanting, and crossing wooden slats. Then changes became rapid. As early as the Tang period, temples, palaces of officials, and more distinguished private houses were decorated with exquisite latticework windows, covered on the inside with rice paper or in exclusive cases, white silk.

Windows became more and more elaborate during the dynasties, as did doors; from the Ming period onward it is hard to tell the difference between them—both fill the façade with latticework. Four doors between every pillar and five smaller windows immediately above them is a common arrangement in larger buildings and temples.

As the walls in traditional Chinese wooden houses do not bear weight, complete freedom exists to use the space between the pillars as desired. Walls can be omitted completely, providing a pavilion where good friends can gather in the evening to play music or

The tall windows of the room open out onto the rock gardens and ponds. Suzhou.

have a meal. A waist-high balustrade may run between the pillars, or the whole section may be filled, with windows and doors designed like patterns of lace. In winter, doors and windows can be kept closed and covered with paper, which insulates almost as well as glass; and when the willow tree's long, sweeping branches begin to bud and the cherry trees bloom again, the windows and doors are opened or quite simply lifted off, leaving a lovely outdoor room for the summer, protected from the sun but open to every cooling breeze.

These beautiful windows and doors can still be seen all over China today, even on quite ordinary houses where they take up the whole long wall. There are usually no other windows. Today the lower part of the window is often glazed, although the upper part is still covered with paper.

There are probably as many patterns for these decorations as there are carpenters in China, but in principle all are variations of ordinary geometric shapes—squares, rectangles, circles, and rhombi— by themselves or alternating in an apparently endless series of combinations. Simpler patterns are often rather like the woven chair seats common in the West, but there are also wavy patterns, S-shapes and U-shapes interlocking with each other, like patterns formed by the cracks made when newly formed ice is stomped on. Others are stylized good-luck symbols for a long life, wealth, dragons, clouds, birds, and flowers—all reproduced in thin wooden slats painted brown or red.

Some examples of ornamental latticework decorating traditional Chinese windows.

I remember many evenings I spent wandering around older quarters of ancient cities such as Beijing, Suzhou, and Anyang. At first the roofs and gray walls stand out, and the lively bustle under the trees along the street—women washing, men with their playing cards and bird cages, and little girls with endless games of jump rope. But as darkness falls and the street empties, all life seems to condense and pour through the doorways into the houses. Not much of what is going on inside can be seen from the street—the construction of the houses, or rather the courtyards, prevents looking straight in—but all the sounds can be heard as if one were right in there oneself: sounds of cooking, children being put to bed, and everything else that happens when people are preparing to settle down for the night. If one looks cautiously in behind the screen by the porch, the long windows look like luminous abstract pictures on which the latticework is drawn in thin lines, the pale light shining gently out over the courtyard and dispersing among bicycles, stools, flowerpots, and cages of chickens. Occasionally, shadows of people moving inside flit across the soft whiteness of the paper, reminding one that despite its mystery, this is a perfectly ordinary window in a perfectly ordinary home.

Windows are never found in walls facing the street, but they are common in walls between the various groups of houses within a traditional Chinese courtyard, as they are in the passages and winding galleries linking buildings in a garden. The windows certainly help to increase the circulation of air, but they also catch the eye, leading it on and arousing expectations about rooms glimpsed on the other side.

When space is too limited, the Chinese have a way of dividing it up even more to create small room spaces, mysterious corners, and surprising views, making one involuntarily slow down, stop, and look around. Behind the tiled latticework of the window is a branch of wisteria with its heavy blue clusters, an unusual stone, or perhaps just a vibrating shadow of bamboo stalks against a white wall. No more is needed to make a gloomy passage into one of the most beautiful spaces in a house or garden. The light plays and leads the eye astray, preventing it from noticing how cramped and dark it really is; and because of the window's limited surface, one's attention becomes concentrated as if on a picture.

One of the most important lessons the first settlers learned was that clay vessels exposed to fire become watertight. In China, that knowledge also began to be used in Neolithic times to protect dwellings against the rain. Loess soil is an excellent building material in many ways, but one weakness is that it easily absorbs moisture, and rain dissolves it. To be useful, it had to be given a waterproof surface.

Latticework windows in a garden in Suzhou, poems carved in black stone behind the panes of glass on the left.

From the remains of houses found in Banpo, Dahe, and other villages, it is known how this was done. Roof, walls, and floors—sometimes the bearing pillars as well—were covered with a layer of clay. When it had dried, a fire was lit and slowly burned along the various surfaces of the house. The clay vitrified from the heat and became as firm and watertight as the surface of a clay pot. The procedure required meticulous care and attention so that the fire did not flare and burn down the whole house; but once done, this firing made the house considerably more protected, not only against the rain but also against rats and insects.

As far as I know, this method is no longer used; the walls are limewashed instead, and the *kang*, the great family bed, is tiled. But a small remnant of early Chinese skill in the use of fire still remains in the cooking done in an ordinary kitchen in the countryside. Stoves are primitive, but by varying the fuel, cooks can adjust the heat and adapt it to whatever food is being cooked. Straw and stems give out gentle heat and so are used for cooking rice, twigs for steamed bread, whole pieces of wood for fried pork that requires a fiercer flame, and so on.

In large parts of northern China where there is little rain, often roofs are still simply covered with a mixture of clay and straw beaten together so tightly that water cannot get through. Further south, roofs are tiled instead. According to ancient writings, tiles were used as early as during the Xia dynasty, the oldest preserved from the beginning of the Zhou period. At the time, they were used primarily on the ridge of the roof and along the outer edges—the most exposed parts of a roof—but after a few hundred years the whole roof was covered from top to bottom with tiles, a further development of the Neolithic roof of burnt clay.

The tiles of the Zhou period were gray, as tiles on ordinary houses have continued to be until today. They were about thirty centimeters long and fifteen centimeters wide. A tube of clay was made first, then cut up into long, narrow pieces. The tile acquired the rounding that is rather like our guttering from the roll of clay. One end was pressed flat to be slipped in under the tile above and then held in place by a small projection. It is thought that the character for **roof tile**, **roofing** stems from tiles of this kind. No earlier character is known, but considering the appearance of the tiles, the explanation seems reasonable.

roof tile

House roof. Suzhou.

According to another theory, the roof tile acquired its shape from the lengths of split bamboo used as roofing material throughout the history of China and still common in southern parts of the country. Thick pieces of bamboo are split, the inner walls removed, and the bamboo halves laid over the roof with the inside facing up, the joints between them sometimes covered with clay or another layer of bamboo placed on top, the outside facing up. Rainwater falling onto the roof is then quickly and effectively drained away.

Among the grave sculptures of the Han period are numerous dwelling houses, watchtowers, granaries, and gatehouses with tiled roofs. From them it can be seen that the bottom part of the tile had begun to be given round or semicircular decorations with impressed pictures of animals and plants. Sometime during the same period, the tiles also began to be glazed, and from the Tang period onward official buildings were decorated with magnificent roofs of yellow, green, and blue tiles. Yellow was reserved for the Imperial Palace, green for the administrative buildings, and blue for temples. Ordinary people kept to their gray roofs.

This is the character for **enclosure**, which appears only in combination with other characters, as has already been mentioned in connection with *vegetable garden*. Together with pig, it forms the character for *pigsty*, and together with millet, the character for the small *granaries* individual peasants have in their homes, as opposed to the 'high' imperial granaries in the capital.

豕	囷	困	囚
pigsty	granary	surrounded by	prisoner

A tree in an enclosure: *surrounded by*, as a tree is surrounded by its enclosure or a man by his friends. But also *to be surrounded, encircled by* and *in difficulties*, and so *under pressure, tired, sleepy*.

A man in an enclosure: *prisoner*. When I see this character, I always think of the square wooden collar that thieves and smugglers had to wear day and night for several weeks or months as punishment for their crime. The crime was written in large letters on the collar; the length of the period of punishment and the weight of the collar depended on how serious the crime was considered. The collar was just big enough for the man to be unable to put food into his mouth, so that he either had to be helped by others or had to try snapping up a little food from the ground like an animal.

A variant of the collar was the slatted cage that grave-robbers and violent criminals were put in. The cages used to be placed out in public in front of the *yamen*, the central official building, or in front of the town gatehouse. Sometimes it was so low that the criminal could not stand upright, sometimes so high that he could not reach the ground and had to stand on bricks. These bricks were gradually removed, one a day, forcing the criminal to stand on tiptoe. When the last brick was taken away, he could try to keep himself up by pressing his feet against the sides of the cage. But as his strength failed, he was mercilessly hanged by his own weight. The procedure used to take about two or three days.

Execution in Shanghai. 1904.

Enclosure is also included in the character for *map*, or does the original picture show the actual map with various villages, roads, water courses, or whatever else they may be?

map

China has a very long history of cartography. As early as the Zhou and Han periods, several agencies were occupied with mapping out the country from various viewpoints, and there were special maps of different areas, of mineral supplies, military resources, and so on. The emperor made journeys of inspection, and the topography and the products of the area were explained to him.

When Qin Shi Huangdi became the first emperor in 221 B.C., he had all available maps collected, and later emperors constantly sent out expeditions to map new areas. The great journeys of exploration during the Middle Ages were a natural continuation of these activities.

The oldest maps preserved were found in 1973 in two graves in Changsha, dated to 168 B.C. They are painted on silk in three colors, two of them showing a mountainous area with rivers, roads, and towns, and the third a purely military map providing a detailed description of fortifications and defenses.

For a long time, I thought I knew what maps were. We had traveled a good deal (sometimes just on the map, one of the prime enjoyments of life). Then one day I went into the big bookstore in Wangfujing, the main street in Beijing, and saw a map that looked very odd. Nothing seemed right—continents floating hither and thither and shapes that since childhood I had been used to regarding as permanent, incorruptible as archetypes, now transformed into amorphous, swelling masses.

Couldn't the Chinese draw maps? They could indeed. But until the day I stepped into that bookstore I had not understood how one-sided my view of the world was, or how dependent I had been on regarding Europe as the center of the world. If the center is elsewhere, in China for instance, shapes of continents swiftly change on the map, large becoming small, wide becoming narrow—a useful lesson.

Another surprise faced me later when I found that older Chinese maps put south instead of north on top, as though the viewer were facing south, as towns and houses in China have always faced, as have their compasses. Nothing remarkable in itself, just a very consistent attitude.

the simplified character for map

Books and
Musical Instruments

The first time one holds a traditional Chinese book, everything seems back to front. From our point of view, not only do we have to start reading backwards—the last page of one of our books is the first in a Chinese book—but added to that, the lines of text run vertically from top to bottom, not horizontally from side to side, and one starts reading in the top right-hand corner of the page.

This arrangement of texts goes back a long time. Writing on the oracle bones and bronzes was generally laid out this way, and the first real books in China continued to be in this form.

The oldest books consisted of thin strips of bamboo. These were made by cutting strong bamboo stems into certain lengths, as short as twenty centimeters, as long as seventy. The cylinders, in turn, were cut into centimeter-wide strips and the outer green skin scraped off. When the strips were dry, the characters were written on their smooth, taut surface with brush and ink. The strips were then tied together with thin hemp or silk cord and rolled up. The 'book' was ready.

Writing script vertically is not as strange as it may at first seem. Modern studies show that people read vertical lines faster than horizontal—possibly something to do with the muscles of the eye. Writing in this way seems to suit the Chinese language particularly well, with each character a freestanding unit.

The drawing on the right is of a section from the *Book of Rituals*, one of thirteen classics that have been the core of Chinese culture from the Han dynasty until the present day. The strips in the book are just over half a meter long, with the rolled-up text on the left and on the right, the sixteen bamboo strips on which it is written.

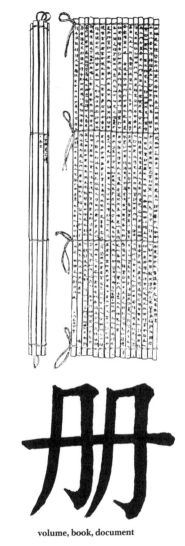

volume, book, document

A book of this kind is seen in the character for **document**, **volume**—bamboo strips bound together with a cord.

Paper book in the form of a scroll. The text is a fourth-century copy of the oldest book on paper in the world, written in the year 256. Reading starts in the top right-hand corner and continues as new text is fed in, roughly like winding a film in a camera. To provide stability for the scroll, both ends of the paper are fixed to a strip of wood. The style of writing is a transitional form between lishu and kaishu.

This text is a historical account of the chaotic period following the downfall of the Han dynasty, when three kingdoms were struggling for power. Generations of storytellers in markets and teahouses used it as a source of material for their adventurous tales, and their stories in turn are the basis of one of China's most famous literary works, the fifteenth-century novel about the Three Kingdoms, new editions of which are still brought out. Right: An extract from the book.

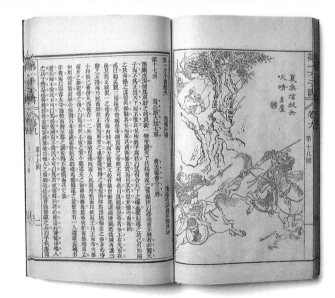

Books made of bamboo are direct predecessors of the traditional Chinese book. They were used from the Shang dynasty until the end of the Han dynasty in the third century—a period of more than a thousand years. Altogether, about forty thousand strips with a great many different kinds of texts have been found—military treaties; works of philosophy, medicine, mathematics, and astronomy; laws and calendars, biographies, and essays.

Bamboo books were both practical and cheap, but heavy and clumsy to handle. During the long period they were in use, society developed a great deal. Trade and other contacts between the various parts of the realm and neighboring states entailed an enormous increase in the number of documents. The purely physical effort required to handle bamboo books became more laborious as each century went by. It is said that the first emperor, a bureaucrat and autocrat, had to plough through over 120 pounds of documents each day to rule and control his kingdom as he desired.

As early as 700 B.C., if not earlier, for practical reasons, scripts began to be written on lengths of silk cloth, the texts arranged in the same way as on the bamboo strips. But silk was expensive and for some time appears to have been used only for important official documents. Eventually, it also became common in more ordinary contexts and continued to be so until the Tang dynasty (618–906) and the transition to paper.

Texts, however, had by then become so long that scrolls became difficult to handle, so paper began to be folded in accordion pleats and sewn at the spine. Thus a book with flat pages arose, outwardly more like books of today than ancient scrolls. But the arrangement of the texts on the paper was not changed. Until today, books continued to be printed with the text—only on one side of the paper—running vertically. Not until recent decades has our kind of book made any headway in China.

Chinese artists have continued to paint landscapes and flower pieces on scrolls of silk or paper, adding atmospheric poems in characters arranged as they were on the old bamboo strips.

The bamboo book, complemented with the character for *stand*, *little table* is also included in the character for *statute*, *code*, *documents*. A variant of the character contains two hands holding out the book as if to read it.

statute, code, documents

Until the middle of the Tang dynasty when printing began, books were all written by hand. According to tradition, the brush is said to have been invented in the third century B.C., but recent archaeological finds indicate that it was in use at least a thousand years earlier, perhaps even during Neolithic times. There are a great many symbols on clay vessels from Banpo, dated 4000 B.C. and written with brush and black ink. The shape of the strokes seems clearly made by a brush. These symbols are strikingly like real characters.

Characters written in black or red can also be seen occasionally on oracle bones. A first draft was apparently often done in color before engraving the characters into the bone. For some reason, certain characters were never engraved, and from these one can tell that a supple, flexible brush was used. The characters are written according to the same principle that still applies—horizontal strokes from left to right, vertical from above downward.

Further evidence of the antiquity of the brush can be seen in the character for **brush**, **pen** on oracle bones as well as bronzes. It shows a hand holding a brush vertically, just as all the rules of the art still dictate today so that the hand and brush will have the greatest freedom of movement when writing.

At present, nothing is known about the appearance of the oldest brushes, but there is much to indicate that they were made of pieces of bamboo, perhaps chewed soft at one end. During the Zhou period, the original character for *brush* was complemented with the character for *bamboo*.

brush, pen

Several brushes have been preserved from the late Zhou period, their construction very similar to those used today. The shaft is usually of bamboo, the head consisting of animal hairs of various kinds, often a hard core of perhaps hare or deer and a softer outer layer of sheep's wool. Together, the different types of hair make the brush at the same time supple and stable, as well as suited to all the different strokes.

brush, pen

Illustration from a 1983 calligraphy textbook.

There is no end to the types of brushes. Different kinds of script and the personal taste of writers require different types of brushes, and for all those dedicated to calligraphy—the supreme art, in Chinese eyes—there are special shops with thousands of brushes of all qualities and prices to choose from. A really good brush costs a month's salary for a teacher or a worker, but if well looked after, may last for many years, even decades. The sizes of brushes vary greatly, from small thin brushes weighing a few tenths of a gram to huge, heavy ones. A calligraphy journal recently published photographs of brushes weighing forty kilos. All have one thing in common— they end in an extremely thin, nicely converging tip from which all brush strokes emanate.

By altering the pressure of the brush on the paper, the width of the brush stroke can be varied. The greater the pressure, the further the brush is forced down onto the paper and the more ink is pressed out of the head of the brush, which acts as a container for the ink. When the hand is again lifted and the brush continues across the paper, thin dreamlike lines are created by the extreme tip of the brush.

During the character reforms of the 1950s, the original picture of *hand* and *brush* was removed and replaced with the character for *hair, down, fur*—not far off, for brushes are still made of animal hairs of various kinds. The simplified form also has a long tradition.

the simplified character for brush

Ink seems to be as old as the brush, shown for instance by chemical analysis of the coloring with which the characters on the oracle bones were written. From early times it was made by the soot formed from burnt wood, and soot is still the main ingredient of Chinese ink. The most famous ink comes from the Huangshan Mountains in Anhui, the same province that produces the famous Xuan paper. That ink is made from pine.

Later, probably sometime during the Song dynasty (960–1279), soot formed in lamps fueled by oil of various kinds began to be used. Lampblack, as it is usually called, is greasier than wood soot and provides a deeper black.

To make ink, soot of various kinds is mixed with glue made of bone, horn, or hide, sometimes with an extra binding such as egg white, and spiced with musk, sandalwood, camphor, or other scented substances.

The ink produced is kept dry in cakes, often beautifully decorated with pictures of creatures that bring luck, such as dragons, deer, or carp, or beautiful flowers and landscapes. To use this cake of ink, it is rubbed against a specially shaped stone on which a little water has been poured. By slowly moving the cake around and around against the stone, the ink required is released—the same ink and the same brush are used for both writing and painting.

For several thousand years, writing in China has been much more than a means of registering facts, leaving messages, or writing poetry. The actual way of forming the characters—providing them with balance and clarity, intensity, force, and life, in short saturating them with all the emotions found within a human being, and yet keeping within the framework of the writing tradition—has long since been regarded as the most supreme of arts. The implements used by the calligrapher—brush, ink, and the ink-stone—were themselves elevated to works of art from very early on and described and discussed in scholarly papers. Both ink-cakes and ink-stones became collectable objects, and even today a beautiful old ink-stone can cost as much in China as a unique porcelain bowl from an ancient dynasty.

It could equally well be a picture of a shaman, a magician who, in association with dances and ceremonies carried out to make contact with the spirits of the dead, painted patterns on their faces and bodies—shamans prepare themselves in this way well into our time.

One of the oldest known depictions of a human being, a head forming the lid of a Neolithic burial vessel, is probably that of a shaman. His face is covered with black lines and at the nape of his neck is something rather like a wriggling snake. Until a few years ago, this head was considered unique, but several pots with similar lids are said to have been found during the 1980s. Unfortunately, I have not seen them, but perhaps they will provide further clues to the interpretation of the character for *black*.

The character for **black** seems at first apparently very simple, but it has become subject to a great many interpretations. The traditional explanation based on *Shuowen* is that it shows soot formed around window openings where smoke from the fireplace emerges. But nothing in the forms of earlier characters indicates that this was the case. Later commentaries suggest that it shows a person whose face and body are covered with spots—perhaps warpaint? Or branding? Or tattooing?

Lid of a Neolithic burial urn in the shape of a head, found in northwestern China.

Black, extended with the character for *earth*, *soil* also means black, but today is used primarily for *ink*—the black, earthy material used for writing and painting (painting oneself?). In some texts, it also means *branding*. Burns are often black.

ink

Whatever the origin of the character for *black*, *ink*, the brush and ink have continued to this day to be the leading implements for writing. Fountain pens and ballpoints have now taken over for everyday notes and memos, but when large-size characters are required, or texts of aesthetic significance, then brushes are used. Schools arrange calligraphy competitions, and exhibitions of nothing but characters are held in art galleries, where calligraphers gather for earnest discussions on individual characters and strokes. Even the big character posters of the Cultural Revolution—those savage wars of words—were written by hand with brush and ink, as are shop and restaurant advertisements of today.

writing, script

This character in the older scripts means *lines*, *strokes*, *ornaments*. But even during the Zhou period it was already used primarily in the sense of **writing**, **script**, **literature** and for **civil** (as opposed to military) and **cultivated**.

On the oracle bones and bronzes the character shows a person standing with arms held out slightly away from the body. As far as can be seen, the chest is what is important in the character, for in most cases it is decorated, either with a heart or a mouth, a cross, a *U*, a *V* or at least a dot.

"Crossing lines," *Shuowen* says.

"Man with tattoo on his chest," say later commentaries, referring to passages in classical scripts describing tattoos used by 'barbarians' of neighboring areas in ancient times to beautify their bodies.

In that case it would be an irony of fate that this character in particular should have such origins, for later in Chinese culture it came to stand for everything concerned with education, sophistication, and elegance, as opposed to anything crude, underdeveloped, and 'barbaric.'

'Educated' men belonged to the privileged class in ancient society. Through their knowledge of the written language and classical works, they were elevated above the 'stupid masses'—the label given to those who could not read. Educated men were those who dedicated themselves to calligraphy, collected inkstones, grew orchids, wrote poems they then read to each other over a cup of rice wine when the bustle of the day had at last subsided, and painted beautiful landscapes on which a little boat slowly moves through the river mists.

The written language they used is usually translated as 'classical Chinese' or 'literary language.'

literary language

It was an artificial language with all the advantages and disadvantages such a language can have—affected and rigid, cliché-ridden, and full of allusions to earlier literature—exciting for everyone who understood, but on the whole impossible to understand for anyone lacking a thorough education in the classical writings.

It was not until the May Fourth movement from 1919 onward that work began in earnest to open up language and literature to a wider public and bring the written language closer to the spoken. The character reforms of the 1950s were part of that work—an attempt, for the first time in two thousand years, to reform the actual written language.

speech, word

This character is now primarily used in the sense of **speech**, **word**, but its basic meaning is *large flute*, and it is generally considered that the character was originally a picture of a flute with a mouth blowing into it. The transfer of meaning, *flute-sound-speech*, is easy to understand.

Speech, word is included in a large number of compound characters, illustrating many situations in daily life in which language and words are used and misused, as in, for instance, *read, recite, comment, instruct, interrogate, oppose, criticize, investigate, spy, doubt, warn, prove, accuse, make a mistake, promise, thank, flatter, boast, tell a lie, swear, quarrel, ridicule, defame, slander.*

Inscription on a stone drum from the late Zhou dynasty.

This is one of my favorite characters, not because it is particularly beautiful but because of its associations. A human being and his or her words: *confidence, to believe in, trust,* and *letter.*

Unfortunately, the world is not always as wise as one would wish: *speech, word* squeezed between two characters for *dog* means *trial, prison*—the unpleasant situation when two warring parties meet and 'bark' at each other like 'dogs,' often ending with one of them landing in *prison.*

confidence . . .

trial, prison . . .

The character for **note**, **sound**, **tone** does not appear in the oracle bones, but on bronzes and other inscriptions from the Zhou period, it is identical or almost identical with the character for *speech, word.* It therefore seems likely that both have a common origin, but gradually two different characters arose with different forms and meanings. Several scholars have demonstrated that the two characters in certain compounds displace each other, and they regard this as evidence of their being originally one and the same.

Note and heart ('the note of the heart'): *thought, idea, meaning, wish.*

note, sound, tone

thought, idea . . .

flute

If flutes of graduated lengths are tied together in a row, they become what is known as panpipes, an instrument known in China since the beginning of historical time. Some scholars maintain that an instrument of this kind is depicted in this character, which means **flute**. The pipes can be seen, the openings or 'mouths,' as well as the binding holding the pipes together.

Some of the bronze characters have an upper part of unknown meaning, and that part is also included in the form that the character was given at the first standardization in 200 B.C.

If the flute pipes are instead fastened together in two rows in a gourd or wooden sound box, they become what is called a mouth organ, one of the oldest and most characteristic Chinese musical instruments, still common among ethnic minorities in the southwest. Their mouth organs are truly impressive, the pipes sometimes over six meters long.

The oldest flute preserved comes from Wuyang, about seventy miles south of Zhengzhou, and is eight thousand years old. It is made of bone, has seven holes, and remarkably, still produces sound. But otherwise few flutes have turned up in archaeological findings. Small bone flutes more like whistles are occasionally found, but most flutes seem to have been made of bamboo, which soon rots, so it is hard to find the exact appearance of the prototype flutes for the characters for *speech* and *note*.

In the *Book of Songs* from the beginning of the Zhou period, musical instruments of various kinds are often mentioned, flutes among them. No flutes of the time have been preserved, but there are two from 400 B.C., and a whole series of twelve bamboo flutes of various lengths from the third century in such good condition that some of them still produce notes.

These flutes were probably never used as musical instruments, but as tuning pipes, to establish the exact notes in the scale of twelve. In ancient China, this was of supreme importance. Music was not just a means of enjoyment, pleasant relaxation, and entertainment, but a sacred institution regulating circumstances between Heaven and Earth and representing the innermost harmony of life. With music, the powers of nature could be influenced, and in a vulnerable area such as the land around the Yellow River, where life balanced on a knife edge between drought and

A small orchestra of painted wooden figures from the grave of the Marquise of Tai in Changsha. The two figures at the back are playing mouth organs, the three in front, a string instrument called a se. 32–38 cm high.

floods, no opportunity was missed. Music was felt to be decisive not only for farming—for the nourishment everyone depended on—but also for the passage of the actual year. At the winter solstice, the critical point when the year turns, one of the most important ceremonies was carried out, and then drums rolled to ensure the transition, the victory of light, and the harvest of the coming year.

But music was decisive not only for the continuation of the state and crops. It also regulated the lives of individual people. Just as a particular note is said to shatter crystal, impure notes imperiled the harmony of life. 'Low music' and 'vulgar sounds' were an insult to Heaven. They not only led to the destruction of old customs but disturbed the correct relationship between man and woman, between prince and subject, and thus undermined the very foundations of the state. Good music, on the other hand, played according to all the rules of the art, could infuse gentleness into a ruffian and restrain the strong from tyranny and lack of respect.

At a very early time music became a means by which a ruler could run the country, and therefore a subject of particular solicitude on his part. It is said that in 2697 B.C., Emperor Huang Di dispatched his minister, Ling Lun, himself a dedicated musician, to acquire bamboo pipes that would correctly reproduce the twelve notes of the scale. In the mountains in the west, Ling Lun found bamboo with fine even stems and cut a pipe from the strongest he could get. When he blew into it, he heard a deep note corresponding to the lowest note he himself could produce. As he sat there with his flute, listening to the murmuring of the stream and the soughing of the wind in the leaves, a pair of phoenix, the mythical bird, suddenly settled in the tree beside him. Phoenix show themselves to people only when great events are to occur, and Ling Lun realized that something remarkable was about to happen.

Twelve bamboo tuning pipes and an embroidered case from the grave of the Marquise of Tai in Changsha, all 0.65 cm in diameter. The longest pipe is 17.65., the shortest 10.2 cm.

The cock bird sang first, and his first note matched the note produced by Ling Lun's pipe. Then he sang five more notes, and Ling rapidly cut pipes to reproduce their sound. Then the hen bird sang six notes, and Ling Lun hastened to cut pipes to be able to remember her song as well. When he then arranged all twelve pipes in the order of the notes, he found that every pipe was exactly two-thirds as long as the one that had produced the last note. His tonal system was, in modern terminology, based on a series of intervals on top of one another.

Everything tallied. It says in the *Book of Ceremonies*: 'Three is the symbolic number of Heaven, two that of the Earth. So sounds that are as three to two are as harmonious as Heaven is to Earth.'

According to the legend, the sounds the twelve pipes produced became the origin of the Chinese tonal system. To preserve the notes in more lasting material, the emperor had twelve bronze bells cast to reproduce exactly the notes of the bamboo pipes, and from then on all other instruments were tuned to them.

Set of bells found in the grave of the Marquis Yi of Zeng from the year 433 B.C.

This is the earliest account in the world of a tonal system based on exact keynotes and exact intervals between notes. What is interesting is that the scale is very close to the modern chromatic scale with its twelve notes, the seven white and five black piano keys in an octave.

The longest bamboo pipe became not only the keynote of the Chinese tonal system but also the standard measure for length—roughly like the meter in Paris—and for volume. The 1,200 millet seeds it contained were called a flute and represented by the character we just met on page 312, which probably depicts a flutelike instrument. When struck, the standard measure had to produce the correct note.

An exact keynote as the starting point to a scale of notes with exact intervals was necessary if the relations between Heaven and Earth were to function. For everyday life on earth, exact measures, coinage, and weights were equally important. If they could be tinkered with, the result was cheating, deceit, and corruption. Trade was threatened, and if things were really bad, disorder and confusion reigned on earth— or 'under Heaven,' as the Chinese call the earth. So when the imperial civil service department of music was eventually established, it became part of the department of weights and measures.

The fate of the bronze bells that the legend says Huang Di had cast is not known—perhaps they are buried somewhere in the soft yellow soil of the Wei Valley. But there are several sets of bells from later periods, the most impressive yet found being those discovered in 1978 in the grave in which the Marquis Yi of Zeng had lain since the year 433 B.C. The man must have loved music—124 instruments were buried with him, among them flutes, mouth organs, and drums, each one of them unique in itself and invaluable in the larger picture of Chinese musical development. Most remarkable of all is the set of bells containing sixty-five bronze bells, the largest weighing over 200 kilos.

The whole instrument is three meters high and almost eleven meters long. The bells hang in three rows: the smallest at the top presumably used to give the note to the other instruments in the orchestra; those on the bottom row producing the bass notes, the backbone of music; the soprano and alto bells in the middle. The bells have no clappers and are played with a wooden club, each one of them producing two notes, depending on whether struck in the middle or on the side of the bell. The notes sounded by the bell are carefully inscribed on the bronze. Altogether, the bells have a range stretching over more than five octaves, from the lowest note of which a cello is capable, to the highest note of the flute. The sequence of notes corresponds to that of the piano.

In cross-section, the bells are not round like our church bells, but elliptical or oval. This construction means that vibrations are swiftly subdued—essential for being able to play them properly. They are tuned with extraordinary precision in relation to each other—many octaves, intervals, and quarters are exactly like those achieved with modern techniques today, as are the notes: the bell that produces C-flat vibrates at 256.4 hertz, as opposed to the ideal 256.0.

All this makes an impressive instrument—and a heavy one. Together, the bells weigh two and a half tons, but the wooden beams bearing them appear to have been designed with eternity in mind, for after 2,400 years, they have still not sagged.

A decoration on a bronze vessel from the latter part of the Zhou dynasty shows a similar instrument. On the left of a long beam ending in a grinning animal head and supported by two birdlike creatures are four powerful bells. Seated musicians play on them with a club.

Further to the right on the beam is another instrument consisting of five L-shaped stone slabs of various sizes, with musicians playing on them in the same way as on the bronze bells. One of the many instruments found in the grave of the Marquis Yi of Zeng is a set of thirty-two such stone chimes, tuned chromatically, just like the bronze bells, their notes pure and crystal clear.

The instrument as a type is ancient and goes back to Neolithic times, but originally it appears to have consisted of only one stone.

The oldest stone chime yet found comes from a place near the Yellow River called Taosi, in the area where, according to ancient records, the Xia dynasty, the first dynasty in the long history of China, had its center. The stone is almost a meter high and as craggy and fierce as the head of an old crocodile. It

stone chime

stone chime

has been dated to 2500–1900 B.C., dates corresponding to existing records on the rule of the Xia dynasty.

About thirty stone chimes from the Shang dynasty have been preserved, generally 30 to 40 centimeters high and 60 to 80 long, some of them decorated with reliefs of animals, as is the one above: a picture of a tiger with its mouth open and tail turned up, reproduced in complete accordance with the conventions of the time.

The stone bears traces of having been used for a long time, and marks of the ropes it was hung by can be clearly seen.

Stone chimes are also found on the oracle bones, where a large slanting stone and a hand about to strike with a heavy club can be seen. The straggly strokes above the stone are usually explained either as a picture of the rope holding the stone or some form of decoration.

This character means **stone chime**.

During the Shang period, this character was already complemented with the one for *stone*, a somewhat unnecessary addition to a picture as clear as that of the hanging stone chime itself.

sound, note

Stone chime and ear together form the character for *sound, note*. In the simplified character often used today, both the hand with the club and the listening ear have been removed, leaving only the picture of the slanting old stone hanging from its rope.

声

the simplified character for sound, note

But is it really a rope? The same straggly strokes above the character can also be found above the character for *drum*, where they are unlikely to show a rope. Drums of the Shang period did not hang on ropes. Heavy and sturdy, they stood on low plinths, at least judging by the drums preserved from that time. Only two drums, however, have been found on which this construction can be seen in detail. Both are made of bronze. Impressions in the soil from yet another drum made of wood long since rotted were found in a grave in Anyang in 1935, but scholars disagree on what it might once have looked like.

The oldest of the two preserved bronze drums from the Shang period is 79 centimeters high and 40 centimeters wide. It is perfectly intact and said still to sound beautiful. It almost certainly originated from a prototype in wood, for the first drums were all made of wood, a fact known from archaeological material and the oldest scripts. This is also evident from the rows of rivets apparently holding down the drumskin—a necessity on a wooden drum but not on a bronze drum cast in one piece.

The 'saddle,' the part at the top of the drum, is still not explained. On the second of the two drums from the Shang period, the top is shaped like two resting birds. Both 'saddles' have holes right through them, so they may have been used when the drums had to be moved with the aid of a rope or a carrying pole—they weigh between 40 and 50 kilos and are not exactly easy to handle. But I think they may also have been used for fastening decorations of some kind. Nothing is as yet known about what those decorations may have looked like, but the *Book of Songs* contains poems describing festivals in which people danced with pheasant or heron feathers in their hands, and the frames of the bells and percussion stones were adorned with tall bunches of feathers. Perhaps the drum was also decorated? According to Xun Zi, one of the leading thinkers of the Zhou period, the instrument was the 'king of musicians' and constituted the focal point in several of the most important rites.

For the ancient Chinese, music was a means of making contact with ancestors and Heaven. Since birds are able to move freely between our prosaic world and the open skies, they were regarded as messengers between people and the supreme powers. Many of the bronze vessels used at religious ceremonies were

Richly decorated bronze drum from the Shang dynasty, found in the province of Hubei in 1977.

shaped like birds. According to myths, the Shang dynasty originated from a black bird, just as the twelve notes in the scale came from the song of the phoenix. The rack where bells and stones were hung, as we saw on page 315, was often shaped like long-necked birdlike creatures with wings and beaks. Birds and music were closely related. These resting birds crowning one of the two preserved Shang drums were not only decorative but of profound symbolic significance.

drum

The powerful type of **drum** of the Shang period can be seen in a number of oracle bone inscriptions. It is sometimes reproduced as viewed from the circular short side where the drumskin is stretched, sometimes from the long side. The character was complemented early with the picture of a hand with a stick or club, as if someone were about to strike and let the dull clang roll out over the plain.

The same squat, heavy drum can be found in the bronze inscriptions.

Until quite recently, almost nothing was known about what this drum's predecessors were like, but then in the mid-1980s, a surprising find was made in the same burial ground in Taosi where the great Xia stone chime was found—two drums, the oldest yet found in China. One of them is a meter high and made of a hollow tree trunk, which was something of a sensation, for wood rots very quickly; but here was a drum that was certainly about four thousand years old and completely intact. In its day, it had had a snakeskin or the skin of some other reptile across the upper opening. It appears to have been painted red, as the drums of China often continued to be, and the remains of the coloring still glow on its surface. According to ancient writings, human blood was rubbed into drums for magical purposes, but the coloring here probably came from another source.

Over time the drum was turned a half revolution and placed horizontally onto a low stand, and a drumskin was fastened over the other opening. That was how the sturdy drum of the Shang period was born.

The other drum from Taosi is made of clay. A pot used as a drum was quite common in ancient times. It says in the *Book of Ceremonies* that the mighty in society use drums of wood or bronze while ordinary people beat clay drums. There are actually two bronze characters for *pot*, *jug*, on which the character for *strike* is on the right, but unfortunately scholars have no explanation for these characters.

Later, clay drums were played in roughly the same way as stone chimes and bells. By filling the vessels with varying quantities of water, they could be exactly tuned. An official in the music department at the end of the Tang dynasty considered that vessels of this kind resounded more beautifully than sheets of metal. I believe him. In Beijing, I once heard a concerto for porcelain bowls filled with water, and the resonance floating out of them was so pure and contained such an unworldly, glowing clarity that it was like listening to the music of the spheres.

In several of the bronze characters from the Zhou period, the drum is raised from the ground on a high plinth, just as it was in reality. In time, drums were raised even higher, perhaps for the simple reason that they were then easier to play. A red drum spiked like a wild strawberry onto a stem of grass was one of the instruments buried with the Marquis Yi of Zeng in his grave in 433 B.C. Similar drums can often be found in decorations on bronze vessels of the time.

A great many lacquered objects were also found in the well-equipped grave of the Marquis Yi of Zeng, one of which is in the shape of a handsome duck, on one side a peculiar scene with two half-human, half-animal figures performing some kind of dance or ceremony.

In the middle, between the figures, is a drum mounted on a long pole and decorated with a kind of

Lacquered object from the grave of the Marquis Yi of Zeng.

Rubbings from Han period burial reliefs in which magnificently decorated drums are being used. The carriage scene on the right comes from the ancestral hall in Feicheng, the oldest preserved building in China.

plume rather like the top part of the character for *drum* found on oracle bone and bronze characters.

Drums are also found on burial reliefs from the Han period, where they are included in portrayals of festivities and processions in honor of the ruler and the state. Many of these drums are decorated with meter-long feathers, others with featherlike garlands. In a lively depiction from the year 193 of jugglers, sword dancers, and musicians of all kinds, we see a large drum adorned with a bird.

From the Han period to the present day carriages full of musicians and other performers often participate in political and traditional festivities. The National Day parades in Beijing in the 1950s and 1960s are legendary; an armada of trucks with huge stages on the back rolled for hours past the Gate of Heavenly Peace, where the supreme leaders of the country were lined up. Scenes were shown from famous operas, beautiful ladies danced with veils, and children with gigantic pumpkins in their hands stood in tableaux in praise of progress in agriculture, while drumbeats rolled out over a sea of enthusiastic blue-clad people.

Several interesting drums are reproduced on reliefs lining the inside walls of the little house in Feicheng—the one built in memory of a son's praiseworthy faithfulness to his mother. One of the suites of pictures is a stately procession in which the ruler is being borne in his chariot followed by lancers, a mounted escort, and a carriage of musicians on two levels, two energetic drummers above and four gentlemen peaceably playing mouth organs below.

During the Han dynasty carts of this kind developed what is called a hodometer, or way measurer. Every time the cart covered a *li*—half a kilometer—a wooden figure beat on a drum, and after ten *li*, another figure struck a metal bell. The mechanism was run by two cogwheels fixed to the cart axle.

禮

abundant, plentiful ...

豐
豆

rite, ritual ...

*Man-high drum
in the Yongzuosi
temple. Taiyuan.*

This character means *abundant, plentiful, luxuriant*. The traditional explanation is that it is a picture of a ritual vessel of the kind called *dou*. But many scholars have pointed out how doubtful that interpretation is. There is much to indicate that it is a picture of a drum. If the early characters for *drum* are compared with the character for *abundant, plentiful*, clear similarities can be seen. The only real difference is that the upper part in the latter character is considerably larger than in the character for *drum* and is also complemented with something as yet unknown.

Together with the character for *omen*, which is concerned with sacrifices and questions to the supreme powers on fortune and misfortune, this character for *abundant, plentiful* forms the character for *rite, ritual, ceremony*, the focal point of political and religious life in ancient Chinese society. At the moment the ruler prepared himself for the year's hunting, as he provided fragrant millet in honor of his ancestors or before the music that opened communications with Heaven began to sound, drums would roll. In the same way, drums today lead the Chinese traditional orchestra. 'Rite' is an abstract concept difficult to portray pictorially. By considering the most important instrument in the ceremony and complementing it with the character for *omen*, clearly stating the purpose of the rite, an expressive character for *rite* was created.

Music was not just a means of ruling the state and communicating with Heaven; it was also closely linked with warfare. When the army assembled for battle, the master of music blew on the pipe, providing a kind of keynote. From this, he ascertained the atmosphere within his own army as well as the enemy's—the 'tone' of the situation—and thus the outcome of the battle. If everything appeared under control, drums gave the signal to attack.

In decorations on bronze vessels at the time of the Warring States, battle drums can be seen, drummers with raised drumsticks urging on the troops, surrounded by fierce warriors with meter-long halberds, banners fluttering and oarsmen in long boats hurling themselves at the oars, while unfortunate soldiers fall headlong, sometimes headless, into the river full of swimming fish and turtles.

The pictures of the various drums are clear. They are the same kind as the red drum from the grave of the Marquis Yi of Zeng, many of them adorned with long, fluttering pennants, others with dagger-axes. But at the foot is a strange and as yet unexplained detail resembling a round ball or disc on a long pole.

For several years I went around China with some well-thumbed pictures of drums of this kind in my wallet, asking anyone who might give me an answer—historians, musicians, linguists, and archaeologists—what that strange ball was, but no one knew.

I began to despair, but when plowing through the old *Zuo zhuan* and *Zhou li* texts in search of clues to quite another question, I found something I had never noticed before: When the signal for retreat was given in battle, bells or metal discs were struck, predecessors of the gong.

Is this the explanation—a battle billowing back and forth, the result never certain? The person giving the signal to attack should also give the signal to retreat, and in order to carry out these tasks as efficiently as possible, he would naturally have had both instruments, the drum and the metal disc, mounted as close to each other as possible.

The drum was the ruler's main instrument for holding the army together in battle. It symbolized his power, and as long as he was successful, it beat on, urging the soldiers to even bolder and more ferocious action. Some old texts say that during the Zhou period the insane were used as drummers; only they had the endurance required to go on drumming to the bitter end, against all odds, without panicking.

middle

Perhaps the picture of the Zhou drum can explain something that has long baffled scholars, the character for **middle**, **center**, which the Chinese have used as the character for their country from 680 B.C. to this day.

The Zhou dynasty, the longest of all the Chinese dynasties, was established in 1028 B.C., and stability and peace reigned for the first two hundred years. The northern and western nomadic peoples were held in check, and the influence of Zhou extended southward. But in time, its power weakened, and the vassal rulers who had until then loyally submitted began to assert their own authority and break away.

In 771 B.C., the nomads raged through the country, the capital was razed, the king was killed, and the old power structure collapsed. The Zhou dynasty lived on in name for another five hundred years, with the king still regarded as the Son of Heaven and the only one to carry out the sacrificial ceremonies on which the state depended. But political power was transferred to the rulers of about a hundred minor states. They nominally acknowledged the king as their superior, but until the fall of the dynasty in 221 B.C., they devoted their energies to bloody struggles for power between each other equivalent to the feuds of the Middle Ages in Europe. Not for nothing is the late Zhou period called the period of Warring States.

In 680 B.C., there was a temporary pause in the civil wars. Threatened by nomads in the north and the increasingly powerful state of Chu in the south, a group of minor states on the central plain joined together in a federation called Zhongguo, the Central Kingdoms. Today this is China's own name for the country, and from that comes our often misleading name, Middle Kingdom.

The character for *middle*, *center* is disputed. According to one explanation, it shows a square with the middle marked. According to another, it shows an arrow penetrating the middle of a target; but for that to be comprehensible, the arrow and target have to be seen on two different levels—hardly likely.

Yet another explanation refers to the 'pennants' that can be seen on the character as it is written on the oracle bones and bronzes. They are said to show a banner or a standard with long streamers fluttering cheerfully in the wind.

As far as I understand, it is evident that the character originally depicted a standard or banner on a pole. This can, for instance, be seen by comparing the forms the character for *banner* has on the oracle bones with the corresponding part of the character for *middle*, *center*.

The same images recur in *clan*, *group*.

Banner is included in many compound words, among them characters for ten or so different kinds of standards or banners: *dragon banners, feather banners, turtle* and *snake banners, oxtail banners, falcon banners,* and so forth. What these concepts consisted of originally is largely unknown. Perhaps they described the ornamentation—the way animals represent families or towns on our heraldic banners; perhaps the banners themselves were shaped like dragons, turtles, or falcons; perhaps they were made of feathers or oxtails. The character is also included in two compound characters meaning *float, flutter like a flag* and in some others meaning *military unit* and *troop, mass.* In the latter, two people are marching along—two of the many anonymous men taking part in the battle—above them a banner flutters as in the character for *middle.*

oracle bone character for troop, mass

The problem with the character for *middle* is not whether it has anything to do with banners and war, for I consider that it must have, considering the similarity with the character for *banner.* The problem is the round or oblong object in the middle of the banner pole, for which no explanation has yet been found. I think it is a drum.

Li ji, the *Book of Ceremonies,* which was assembled during the late Zhou period, says that drums during the Shang period were mounted on a pole. This does not correspond to archaeological finds, of which, however, there are very few. The only drums preserved from the Shang period lie like heavy wine kegs on a low stand, and that is the type of drum found in the character for *drum.* But there are other characters for drums of other kinds: the great battle drums used by riders on horseback, and the small hand drums mounted on a pole used in religious rites, as well as at more profane festivities. These can be seen depicted on burial tiles from the Han dynasty. Drums of the latter kind have survived to this day. I have heard them played by traveling salesmen and craftsmen, who use them to drum up customers.

But to return to the character for *middle, center.* In one of the oracle bone characters, banners are fluttering as usual, and alongside the object on the pole, which I think depicts a drum, are two strokes apparently somehow coming from it.

Similar strokes can be found in a character that in older texts means *forceful, sound of a drum* and the onomatopoeic word *bang*. The solid old drum of the Shang period is surrounded by a cloud of thin strokes—a picture said to depict the drumming or the twirling of the drumsticks, but which any habitual reader of comics at once interprets as the forceful sound pouring out of the drum.

In the oracle bone characters, the strokes are all over the place, sometimes on the left, sometimes on the right, sometimes on both sides, sometimes three, sometimes five. But like the three strokes in the bronze character, they all vibrate out from the drum in the same way as the strokes in the oracle bone for *middle, center.*

It is easy to imagine the strokes as sounds when one sees the intensity with which the drummers on the bronze vessel from the days of the Warring States attack their instruments. They are in the thick of the battle, a long banner fluttering above one of them and the much-feared dagger-axe with all its sharp blades threateningly raised above the other.

The drum embodied the power of the ruler and the destiny of the army. Before battle, it was consecrated by rubbing in the blood of sacrificed prisoners of war, and as the fighting continued, everyone followed the drum with great attention as it stood on the command ship or war chariot. The eyes and ears of the army adjusted to the flag and the drum and advanced or retreated as they did, according to *Zuo zhuan*, the ancient book from the late Zhou dynasty.

Just as the bundle of rods and the axe symbolized the Roman state, and the hammer and sickle represented the new state that workers and peasants were together to build in Russia after the 1917 revolution, the character for *middle, center* came to be the symbol first for a group of minor states, which during the last centuries of the Zhou period were fighting for their very existence, then later for the whole of the vast Middle Kingdom. The people who lived there regarded themselves as the center of the world, surrounded—like the Greeks and Romans—by 'barbarians,' crude fellows sitting around campfires and eating their food with knives, encircled by howling dogs, with no inkling of the solemn ceremonies and elevated thoughts that guided 'civilized' people.

Just as the expression *Douce France* gives a hint of the way early French civilization regarded itself in relation to a harsh outside world, *middle*, *center* also stands for *moderate* and *upright*, and the character for *loyal*, *faithful*, *honest*, *patriotic* is composed of middle and heart: what a man has at heart—his country—the Middle?

loyal, faithful

The character occurred late, appearing for the first time in inscriptions from the period of the Warring States, the time when, from being primarily a determination of position, *middle* became the symbol for the country and for an intellectual way of behaving that supported the new regime.

The name Zhongguo, the Central Kingdoms—Middle Kingdom—became integrated in symbiosis with Zhongyuan, the Central Plain, the name of the areas constituting the cradle of Chinese civilization, the loess plateaus of Shanxi, Shaanxi, and the flat, fertile northern Chinese plain around the Yellow River. Together the two names constitute a metaphor for China—geographical, political, and moral.

The drums went on guiding people's lives for a long time. Just as church bells in our towns rang out the passing hours and summoned inhabitants in the event of war or fire, so the Chinese had their drum towers; and every other hour, starting at seven in the evening, the sound from the drums rolled out over the low dwellings, over markets, temples, and walls, to say that the day had ended and the city gates were closed. The drums started slowly, with quite faint taps, rose to a crescendo of sound, then suddenly ceased, the sequence repeated over and over again.

Every other hour during the night, the sound recurred as a signal for the nightwatchmen patrolling the alleys to change shifts, and in the morning the drums sounded again to wake up the inhabitants and tell them the day had begun, the city gates were open, and activity in the markets could begin.

In old cities like Beijing, Xi'an, and Nanjing, the drum towers are still there in their ancient magnificence, but now they are museums, and nothing but swifts fly in and out of the vents.

As an aid to measuring time, what was called a clepsydra was used—a water clock in which water, like the sand in an hourglass, slowly ran from one vessel into another. The clepsydra came into use sometime in the middle of the Zhou dynasty and was developed under the Han dynasty into a whole series of vessels on which the time could be told almost as accurately as on the clocks of today. The water clock in Guangzhou that functioned from 1316 until the fall of the empire in 1911 is famous.

The drums were also used occasionally to warn inhabitants in the city of danger, a custom that seems to go very far back. It is said that one of the kings of the Zhou period placed a drum in a high tower to be able to mobilize his people rapidly and ward off attacking enemy armies. There is a character, now changed out of all recognition, that means *problem*, *misfortune*, *disturbing news* and shows a person beside a large drum. The character recurs very often in oracle bone inscriptions.

The drums of the drum towers have now fallen silent, but the sound of drums continues to roll through Chinese towns. They are red, as always, often decorated with fluttering silk ribbons and rosettes. They are brought out whenever there is a ceremony or festivities, for weddings and funerals—all ceremonial occasions demand the insistent beat of drums.

Papercut with the character for double joy surrounded by a dragon and a phoenix, symbols of the emperor and his consort.

joy   double joy

When retired workers leave their workplace for the last time, they are accompanied home by their workmates, friends, and acquaintances crammed onto the backs of trucks with drummers and other musicians, just as the Han period nobles once did on their chariots.

While music has indeed been a serious matter in China since the beginning of civilization, at the same time, music has also meant joy. This can be seen in this character, which means *joy*, *rejoice*, *delight* and consists of drum and mouth. Doubled, it means *double joy* and is used at joyful festivities such as weddings when two people and two families are united. Then great red papercuts of the character are glued to the street door, often to lamps, windows, and mirrors as well, and any passerby can at once see that festivities are taking place. The character is also common as a pattern for jewelry and cloth and as mother-of-pearl inlays in old-fashioned rosewood and ebony furniture.

Finally, here is a character meaning both **joy** and **music**, the traditional explanation of which is a picture of a large drum surrounded by four small drums mounted on a wooden stand.

joy, music

At first this explanation seems obvious. Instruments of the kind were common during the Han dynasty, used on horseback by mounted drummers, and are found on burial tiles of the same period. Many bronze characters are strikingly like them.

But if one goes back to the ora-cle bone characters and the oldest bronze characters, doubts arise—there is not a hint of any drums, and only the character for *tree, wood* and  two elements rather like the character for *silk* or the character for *small, tender*, originally concerning silk. I wonder whether the explanation for the construction of the character is to be found here.

Since the Zhou period, Chinese instruments have been divided according to the material they are made of, what are called The Eight Sounds:

stone—stone chime
metal—bell
silk—string instrument
bamboo—flute
wood—'mortar' (wooden box out of which sounds were thumped), 'wooden fish,' 'wooden tiger,' castanets
skin—drum
gourd—mouth organ
earth (pottery)—ocarina

All through the history of China until today, *silk and bamboo* has been used as a generic term for 'music.' Perhaps only two in the row of The Eight Sounds were taken and made to represent them all—although in that case it would have been more logical to choose the first two, stone and metal. Perhaps another thought lay behind it: string instrument and flute have always been a very common combination in Chinese music, especially at musical gatherings in the pavilions and study chambers of the educated classes.

A common earlier term for 'string instrument' was *silk and wood*. During the Zhou dynasty, there were two string instruments, *qin* and *se*. Both were made of curved pieces of wood just over a meter long, which together formed a sound box, and both had strings of tightly twisted silk. *Qin*, which is usually translated as 'zither' or 'lute,' soon became the leading instrument of the intellectuals—Confucius and other learned men are said to have written pieces for it—and through the millennia after his day, it developed into one of the most sophisticated implements for quiet, almost sacred meditation.

the simplified character for joy, music

There is still no evidence that *qin* and *se* were in use as early as the Shang period—the oldest known example yet found comes from the grave of the Marquis Yi of Zeng from 433 B.C.—but they are mentioned in several places in the *Book of Songs*. And the character for *joy, music* may well provide a clue to whether they already existed at the time the character was created. In that case, the character would not be a concrete description of an instrument with drums of various sizes on a stand, but a compound character in which silk and wood together provide the associations needed to clarify the concept of *music, joy,* and *to rejoice.*

Then the problem is, what are the round or oval objects included in the latest bronze characters, which are usually interpreted as a drum? A question still unanswered.

That the character for *music* can also mean *joy, to rejoice* is close at hand for most of us—all this may have been so to an even greater degree for the ancient Chinese. For those who lived with no access to radio, television, stereo equipment, and the various musical instruments we regard as natural ingredients of daily life, the dance songs when praying for rain and good harvests, the magical religious invocations to the spirits of the shamans, and all the collective festivities accompanied by music must have been moments of light in a monotonous and exhausting daily life, providing it with a glow and meaning through their rhythmical recurrence.

And to the learned who once constructed the characters and engraved them into the oracle bones and bronzes, the religious rituals, and especially the great ceremonial orchestras, must have been a tremendous experience. As the quavering notes of bamboo flutes, the gentle drone of mouth organs, the ringing of bronze bells and stones—'pure as running water,' as the philosopher Xun Zi expresses it—merged with the muffled beat of the drums, and everyone present knew that the notes were just then rising, together with the scent of sacrificed animals, wine, and grain, into the skies and making contact with Heaven and ancestors—at that moment it certainly must have been easy to feel that music, joy, and rejoicing were one and the same.

Numbers
and
Other Abstract Characters

Characters I have so far covered have either been simple pictures of objects or phenomena from everyday life, or combinations of images standing for more composite concepts. But there is also a small group of purely abstract characters. These include two, meaning **over** and **under**.

over   under

On the oracle bones, the pictures are quite clear, a simple description of position provided by two strokes, one shorter, the other longer.

Sometime during the Zhou period, a vertical stroke began to be added, perhaps to prevent the short stroke, truly the most important in this context, from being obscured.

The character is now used for numerous different meanings having to do with *over* and *under*, such as *go up–go down, go on–go off, begin–end, higher–lower, finer–worse, first* (part of a book)–*second* (part), *last* (month)–*next* (month), and so on.

convex   concave

Two characters constructed on a similar principle are **convex**, **protrude** and **concave**, **sunken**. These did not come about until the Tang dynasty, and so lack ancient forms.

The character for *large* is a picture of a man who was or made himself large, or anyhow made a large gesture. But the character for *small* is not a picture of a small person or a child; it is three small strokes or dots, and what they stand for is very uncertain. The old character dictionary *Shuowen* says the character shows something divided up into small parts. Maybe so. But it is more likely to be a purely abstract character, which is how modern Chinese linguists describe it.

Perhaps what the three dots stand for is of minor importance. Anyone can see it is **small**.

small

Apart from these and a few others, the majority of abstract characters are either numbers or numerals or cyclic characters used to divide days and years into manageable units.

Europe took over arabic numerals at a very early stage, but throughout their history until the early 1900s, the Chinese have used their own numbering notation. This seems to have stemmed from thin, fifteen-centimeter bamboo strips or rods placed in various formations on a flat base and representing numbers.

The oldest calculating rods yet known were found in the early 1970s in two Han graves, but the rod-numeral system is mentioned in several places in literature of the fifth century B.C. and seems to have already been in use during the Shang dynasty. Even at this early stage it was based on the decimal system. At that time, units, hundreds, and tens of thousands were represented by vertical rods; tens, thousands, and hundreds of thousands by horizontal rods.

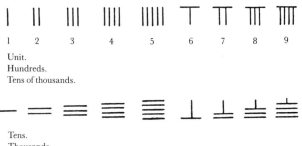

Unit.
Hundreds.
Tens of thousands.

Tens.
Thousands.
Hundreds of thousands.

From the latter part of the Zhou dynasty, zero was simply a space, but from the 1200s onward, it was written with a circle.

This is the number 6,708:

The system may seem primitive, but from a mathematical point of view it is more advanced than the numeral systems used in the old realms of Babylon, Egypt, Greece, and Rome—all famed for their high mathematical standards. While in these cultures both addition and subtraction were necessary to express certain higher numbers for various tens and hundreds—the Romans wrote 19 as XIX (10+10−1), 50 as L and 100 as C—the Chinese, with their nine vertical or horizontal numerals, could express any desired number, however large. In this, according to Joseph Needham, they were probably the first in the world. The value of the numerals depended entirely on their placement in relation to the other numerals in the number, rather like the numeral system of today.

Sometime during the Ming dynasty, the standing and lying numerals were joined together into one single system:

In that form, the numbers have lived on until the present day, and they are still used by businessmen when pricing their goods. But in most other contexts, arabic numerals have now reached China, and schoolchildren learn mathematics with their help.

Calculating rods were in general use for at least two thousand years, but when the abacus appeared in the 1300s, their time was up, just as the abacus will now be superseded by the calculator.

An abacus consists of an oblong wooden frame, a series of thin wooden rods fixed between the long sides, and seven slightly flattened wooden spheres threaded onto them. They are separated by a crossbar, with two spheres above, five below the crossbar. Each of the upper spheres corresponds to five of the lower ones. Everyday frames often have eleven or thirteen rows of spheres, although they can have considerably more, for instance, if very high numbers are

Mathematics lesson in Huwan School in Shanghai.

to be counted or if several people are to use the frame at the same time, which is quite possible. One can begin anywhere on an abacus, but before starting, the location of the unit column must be decided. Schoolchildren often mark the frame with a chalk line.

The longest abacus in China is now in the Tianjin Historical Museum. It is 3.5 meters long and in its day ran along the counter of an apothecary, where it could be used by five or six assistants at once. Another amusing abacus is in the Military Museum of the Chinese People's Revolution in Beijing. It has spheres of hickory nuts and was made in the 1940s during the civil war by students in Yan'an, who had to use whatever materials were available.

Chinese and Japanese children are given a thorough training in how to use an abacus. Calculators are not allowed because pupils are thought to become far too easily dependent on them, so the school authorities say they must first learn to use their heads and hands.

Perhaps the abacus will survive after all, brilliantly simple and dependable as it is. It needs no electricity or batteries, so is almost invulnerable, and it is quicker than the calculator at addition and subtraction, and usually cheaper. Anyone with a few sticks and a handful of nuts can make an abacus; then all there is to do is to start to use it. Numbers up to a billion can be managed without blinking, and it is quick.

Just as we have numerals written in letters (*one*, *two*, *hundred*, *thousand*, etc.), the Chinese have numerals written in characters. It is easy to guess that the three top lines on the right here mean **one**, **two**, and **three**, and the characters have looked like that since the days of the oracle bones until today. Their form may well have come from the old counting rods.

The character for **four** in ancient times was written with four horizontal strokes, but in the third century B.C. it was increasingly replaced by a square form, which then took over.

On the oracle bones, the character for **five** was also written with horizontal strokes, but even there all strokes had begun to be compounded into an X, except the top and bottom—so the character was given the form corresponding to the roman number *ten*. This X developed into the final form of the character for *five*.

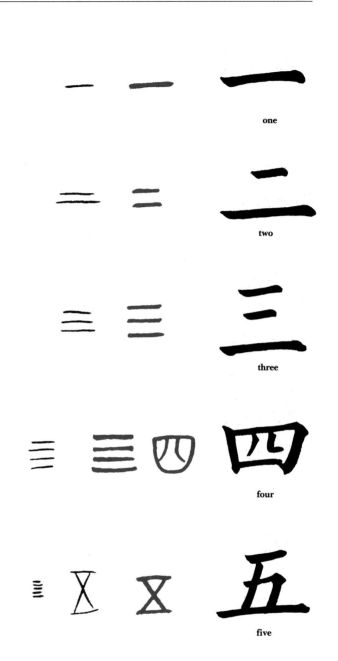

one

two

three

four

five

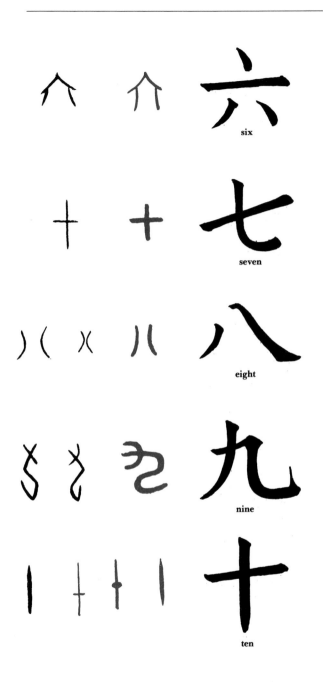

The characters for the numerals **six**, **seven**, **eight**, **nine**, and **ten** are much discussed, but at present there is no generally accepted explanation of their forms. Like the characters for *one* to *five*, they probably stem from the counting rods. In addition, the characters for *six*, *seven*, and *ten* in their oldest form were written with perfectly straight strokes of the same length and type as those included in *one* to *five* — a clear indication that they have the same origin.

There are really only two problem characters, the *eight* and the *nine*. In the original forms of both characters we see gently curved lines that could hardly have originated in the counting rods, for as far as is known, they were all straight and the same length. So there is nothing to be done except await new archaeological finds.

The numerals *eleven* to *ninety-nine* are made with various combinations of the characters for *one* to *ten*. The characters for *eleven* up to and including *nineteen*, like those for *twenty-one* up to and including *twenty-nine*, and so on, are formed by addition of tens and units, the tens by multiplication of units and tens.

Eleven: 十一 Twelve: 十二
Twenty: 二十 Twenty-one: 二十一 and so on to Ninety-nine: 九十九

To count, calculate is composed of the character for *word* and *ten*: to be able to count to ten, 'say ten.'

to count   old

Ten and mouth together means *old*: what passes through ten 'mouths,' ten generations — that is, a tradition that goes back a long time and really can be regarded as old.

There is a special character for a **hundred** that appears to depict a clay pot; though what it actually is, is as yet not known.

hundred

A **thousand** shows a person with a transverse stroke across the legs. What is behind this is also unclear. It might be something to do with military organization.

thousand

The character for **ten thousand** is a loan word. It actually means *scorpion* and provides an extraordinarily clear picture of the creature, its claws (with which it tears its prey apart) and the poisonous sting in the curved tail (with which it kills).

In ancient times, the two words were pronounced identically, and for some reason the picture of a scorpion was also allowed to stand for *ten thousand*, *innumerable*, *myriad*—numbers so great that they are beyond ordinary people's understanding. The cli-

mate around the Yellow River was much wetter and hotter in ancient times than today, so perhaps there were myriad scorpions there at the time—an unpleasant thought.

ten thousand

Until today, this character has actually functioned as the highest number in everyday use. *A hundred thousand* is expressed as ten times ten thousand, a *million* as a hundred times ten thousand. A foreigner can easily make mistakes when visiting factories or farms and a barrage of production results is offered, but for the Chinese this is the natural way to express high numbers.

When we wish to congratulate someone on a birthday, we usually sing or say 'many happy returns of the day' and 'may you live to be one hundred.' For an emperor or Mao Zedong, the Chinese go one better and say 'ten thousand years'—*Wan sui! Wan sui! Wan wan sui!*

万

the simplified character for ten thousand

Over the years, many of the numerals were given magical-symbolic significance. They were used not only to depict numbers and units but also to classify and explain reality.

As mentioned earlier, Yin and Yang were the fundamental principles of the universe or primeval forces, perpetually relieving each other in succession. Yin was perceived as the earth, feminine, dark, passive, and receptive. It was found in even numbers, in valleys and rivers, and was represented by the tiger and the broken line. Yang was in the odd numbers and perceived as the heavens, as manly, light, and active, and was represented by the dragon and the unbroken line.

There are no undertones of good and evil in this division. Yin and Yang were indeed opposites, but the universe was not static—it was alive and constantly subject to change. An eternal growing and diminishing, contraction and expansion kept the universe in movement. Yin and Yang, like the positive and negative forces used to try to explain the universe in modern science, were a prerequisite for each other's existence, and through their cyclic interplay everything was constantly renewed.

Harmony was regarded as the ideal state, and the universe could function only if the forces were in balance. Then happiness, health, and order in society could be achieved on earth. The universe, as the Chinese saw it, was a huge organism in which sometimes one, sometimes the other part took the lead for a time, and in which all parts, large and small, played according to their own conditions, as in a vast orchestra, though with no conductor.

Everything had its place and its time in relation to everything else, and everything belonged inexorably together.

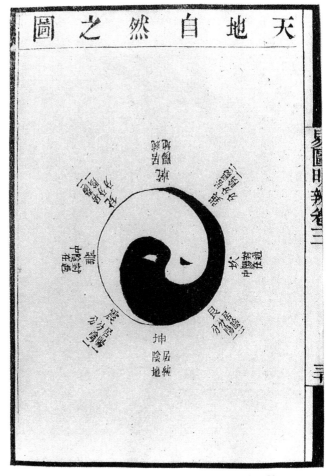

Symbolic representation of the two fundamental principles of the Universe. Heaven, Yang, in white. Earth, Yin, in black. At the top and at the bottom are the points where one force starts diminishing, the other expanding. The characters around the circumference explain the phases.

This way of perceiving reality has much in common with the teaching of *The Five Elements* (wood, fire, earth, metal, and water), also to be regarded more as processes or metaphysical forces than concrete substances.

五 行

The Five Elements

Like Yin and Yang, they acted on each other reciprocally and reshaped each other in a perpetual flow, at the same time 'producing' and 'destroying' each other.

Wood engenders fire. (*Wood burns.*)

Fire engenders earth. (*Ash is fertile.*)

Earth engenders metal. (*Ore is in the bowels of the earth.*)

Metal engenders water. (*A strange idea, probably going back to certain nightly rituals when dew was collected on metal mirrors. Molten metal was also regarded as a liquid.*)

Water engenders wood. (*Growing trees need water.*)

Wood overcomes earth. (*Wooden plows break up the ground, and trees grow up out of the earth.*)

Earth overcomes water. (*Dams can stop water, and soil can absorb it.*)

Water overcomes fire. (*Is an explanation necessary?*)

Fire overcomes metal. (*Fire makes metal melt.*)

Metal overcomes wood. (*Man cuts down trees with axes.*)

In time, a number of other categories were coordinated with the theory of The Five Elements: 'The Five Cardinal Points,' 'The Five Planets,' 'The Five Grains,' 'The Five Senses,' and so on. Together, these formed a magnificent system of symbolic correlations by which it was thought every course and thing in Heaven and on Earth could be explained.

Some of the correlations appear fairly natural, such as *summer, fire, south* or *earth, middle, yellow* — the yellow earth in the middle, the Middle Kingdom — while others seem very far-fetched according to Western ways of seeing. But they have obstinately lived on and are still used as models of explanation, for instance, in traditional Chinese medicine.

Older Chinese books often contain graphic descriptions in which The Five Elements and the various phenomena considered to be associated with them have been brought together inside a circle. In the middle, above, we see *earth*, surrounded by its opposite correspondences, and the four other elements — *wood, fire, metal,* and *water* — with theirs.

The Five Elements	Wood	Fire	Earth	Metal	Water
The Five Cardinal Points	East	South	Center	West	North
The Five Planets	Jupiter	Mars	Saturn	Venus	Mercury
The Five Senses	Eye	Tongue	Mouth	Nose	Ear
The Five Tastes	Sour	Bitter	Sweet	Acrid	Salty
The Five Grains	Wheat	Beans	Millet (Panicum)	Hemp	Millet (Setaria)
The Five Domestic Animals	Sheep	Chickens	Ox	Dog	Pig
The Five Colors	Azure	Red	Yellow	White	Black

Number mystique and numerology have existed among peoples in various parts of the world, but probably nowhere so persistently as among the Chinese, who have dedicated themselves so long to sorting reality under various numbers. Sun Yat-sen called his and the National party's program 'The Three Principles of the People': nationalism, democracy, and a good living for all. Although the program turned out to be impossible to carry through, it functioned from 1912 to 1949 as a lodestar for official policies in China.

The history of the Communist party is studded with similar slogans summarizing political directives into groups of three, five, eight, and so on. One of the most famous is 'The Three Rules of Discipline' (later extended to eight) for soldiers in the Red Army during the 1930s and 1940s.

1. Speak politely.
2. Pay honestly for what you buy.
3. Return everything you borrow.
4. Pay for everything you destroy.
5. Do not swear at people or hit them.
6. Do not walk on growing crops.
7. Take no liberties with women.
8. Do not treat prisoners badly.

In 1951, when the revolution had been carried out but a great deal of work remained to get the country functioning again after decades of war, not least to make the bureaucracy adapt to the norms of the new society, a fierce campaign was begun against *The Three Evils*: corruption, waste, and bullying by officials.

三 反　　　　五 反

The Three Evils　　　　The Five Evils

The following year, another campaign was begun against *The Five Evils*, primarily aimed at the unsatisfactory state of business and trade: bribes, tax evasion, dishonest contracts, theft of state property, and theft of financial information.

When Sun Yat-sen drew up his program and the Communists their campaigns, they drew upon the tradition to which the concepts of Yin–Yang and The Five Elements belong. This probably had its origins as early as during the beginning of the Zhou dynasty and was summarized in the third century B.C. in the classic work *Shujing*, the *Book of Records*. The tradition had begun as a systemization of observations regarding the changes in nature and human life, but during the dynasties that followed, it was watered down with quantities of new material, not least from Taoist and Buddhist perceptions of the world and Confucian rules of morality. Since all of this could not be compressed into the number five, new groups were constructed, for everything preferably had to belong to some group.

One such new group was 'The Four Heavenly Kings,' who defended Paradise Mountain against evil spirits. Statues of them can be found in the entrance halls of Buddhist temples, and their size and hideous appearance would make any rogue have second thoughts.

Other groups were 'The Four Treasures,' or the leading tools of the intellectuals—paper, brush, ink, and ink-stone—and *The Four Books*—the philosophical works that were the foundation of all education until 1905.

Apart from the groups of five already mentioned, there were many others. One of the most important was 'The Five Relations,' which guaranteed prosperity in the country if they were upheld in the correct manner; namely, relations between sovereign and subject, father and son, man and wife, older and younger brother, and friend and friend.

There were also 'The Five Virtues,' 'The Five Poisonous Animals,' 'The Five Internal Organs,' and 'The Five Punishments': branding, cutting off ears, amputating feet, castrating, and decapitating. These last disappeared at the fall of the empire. Since then the condemned have been executed with a shot in the back of the head and ordinary rogues imprisoned.

One group of five still in existence is found in many kitchens—'The Five Spices,' a mixture of aniseed, cinnamon, fennel, cloves, and Sichuan pepper, often used for pork or duck dishes. 'The Five Blessings' constantly recur in New Year pictures, summing up everything a person could possibly wish for: long life, wealth, health, virtue, and a natural death. These wishes were sometimes limited to three, namely, sons, wealth, and a long life—more than enough for most, perhaps.

This New Year picture contains a bowl of goldfish—a symbol of plenty—surrounded by five fat children with lucky symbols in their hands. The coin stands for wealth, as does the peony; and the scepter, the curved object the girl on the right has resting on her arm, stands for love of virtue. As a concession to the values of a new era, two of the children are girls, but as is proper, they stay discreetly in the background.

'The Seven Ways Out' sum up the reasons a man gives if he wishes to get rid of his wife: infertility,

New Year picture from Xiamen in the province of Fujian. 1982.

wanton conduct, neglect of in-laws, shrewishness, thievishness, jealousy, and malignant disease. In reality, divorces were rare. A poor man and his parents found it difficult to finance the acquisition of another wife; and in wealthy homes, heads of households always had subsidiary wives of varying status and primarily used 'The Seven Ways Out' to frighten their wives into submission. Husband and wife were not regarded as equal, a situation improved by the 1950 marriage legislation.

Eight was also an important number. *Ba gua*, or 'The Eight Trigrams,' was one of them, the basis of the sixty-four hexagrams with which it was considered possible to explain the world and life as well as to predict the future.

'The Eight Immortals' were a group of Taoists. Through their studies of nature, they had gone so far as to have become immortal, but fortunately had not lost their humanity. They liked a glass or two, as well as a number of other somewhat inappropriate things, but they were holy and floated about in the clouds. It is worth pointing out that two of them were women—like so many of the magicians or shamans of ancient times. They can often be seen in decorations on porcelain, for instance, and they are much loved in popular art, particularly because of their humanity.

Since the most ancient times, nine has been a very important magic number. According to legend, about four thousand years ago when Yu the Great had managed to steer the water away after the great flood to make the land habitable again, he divided the land into nine provinces and had nine bronze vessels cast as symbols for them. Those bronze vessels symbolized the power of the state and were inherited by subsequent dynasties.

There were nine sacred mountains (five Taoist, four Buddhist), nine heavens, and nine grades for officials. Nine swirling dragons—symbols of imperial power—decorated many of the walls previously built in front of temples and administration buildings to ward off

evil spirits. A wall of this kind can be seen in Beihai Park in Beijing. The most handsome of all is in Datong, in northern Shanxi. With brilliant glazed tiles in five different colors, it was built in the late 1300s and is 45 meters long, 8 meters high, and 2 meters thick. Against a background of clouds and a frothing sea, nine yellow dragons fight over glowing spheres—symbols for sun, manliness, and just administration.

The great gates of the Imperial Palace are adorned with nine times nine hemispherical bronze or brass knobs. Their practical purpose was to hide the pegs holding the wide planks of the gate to the transverse beams at the back, but the number was no matter of chance. Nine was regarded as the highest number—after it, one reappears. Nine times nine is eighty-one, and if eight is added to one, nine is back again.

The Altar of Heaven in Beijing, probably the most beautiful and well-thought-out building in China, is constructed with the number nine as a basic principle. The altar consists of three circular terraces surrounded by marble balustrades. From east, west, north, and south, stairs lead to the uppermost terrace, where during solemn ceremonies at every winter solstice, the emperor established contact with Heaven and accounted for what had occurred over the past year.

This uppermost terrace is ninety feet wide; the floor is laid with marble blocks in nine concentric circles, as are the other terraces. The balustrades around the top terrace have 72 tall pillars with clouds carved on them, the middle terrace has 108, and the bottom terrace 180, making a total of 360, as many as the degrees in a circle. Count up three, six, and zero, and there is nine again.

One could go on and on. Campaigns waged within various fields such as agriculture, cultural life, and health services and more general political debates are grouped according to various numbers. From the 1950s onward, the Chinese have discussed how to

The Temple of Heaven, Beijing. In the foreground, the altar where the emperor accounted to Heaven for the past year.

reduce 'The Three Great Differences': between town and country, workers and peasants, intellectual and physical labor. They have been urged to partake actively in 'The Three Great Revolutions': the class struggle, increased production, and scientific research, and to rally around 'The Three Great Banners': socialism, the Great Leap Forward, and the collectives.

Since the campaign against 'The Gang of Four' in the 1970s, when Jiang Qing, Mao's widow, and her collaborators were held responsible for the disturbances in the country during the Cultural Revolution (or 'The Ten Years of Disaster,' as the period is now called by most Chinese historians), China is now experiencing 'The Four Modernizations.' According to the plans, a conscious concentration on industry, agriculture, defense and science and technology will, by the year 2000, raise the country to the level of the industrial nations.

During the Shang dynasty, the Chinese used a time cycle embracing sixty days. The names of the days were made with two characters, one from a group of ten cyclic characters called 'The Ten Heavenly Stems,' the other from a group of twelve characters called 'The Twelve Earthly Branches.' Opinions on what the characters actually mean are extremely diverse, and this is not the place to go into them. The Ten Stems were probably names used for the ten-day week, and The Twelve Branches, names of the twelve lunar periods and the twelve hourly shifts in a day.

By putting together six groups of The Ten Heavenly Stems with five groups of The Earthly Branches, the result was sixty different combinations. During the Shang dynasty, these were used to denote days, and they can be found constantly in the oracle bones, where they indicate at which point in time the ruler put a question to his ancestors. After 100 B.C., they

The Ten Heavenly Stems		The Twelve Earthly Branches
甲	1	子
乙	2	丑
丙	3	寅
丁	4	卯
戊	5	辰
己	6	巳
庚	7	午
辛	8	未
壬	9	申
癸	10	酉
	11	戌
	12	亥

also described the year, and from that time until the present day the years have been divided into periods of sixty years.

From a practical point of view, coordination between the groups of characters functions roughly like that of two cogwheels of different sizes united in a common movement. The description of the first year in the sixty-year cycle is produced by putting together the first of The Ten Stems with the first of The Twelve Branches, then continuing until the stems come to an end. Then there are still two of The Twelve Branches left. So The Twelve Stems are allowed to start again. The eleventh of The Twelve Branches is put together with the first of The Ten Stems, and so the whole continues until all the sixty possible combinations have been made, and the starting point is back again—time for another cycle of sixty years.

Each one of The Twelve Branches is symbolized by an animal—the rat, the ox, the tiger, the hare, the dragon, the snake, the horse, the sheep, the monkey, the cock, the dog, the pig—which thus come to symbolize a year.

This system is still used in China alongside the Western calendar, and most Chinese know perfectly well under which animal sign they were born and in which they are now living, even if they no longer believe it is of any significance to their lives.

There are problems in arranging years into sixty-year periods. The placing of individual years into the time cycle is clear, but since the various periods were not numbered until rather late, it could be difficult to know whether what was being related happened in ancient times or a year or two ago. It became custom-

ary to write the name of the ruling emperor first, then the animal of the year when the incident occurred, so as to avoid all misunderstandings.

On the back of the 1985 calendar, below, is the whole cycle of animals and a summary of the years the animals symbolized since 1878. The dog is barking and the cock crowing as wildly as on the bronzes.

The ox, the horse, the snake, the dragon, and the tiger look like their prototypes on tiles and stone reliefs from the Han dynasty, but the rat and the pig look more as if they came from a comic strip.

丑牛			子鼠			亥猪		
1 岁	乙丑	1985年生	2 岁	甲子	1984年生	3 岁	癸亥	1983年生
13 岁	癸丑	1973年生	14 岁	壬子	1972年生	15 岁	辛亥	1971年生
25 岁	辛丑	1961年生	26 岁	庚子	1960年生	27 岁	己亥	1959年生
37 岁	己丑	1949年生	38 岁	戊子	1948年生	39 岁	丁亥	1947年生
49 岁	丁丑	1937年生	50 岁	丙子	1936年生	51 岁	乙亥	1935年生
61 岁	乙丑	1925年生	62 岁	甲子	1924年生	63 岁	癸亥	1923年生
73 岁	癸丑	1913年生	74 岁	壬子	1912年生	75 岁	辛亥	1911年生
85 岁	辛丑	1901年生	86 岁	庚子	1900年生	87 岁	己亥	1899年生
97 岁	己丑	1889年生	98 岁	戊子	1888年生	99 岁	丁亥	1887年生

戌狗			酉鸡			申猴		
4 岁	壬戌	1982年生	5 岁	辛酉	1981年生	6 岁	庚申	1980年生
16 岁	庚戌	1970年生	17 岁	己酉	1969年生	18 岁	戊申	1968年生
28 岁	戊戌	1958年生	29 岁	丁酉	1957年生	30 岁	丙申	1956年生
40 岁	丙戌	1946年生	41 岁	乙酉	1945年生	42 岁	甲申	1944年生
52 岁	甲戌	1934年生	53 岁	癸酉	1933年生	54 岁	壬申	1932年生
64 岁	壬戌	1922年生	65 岁	辛酉	1921年生	66 岁	庚申	1920年生
76 岁	庚戌	1910年生	77 岁	己酉	1909年生	78 岁	戊申	1908年生
88 岁	戊戌	1898年生	89 岁	丁酉	1897年生	90 岁	丙申	1896年生
100 岁	丙戌	1886年生	101 岁	乙酉	1885年生	102 岁	甲申	1884年生

未羊			午马			巳蛇		
7 岁	己未	1979年生	8 岁	戊午	1978年生	9 岁	丁巳	1977年生
19 岁	丁未	1967年生	20 岁	丙午	1966年生	21 岁	乙巳	1965年生
31 岁	乙未	1955年生	32 岁	甲午	1954年生	33 岁	癸巳	1953年生
43 岁	癸未	1943年生	44 岁	壬午	1942年生	45 岁	辛巳	1941年生
55 岁	辛未	1931年生	56 岁	庚午	1930年生	57 岁	己巳	1929年生
67 岁	己未	1919年生	68 岁	戊午	1918年生	69 岁	丁巳	1917年生
79 岁	丁未	1907年生	80 岁	丙午	1906年生	81 岁	乙巳	1905年生
91 岁	乙未	1895年生	92 岁	甲午	1894年生	93 岁	癸巳	1893年生
103 岁	癸未	1883年生	104 岁	壬午	1882年生	105 岁	辛巳	1881年生

辰龙			卯兔			寅虎		
10 岁	丙辰	1976年生	11 岁	乙卯	1975年生	12 岁	甲寅	1974年生
22 岁	甲辰	1964年生	23 岁	癸卯	1963年生	24 岁	壬寅	1962年生
34 岁	壬辰	1952年生	35 岁	辛卯	1951年生	36 岁	庚寅	1950年生
46 岁	庚辰	1940年生	47 岁	己卯	1939年生	48 岁	戊寅	1938年生
58 岁	戊辰	1928年生	59 岁	丁卯	1927年生	60 岁	丙寅	1926年生
70 岁	丙辰	1916年生	71 岁	乙卯	1915年生	72 岁	甲寅	1914年生
82 岁	甲辰	1904年生	83 岁	癸卯	1903年生	84 岁	壬寅	1902年生
94 岁	壬辰	1892年生	95 岁	辛卯	1891年生	96 岁	庚寅	1890年生
106 岁	庚辰	1880年生	107 岁	己卯	1879年生	108 岁	戊寅	1878年生

Meaning and Sound

From pictographs to phonetic compounds

The characters mentioned so far—from the character for *sun* to the character for *music, joy*—are, on the whole, all fairly clear and easy to understand. But the Chinese written language is not as simple as it may seem from what has appeared earlier in the book. I haven't yet mentioned anything about characters that as early as the Shang period began to be used as a kind of phonetic language. This is how it came about.

Pictographs

As is evident from the previous chapters, the characters were originally simple pictures of various objects and phenomena, often very expressive in their oldest forms, and many of them have kept their character as pictures until the present day. According to a recent calculation, there are 227 different simple pictographs on the oracle bones, of which I've mentioned only about half. In *Shuowen*, Xu Shen's dictionary from the year 121, the number has grown to 364. They are the basic characters, equivalent to the basic elements in chemistry.

The pictographs functioned excellently as long as it was a question of reproducing concrete objects such as sun and moon, woman and child, chariot, field, dagger-axe, and so on. They were considerably less good when it came to reproducing abstract words. Some of the abstract words—numerals, for instance, and concepts such as 'over' and 'under'—could be expressed through simple schematic depictions. In other cases, a pictograph for a concrete object could be used in a 'transferred meaning' for an abstract idea. For instance, the picture of the sun also stood for *day*—the time of the day when the sun shines. The character for *moon* also stood for *month*—the orbit of the moon took a month. *High* was reproduced with the picture of a high building, and so on.

日　月　高
sun, day　　moon, month　　high

Compound Pictographs—Ideograph

But many words could not be expressed by such simple means. At a very early stage of the development of writing, two or more identical characters began to be put together to form another character. For example, two characters for *tree* mean *forest*; three characters, *thick forest, many trees, dark, serious*.

林　森
forest　　thick forest, dark, serious

Several similar doublets or triplets using one and the same character exist, but the possibilities of continuing in that way turned out to be limited. A more productive method was to combine several quite different characters with one another. Sometimes the parts included in the character have a common characteristic; sometimes one part of the character is an attribute of the other.

Sun and moon, both distinguished for their clear glow, together stand for the concept *clear, brilliant*.

明
clear, brilliant

Woman and child together form the character for *good, well, like*.

好
good, well, like

Man, person, and speech, word together form the character for *to believe in, trust*.

信
to believe in, trust

There are 396 characters constructed on this principle on the oracle bones. In the *Shuowen* dictionary, there are 1,167. Characters of this kind are called compound pictographs or ideographs. Most of them are abstract, but there are some concrete ones such as *prisoner* and *home, family*.

prisoner   home, family

Writing in the Shang period was primarily used when the ruler and his diviner put questions to ancestors on important matters concerning the religious–administrative government of the country. However, there was no reason to consult the supreme powers on most matters of everyday life, so written characters concerning that part of reality were not constructed.

But the words existed, used daily in the spoken language, and as the political, economic, and social organization of the country changed over the years, the need for the written language to be able to express more of the many existing words increased. Contracts and trade agreements had to be recorded, as did taxes, tributes, and day work. New implements and production processes, as well as new scientific and philosophical concepts, brought with them an increase in vocabulary. The limited number of characters that had been adequate in the early days of writing turned out to be insufficient for the demands of new eras.

Inventive creators of characters composed many new and easily understood compound characters with the aid of simple pictographs. During the Shang dynasty, these already constituted over 40 percent of all characters. But sometime during the Zhou period, such new characters ceased. There was probably a limit to how many meaningful combinations could be formed by combining already available simple characters. It was also almost impossible to construct a comprehensible character for a great many abstract words, however many different pictographs there were to put together.

Loan Characters

To get out of this cul-de-sac, characters were quite simply borrowed and allowed to stand for similar-sounding words that had no characters.

Same-sounding words, called homonyms, are common in many languages. For instance, *bat* can be a flying mammal or a cricket or baseball bat; *pole* can be a long staff or a place on the globe; a *firm*, a commercial company or firm ground; *well*, a well or 'do well,' and so on.

In the Chinese language, the number of similar-sounding words has always been unusually large. When their imaginations started failing them, the creators of characters resorted to this method. In archaic Chinese, in a classic example, there were two words pronounced the same: one, a kind of cereal (*Triticum estivum*), a species of wheat; the other, meaning *to come*. There was already a character for the species of cereal, a picture of the actual plant and rather like the character for *wheat* already mentioned, but no character for *to come*.

wheat, to come

Instead of constructing a character of its own for *to come*, ancient scribes simply borrowed the character for the type of wheat, leaving the reader to decide which meaning was appropriate in the context.

scorpion, tens of thousands

In the same way, the character for *scorpion*—a picture of the insect with its tail up ready to strike—was used for the similar-sounding words *innumerable, tens of thousands*; and the character for *basket, winnower* was used for the almost similar–sounding demonstrative and possessive pronouns: *this, that, his, hers, its*.

basket, winnower, this, its

This was a practical way of temporarily solving a difficult problem, and the method became common for a while. But it was hardly conceivable that in the long run characters could go on being borrowed. Texts ran the risk of being turned into incomprehensible puzzles if every or every other character had one basic meaning but was used in different ways independently of each other. How would anyone know when the character was being used in its original meaning or when it was just functioning as a borrowed sound?

Enlarged Loan Characters

In some cases, the character used as a borrowed sound had already become obsolete, and then the borrowed sound functioned with no real problems. In time, the original meaning of the character was simply forgotten, and the new meaning took over.

But in many other cases, the character went on being used both in its original sense and at the same time as a borrowed sound, which led to constant misunderstandings. To limit this confusion and differentiate between the two, an explanation was added to the original character that gave the reader a hint that it was being used in its basic meaning.

The character for *basket, winnower*, for instance—in itself a perfectly satisfactory picture of a woven basket—was thus expanded with the character for *bamboo*, the material of which the basket was generally made, and the original character for *basket, winnower* continued to be used for the demonstrative and possessive pronouns, for which it was difficult to construct a character of their own.

the enlarged character for basket, winnower

The same fate afflicted many other old concrete pictorial characters. The additions may seem superfluous, considering the clarity of the original characters, but nevertheless, the result was that the clarity of language increased, as did the number of characters.

Characters with Derivative Meaning

Other problems arose. Over the centuries, the meanings of many characters changed, sometimes expanding, sometimes becoming specialized. Many characters had also acquired a metaphorical, transferred, or derivative meaning. For instance, the character for *lines, strokes, ornaments* was also used for *writing, script, literature*. Although the Chinese language on the whole consists to a great extent of 'strokes' and 'lines,' the two meanings were so far away from each other that misunderstandings easily arose in a text. To make it easier for the reader to differentiate between the literal and the figurative meanings, the character for *lines, strokes, ornaments* was complemented with the character for *silk* on occasions when it was used in its literal sense, and the original character was reserved for the transferred figurative meaning *writing, script, literature*.

writing, script, literature   lines, strokes, ornaments

The reason why the creators of the characters decided on *silk* is unclear, but their choice is in its way quite logical. The unusually varied patterns of silk cloth and the thousands of threads—'lines'—together making those patterns, lacks any equivalent in other materials. A reference to *silk*, *silk cloth* reinforced in an understandable way the meaning of the character: *lines, strokes, ornaments*.

The character for *to fill*, and *fullness (abundance)* is also used in the oracle bone inscriptions for the concept of *happiness, luck, blessing*. The meanings are related—satisfaction, plenty, happiness—nevertheless, as early as during the Shang period, the need arose to separate them. By adding the character for *omen, prediction*, having to do with predicting fortune or misfortune, a new character was formed that indicated in a useful way the two meanings intended.

to fill, fullness (abundance)   happiness, luck, blessing

The many new characters thus arrived at may initially seem constructed on the same principle as the compound characters of the *clear*, *good* and *believe in* type, in which the parts included have either a common characteristic or one part forms an attribute of the other. But that is not the case. They all start out from a 'mother character' and indicate definitions of various meanings for it. The characters included in the respective word families are etymologically and semantically closely related and thus remind us of derived words and metaphors that are so important in the Indo-European languages.

Radical plus Phonetic Compounds

All these various methods were used to form a number of new characters, but in the end, the character makers were still faced with the fundamental problem: How were characters to be found for the tens of thousands of words in the spoken language?

The task may well seem insoluble, but by borrowing characters and differentiating between the various meanings some characters have acquired imperceptibly, a revolutionary new principle for the construction of characters had been found—a compound character in which one part gave the meaning, another the pronunciation. By ignoring which particular meaning a certain character had, this part began to be used entirely for the sound it represented. For instance, there was no character for the words *to brush off* or *to tangle*. Instead of trying to construct appropriate pictographs for them, the character for *writing, script, literature*, which was pronounced the same way, was quite simply complemented with different additions that hinted at the meaning, and two new characters were soon formed.

to brush off

To brush off. On the left is a hand, on the right, writing. The word is pronounced as 'writing' and concerns *hand*—the hand that brushes the dust off coats and trousers.

紊

to tangle

To tangle. Writing above, silk below. The word is pronounced as 'writing' and concerns *silk*—those thin threads that have such an irritating habit of becoming entangled and making a mess.

The semantic part of these characters is usually called radical, the sound part, phonetic. When characters constructed in this way are mentioned, they are generally called radical or phonetic compounds, or ideographs. Other terminology exists, and a great many heated opinions regarding terminology have been exchanged, but that is irrelevant here.

Instead, consider what can be achieved with this new principle of construction.

There were no characters for the words *spokes in a wheel, the medicinal plant Phytolacca* (pokeweed), *cloth width, to help/assist,* and *wealth.* But they were all pronounced in the same way as *to fill, fullness,* and with the starting point of that character, new characters were made.

Radical = *meaning*	Phonetic = *pronunciation*	New Character
輻 Cart	fill	spokes in a wheel
葍 Grass, herbs	fill	medicinal plant *Phytolacca* (pokeweed)
幅 Cloth	fill	cloth width, length
副 Knife	fill	help, assist
富 Roof	fill	wealth, prosperity

At first, phonetics were chosen with great sophistication, and there is often a certain agreement in meaning between characters with the same phonetic part. So sometimes it is difficult to decide whether a certain character is to be considered an ideograph, an expanded pictograph, or a phonetic compound. Scholars often have widely different opinions.

The character for *wealth, prosperity* is an example of this. Wine was a valuable possession and was often used as a gift. A character showing a large wine jar beneath a roof, that is, a house, is a picture as good as any for the concept of 'wealth and prosperity.' So the suggestion has been made that the character is a compound character in which the two parts together provide the meaning. But the character did not occur before the latter part of the Zhou period when new ideographs were no longer made, and so it is likely to be a phonetic compound, in which the roof indicates the meaning (*a rich house*) and the rest of the character indicates the sound that is produced.

The situation is, therefore, rather complicated:

There are pictographs, simple and compound.

There are phonetic compounds.

Between these clearly defined groups are several different types of characters that are transitional forms.

There are loan characters, which have lost their original meaning and began to be used for their sound only.

There are old pictographs complemented with a semantic part to make it clear that the pictograph is to be used in its original literal form.

There are characters that are metaphorical expansions of an old pictogram and are complemented by an explanatory addition.

There is no problem with the majority of characters. They are phonetic compounds in which one part provides the meaning, another part the pronunciation, and that is that. Here is an example of what can be done with the character for *square* which was also used, that is, in the sense of *region, place, occupy an area, to sacrifice to the spirits of The Four Quarters, side by side, in all directions.* The character often occurs in oracle bone inscriptions and is included as part of names of the many 'barbarian' tribes and peoples who lived on the boundaries of the Shang kingdom, *outside* civilization.

square, four-sided

Scholars have quite different opinions as to what the character was originally a picture of, but that is of no importance here. What is interesting is how easy it would be to create a whole new series of characters with this character as a basis. For some words that had no character of their own but were pronounced in the same way as the word for *square*, the word *square*, or *four-sided*, had previously been used in the hope the reader would nevertheless understand what was meant. Here are some examples:

two boats tied together side by side
a kind of tree
a kind of strong ox
bream
room, house
place
bright dawn, appear, just then, at that time
fragrant
to spin
to resemble, imitate
to find out, inquire
to loosen, let go, drive away
to injure, hinder, disturb

I would now like to ask the reader to cover the following text and for a while try to work out just how, with a starting point in the character for *square* as a phonetic element one could form new characters for the words in the list just provided. What semantic element would be needed for the meaning of the new character to be absolutely clear?

For some of the characters, the semantic element is fairly obvious. The character that means a kind of *boat, tree, ox,* and *fish* ought preferably to contain the character for *boat, tree, ox,* and *fish*. Even a beginner at construction of characters would realize that.

For *room, house,* the character for *roof* could be a good semantic element; another possibility would be the character for *household/family,* originally a picture of a single door leading into different rooms in a house, as opposed to double doors onto the street.

It is hard to think of a better semantic element for *place* than *earth,* the material that everything was built with in the old days—embankments, walls, houses, pigsties, and workshops, as well as the streets between them. The open places for threshing, and where markets were held, were also of earth, beaten down and as smooth as a floor. From early times, the character was also used for *marketplace,* for *village,* and for the various *quarters, neighborhoods* into which the town was divided.

Bright dawn, appear, just then, at that time. This must surely be primarily about the sun. A peaceful gray light first appears, then—blinding in its force—the first rays directed straight into the eyes, that short moment when the sun appears, at that moment, then.

Fragrant. Something providing truly pleasing associations is needed here, a bouquet of flowers, the smell of a sleeping infant's hair, a pan simmering on the stove, flavored with onions and good herbs. The character for *food, eat* or better, *nose* would work well as a semantic element, though perhaps *grass* would be even better, for *grass* also stands for *herbs*, among which there are many with strong scents in China.

For those who created the characters, nature was never far away—where they lived was still half countryside with fields and vegetable plots between houses, and the scent of crushed leaves from varieties of artemisia, mint, chrysanthemum, and allium growing among wild varieties of millet and grass surrounded them as they walked along the small roads.

Several of these are still well-known medicinal plants used year-round for people's chills and stomach troubles.

Artemisia—mugwort and wormwood, well known both here and in China—was useful in various contexts. Smoke from smoldering artemisia leaves was used to drive out mosquitoes and flies, silverfish, beetles, and other insects—a predecessor of today's mosquito repellants—and grain stores were protected against insects with dry artemisia leaves, one handful per fifty kilos of grain. Vegetables and flowers were watered with a decoction of artemisia against aphids and larvae. For rheumatism and urinary infections, a cone of finely pulverized artemisia leaves was lit on the acupuncture places needing activating for the illness to be driven out of the body. The powder burned without a flame, but the heat spread inward and the room filled with its strong aromatic smell. This method, called moxibustion, is still in use, not only in China but all over the Far East.

To spin. The choice here is primarily between *hemp* and *silk* as the semantic element, for cloth was woven mainly from them. Considering the central role silk played in ancient society—not least as a means of payment—and the beauty of the cloth woven with it, the choice is easy: *silk*.

To resemble, imitate—several alternatives here. *Hand* would work well, for in imitating what others do, the right grip is learned for playing a musical instrument, for instance, or chopping onions or planing wood.

Foot is also conceivable; the metaphor 'to follow in someone's footsteps' often entails wanting to be like someone else, and so choosing to continue in a certain occupation. But perhaps *man, person* would be best. Who hasn't heard relatives saying 'You're just like so and so'? Who hasn't dreamed of being like the person at the top of the class, equally excellent, or having so many friends?

To find out, inquire is more difficult, for inquiries can be carried out in so many different ways. One possibility would be to add the character for *hand*, for when rummaging around in drawers looking for something, the hand is primarily in action, just as it is when taking apart a broken article to see if it can be mended. But *to find out, inquire* also often involves intellectual activity, looking up in books and talking to knowledgeable people to try to find out the circumstances of a given problem. If the character has that content, then it would be better to add *speech, language*.

To loosen, let go, drive away. In this case *hand* would be one of the first meaning indicators to come to mind. The hand is used to untie a boat or the tether of a domestic animal or the rope binding a prisoner. But the meaning of *drive away* implies greater force, so perhaps *hit* would be better. That character shows a hand with a mattock or axe held aloft, and with such an implement or weapon, many problems could surely be solved—remember the Gordian knot—and anyone driven away.

To injure, hinder, disturb. To me, the word *injure* is primarily associated with weapons, violence, and physical force. *Axe, knife* and *dagger-axe* are some of the characters able to function as semantic elements if violence is to be emphasized. But then there are words that hurt. Lack of understanding and respect, conscious exploitation, nonchalance, and bullying—people have many opportunities to wound, hinder, and upset each other. From that point of view, *speech, language* or perhaps *man, person* would be the best characters for that meaning. In that case, other semantic elements must be found for *resemble, imitate* and *find out, inquire*. What can be done about that?

This is what the ancient character makers chose:

two boats tied side by side 舫 (*boat*)

a kind of tree 枋 (*tree*)

a kind of strong ox 牥 (*ox*)

bream 魴 (*fish*)

room, house 房 (*household, family*)

place 坊 (*earth*)

bright dawn, appear, at that very moment 昉 (*sun*)

fragrant 芳 (*grass*)

to spin 紡 (*silk*)

to resemble, imitate 仿 (*man, person*)

to find out, inquire 訪 (*speech, language*)

to loosen, let go, drive away 放 (*to hit*)

So far it has been quite possible to understand the way the character makers reasoned in their day when choosing semantic elements. So it is surprising when one comes to the character for *injure, hinder, disturb*. What lies behind this choice of semantic element?

to injure, hinder 妨 (*woman*)

Was it common that women were injured, hindered, or disturbed? Or was it the women themselves who were so troublesome, by injuring, hindering, and disturbing other people?

There is rarely any mention of ordinary women's lives in the scholarly literature on ancient China that would explain the way they appeared to their contemporaries. But it does appear that the widespread economic and social changes that occurred during the Zhou dynasty resulted in women's opportunities to work becoming increasingly limited to the home and family. The important activities for which they had been responsible since Neolithic times, such as pottery manufacture and agriculture, were successively taken over by the men.

The pottery wheel and the iron-clad ox-drawn plow increased productivity, but at the same time made the work heavier. It 'required a man' and could no longer be carried out as a subsidiary occupation. The increase in population brought with it increased pressure on the land, and hunting, previously undertaken by men, lost its importance to people's livelihoods. The land became the primary means of production and rather than being owned by sovereign and clans, toward the end of the Zhou period it became privately owned. The individual family became the normal production unit, steered by the man, the head of the household. How this affected the position of Chinese women has not yet been studied.

Nor has there been any analysis of the effect of these great changes on the construction of the characters. Until recently, language scholars have rarely made use of the results that archaeologists, historians, economists, sociologists, ethnographers, and others have arrived at. Just the same, one thing is quite clear: it was never a matter of chance just which semantic element was chosen for the various characters. The intention was to give the reader as simply and clearly as possible some hint of the content of the character, and so the prevailing general experiences, values, and conventions at the time the character was constructed were the basis for the choices.

To try to form a picture of the way the character for *woman* was used as a semantic element, I went through the 222 characters registered under the radical *woman* in the *Shuowen* dictionary. About a quarter of them turn out to be terms used either for many female members of a family, such as *mother, aunt, older* and *younger sister, sister-in-law, stepmother,* and so on, or for other women also in and around a home: *servant girl, concubine, matchmaker.*

Another quarter concern *marriage, matrimony, pregnancy* and *childbearing* or *pleasures,* alongside concepts such as *illegal intercourse with servant girl, debauchery,* and *visit to prostitute.*

The remainder of the characters—that is, half of them—are either very positive judgments on the beauty of women and attractive ways of behaving, such as *beautiful, pretty, elegant, gracious, handsome, slim, fascinating, pleasing, delicate, attractive, quiet and friendly, amenable,* and *accommodating,* or very negative judgments such as *false, disloyal, horrible, deformed, troublesome, flighty, envious, jealous, bad-tempered, foolish, suspicious, lazy, ugly,* and *worn out*—a depressing catalogue.

The negative characters appear primarily to concern the element of irritation that a discontented and perhaps unhappy woman could cause her husband and the rest of the household. With no possibility of influencing her position, perhaps she became so *bad-tempered* that she *hindered* and *disturbed* others.

The characters that we have seen used as semantic elements—*man/person, woman, hand, to hit, sun, omen, earth, tree, grass, bamboo, silk, fish, ox, cart, knife, cloth, household, roof,* and *speech/word*—are also included as semantic elements in a large number of other characters. All other pictographs previously mentioned in the book are used in the same way, each character with its special area of use. *Heart* shows that the character concerns either emotions and experiences or haste—the regular or uneasy beats within the body; *food/eat* indicates dishes or cooking methods, *cowrie shell* economic values, trade, wealth, bribes, alms, or theft.

Mouth is included in the many characters for sighs, groans, and shrieks emerging from the mouth, ranging from the whimpering of an infant to the shuddering speech of someone freezing cold, as well as the unlikely sounds of someone snoring, spitting, hiccupping, slurping, coughing, whistling, kissing, spewing, or calling to the pigs, as well as the sounds of animals—humming of bees, twittering of birds as a flock settles in a tree before nightfall, and howling of dogs.

Water—the radical used most of all—is included in characters either concerning liquid of some form or with life in and around a river. There are characters for *level riverbanks* and *marshlands*, *tides* and *the sound of waves*, swift crystal-clear *streams* and muddy *backwaters*, *bubbles* slowly plopping out of the mud, *sand*, *mist*, and *heavy rain*. In all these characters, the lives of people are evident, all those living by the river, fetching water, washing clothes and themselves, then sitting down in the evening feeling the cool scent of the water streaming toward them.

The method of putting characters together with one part providing meaning and one part sound turned out to be extremely productive. At one blow, it was possible to produce almost as many characters as were needed. And that is what happened. During the Shang dynasty, phonetic compound characters constituted about 30 percent of the characters used at the time, and during the following dynasties, they steadily increased. In *Shuowen*, which contains 9,353 characters, they constitute about 80 percent; in Zheng Qiao's historical work of the 1100s, which uses over 23,000 characters, about 90 percent, and in Kang Xi's great dictionary of 1711, containing 48,641 different characters, 97 percent. Many of them are names of people, places, and implements that have long since disappeared, but the characters remain.

New characters are still being created. If a character that does not exist is required, all that has to be done is to construct it. A Swedish friend once asked me to help her have a seal cut, and the problem was how she was to put her long and complicated name into Chinese, preferably no more than three characters, as it should be in China. We must have spent at least an hour over the counter at the seal engraver's shop, discussing what her name really meant, which sounds it was composed of, and which appropriate character we should choose. Finally we found three characters that fit really well, both in sound and meaning, but the seal engraver shook his head.

"In itself, that's all right," he said. "But the trouble is, the impression given is of a man's name."

The discussion went on until one of the assistants suggested adding the character for *woman* to one of the characters for my friend's personal name. That solved it. The character as such 'doesn't exist,' but anyone seeing it would immediately grasp how it should be pronounced, as well as the fact that it is the name of a woman.

I think that was the first time I really understood what actually happened when the phonetic compound originated as a principle of construction.

It would be leading the reader astray if I were to end here. There is actually a considerable problem concerning pronunciation when it comes to phonetic compound characters. During the Shang dynasty when characters began to be constructed with one part indicating sound, another meaning, no one could have foreseen the widespread changes in sound that the spoken language was to undergo during the following three thousand years.

Although little thought is given to it in everyday life, spoken language changes very quickly: sounds are contracted or change their nature, other sounds are inserted, endings disappear, and so on. In a language written with letters, this does not cause many problems, for after a time lag, the written and spoken language adapt to each other, and expressions and forms previously regarded as wrong or inappropriate become generally accepted.

The Chinese spoken language, like any other language, has also undergone great changes, but the characters have maintained the form they were once given, so in some ways, the idea of phonetic compound characters has been lost. With a key, it is possible to establish that many characters once perfectly suited to act as sound elements in a character do not today provide the reader with any correct information at all on how the character should be pronounced.

I have so far consciously avoided taking up the pronunciation of the characters, for the purpose of this book is different. It would take another book to go into the subject more deeply, interesting as it is. But here briefly is an example of what has happened to many phonetic compound characters.

During the Shang dynasty, the character for *work* was used in several different closely related meanings, all concerned with the way in which the work was carried out. By complementing *work* with the character for *strength*, a character was produced for the concept of *effort, achievement, result*. By complementing that with the character for *hit*, a hand with a mattock or axe held aloft, the character meant to *attack, set about, work at*.

When this was done, yet another number of words were soon made, in principle pronounced in the same way as 'work,' some of them distantly connected with the concept of work, but most concerned with quite different activities or subjects. In ancient times, they were all pronounced almost exactly like 'work,' but over the years differences in pronunciation became greater, in some cases confusingly so. Is it really possible to state that the character for *work*, pronounced 'gong,' is a sound element in *river*, pronounced 'jiang'? Yes, it is. That has been so since the Han dynasty, when people still remembered what happened as phonetic compound characters were formed and pronunciation was still more or less agreed upon. But the way in which all this coheres was never clarified until research done by Bernhard Karlgren, most of all through his *Grammata Serica Recensa*, was published in 1940.

Radical		Phonetic		Meaning		Modern Pronunciation
力	strength	工	work	功	result	gong
攵	hit	工	work	攻	attack	gong
穴	cave	工	work	空	empty, hollow	kong
絲	silk	工	work	紅	red	hong
木	tree	工	work	杠	log, pole	gang
水	water	工	work	江	river	jiang

Karlgren started his career in research as a school-boy, almost for fun. His older brother, Anton, was reading languages at Uppsala University and returned home one summer holiday, bringing with him a vocabulary of over three thousand representative Swedish words.

Systematic investigations into Swedish dialects had recently begun, and just as Carolus Linnæus once sent his apprentices out to collect information on the flora and fauna of Sweden, young language scholars were being sent out to collect words, expressions, and pronunciation of Swedish dialects. Starting out with the material collected, the intent was to reconstruct an earlier stage of language and explain relationships between the various dialects.

For a few summers, Bernhard Karlgren walked around farms in the Taberg area of southern Sweden, where the Karlgren family spent their summers. With the aid of the 'characters' of the particular phonetic alphabet for local dialects, he noted on the word list the way farmers and old country people pronounced the words. In 1908, when he was only eighteen and still at school, his notes were published in a respected scholarly journal.

After some intensive years reading languages at Uppsala University and now twenty, Karlgren found himself in Taiyuan, the capital of Shanxi province, on a high plain in the middle of the huge loess soil area. As soon as he had learned Chinese, he did just what he had done at home in the south of Sweden: he set off around the countryside, noting dialects, starting out from a word list of over three thousand representative characters, and in villages and towns sought out people who had lived there all their lives and had an authentic pronunciation. With the help of the phonetic symbols of the Swedish dialect alphabet, he registered the way the Chinese pronounced the characters. However remarkable it may seem, this worked extremely well.

He found time for seventeen dialects before the 1911 revolution broke out and put an end to the two-thousand-year-old empire. Karlgren experienced the fighting in Taiyuan at close quarters, then returned home via the Trans-Siberian Railway. With the help of the dialect material he had gathered and a copy of a rhyming dictionary from the 600s, which later proved invaluable for his research, Karlgren set about trying to reconstruct the common origins of the dialects—in fact, medieval Chinese. How he did this and the way he later succeeded in reconstructing the pronunciation of the beginning of the Zhou dynasty, thus explaining the construction of the characters, is a very long and fascinating story requiring far more space that I have at my disposal here.

It may appear that I have now moved a long way away from the subject—the Chinese characters and their connection with reality—but that is not the case. On the contrary, despite the huge changes the written language has undergone, the foundation of the written language is still the original characters. *Man* and *woman*, *water* and *mountain*, *tree* and *silk*—all keep recurring individually or in combination, as in Hesse's 'Glass Bead Game,' in which the different parts interplay, affect, complement, and comment on each other. Regardless of which function these basic characters have in the various compositions, they keep their identity, their pictorial clarity. Once one has learned to recognize and understand them, they provide a key not only to the written language but also to the reality from which they once came, as well as to life lived today.

Empire of Living Symbols

Characters are the focal point of Chinese culture. In them the experiences and observations of thousands of years of human life are summarized, and within them can also be found the Chinese countryside, its mountains and rivers, plants and animals. From the angular strokes on the oracle bones, to the smooth yet forceful lines of the bronze characters, to the written characters of today, at first glance these steps may seem very long, yet it is the continuity that is so striking. Methods of writing have changed, but the way of perceiving and reproducing reality still lives on, and the reality itself—for all the length of time that has passed since the first characters were created—has changed less than it is possible to believe.

Oracle bone with questions to ancestors and the Supreme Ruler. The answer was read off in the cracks—prototype for the character for predict. *Shang period. 20×12 cm.*

Inscriptions are also found on bronze vessels used by the ancient Chinese when offering meat and wine to the spirits of their ancestors. Right: On older vessels like this three-legged Shang period ding, decorated with birds, cicadas, and whirlwind patterns, the inscription often consisted of one single character, probably a name. Long descriptive texts are found on later vessels such as the lid above, from the end of the Zhou period.

One has only to go out into the street to see prototypes of many of the oldest characters concerning mankind. Eye and ear, nose and mouth, the characteristic stance of a person sauntering away across the street, or in all simplicity, someone just standing looking around.

The still flow of the waterfall down the cliff, an oft-recurring theme in Chinese art, also found in the character for spring, origin, source. Painting by Li Keran (1907–1989).

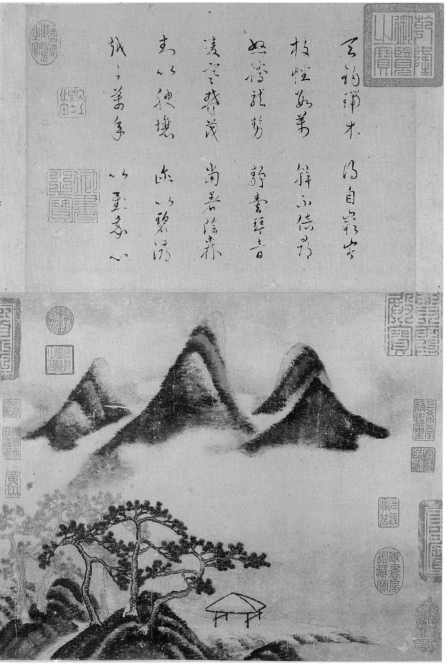

Mountain peaks covered with thick, close foliage, rising dreamlike out of the valley mists, a pavilion in the foreground in the shelter of a few old pines, in which to seek refuge and quiet contemplation of the force and beauty of nature. Painting by Mi Fei (1051–1107).

The poem in praise of these trees was written by Emperor Qian Long (1736–1795) in his own hand. Several of the seals, including that on the top right, are his.

The Yellow River cutting a winding furrow on its way south through the fertile soil of the valley, a picture as clear as that of the characters for water, river *and for* island, area, *on the left. The huge loess soil area lies all around with its almost bare, treeless mountains, eroded by water and wind, sometimes like gigantic sand dunes, sometimes angular, flat-topped mountains where the surface plateau runs over into a precipice. The soil is loose; the steep ravine walls, prototypes for the character for* cliff *to the right, give way easily and collapse, as here in the Fen Valley in Shanxi.*

"There were two sorts of tigers," an old woman in Yan'an told me a few years ago. "The dangerous ones in the mountains and the good ones. If you meet a dangerous one, you shouldn't look at it, or say anything, just walk on. Otherwise, it will attack you."

"Are there tigers here in Yan'an?" I asked in surprise.

"Oh no. There are only ordinary good tigers here, and they protect us from all evil."

A Shang dynasty wine vessel on the left; a chest from a peasant home, top right; and below, a toy tiger at the Beijing Zoo, where fathers have their photographs taken with their sons so that the sons will be as strong and brave as a tiger.

In Yang Xixian's dark kitchen, above, every bit of the walls is decorated with pictures. New Year pictures of chubby children surrounded by lucky symbols such as peonies, phoenix, and dragons compete with homemade papercuts of birds and scenes from famous stories such as 'The Wedding of the Rat' and 'The Monkey King.'

The boy on the right, riding on the red carp with nuclear energy as a flower in his hand, symbolizes the campaign for modernization introduced in 1978. The carp—ancient symbol of plenty and effort rewarded—is leaping, full of energy, up the Yellow River as it rushes through the Dragon Gate. Thus China will also overcome all difficulties and develop the country. The cranes in the background mean long life.

On the far left is Ji Lanying, beside her Yang Xixian, who made the papercuts above.

One of the new China's most famous pictures is a 'peasant painting' from the village of Huxian, some miles from Banpo. It is called 'Commune Fish Pond' and was painted in 1973 by Dong Zhengyi. Trained as an artist, he went to live in the country in the 1950s as a teacher, to take part in the widespread popular art movement encouraged in the villages at the time. In a golden cascade, the huge carp flow over the surface of the water and the surface of the picture, the net heavy and full of fish, the men hauling in the catch as hard as they can. The message is that the catch can be as plentiful as this if everyone pulls together. Abundance and wealth are possible to achieve, but require hard work. The picture was painted during a period when collective work was emphasized, whereas today individual effort is being encouraged. The difference is not all that great. In either case, everyone puts his or her shoulder to the wheel, and the prosperity of the nation increases. The three characters on the left mean to fish.

Boat with vegetables on a Suzhou canal. Straight prow, straight stern, transverse walls dividing the boat into sections—a construction unique to China. As can be seen from the characters on the left, it has been used since the Shang period.

舟

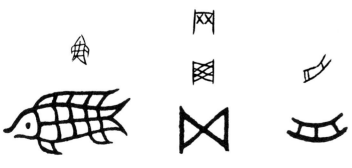

A boat in a lotus pool, large-scaled fish, a net in the background—all as clearly reproduced as in the oracle bone and bronze characters below. Peasant painting from Jiangsu. 1979.

In the thin morning light, the coal carts creak through icy-cold Datong. Dust whirls. Men half-asleep under their black fur caps, their whips exclamation marks in the crackling, parched yellow air.

The predecessor of the carts — military chariots of early history — are nowadays seen only as copies in museums. This one on the left is in Beijing; the bronze character is from the Zhou dynasty.

When I was to leave China in 1962, the old qin master, Guan Pinghu, painted the album page above in classic style to remind me of the summer melons and pumpkins that covered the house where we had our music lessons. His father had been court painter at the Imperial Palace, and he himself also trained as a painter. But the empire fell in 1911, and Guan Pinghu devoted the rest of his life to the gentle, meditative music that since Confucius has been written for qin, the seven-stringed Chinese lute. On the right is the character for melon, pumpkin, gourd.

On the left — 'Land of milk and honey' is our biblical term for beautiful, prosperous agricultural areas. 'Land of fish and rice,' the Chinese say, referring to the fertile areas of central China, where rice thrives in the steamy, humid fields and fish leap in the waters of rivers and canals. Painting from 1976 and next to it, the character for field.

Burial urn from Neolithic times on the left, and storage vessels for soybeans, pickles, and so on, above, from the village of Dayudao—five thousand years of unbroken tradition. But clay pots are expensive. Dry goods can just as well be stored in homemade papier-mâché jars . . .

A mash of old newspapers and glue is dried around a clay vessel, which is then carefully eased out, and an excellent container remains, to be decorated with pretty paper.

Silk production is an extremely complicated process. On the left, women gather cocoons off the twigs where the silkworms settle when cocooning. Below, hands gather the thin threads out of the water to twist them together into one thread, the character for this is on the right.

On the far left, a burial figurine in her silk gown and beside her an embroidered cloth, both from the grave of the Marquise of Tai, 165 B.C. Below, a loom and the character for it on the right.

On the right, two cheerful ladies from the sixth century, their hair done up in the traditional way. Except for the long 'modern' sleeves, the gowns look the way the Chinese costume has looked since the Shang period. A bronze character for clothes is in the corner.

Residential streets in Hangzhou, cathedrals of shimmering green light. The plane trees were once imported from France. Inhabitants of the town stroll and cycle in their shade, protected from the heat of summer. Behind the whitewashed walls are residential areas and leafy gardens, a privileged, peaceful environment where everything is designed in human proportions and reflects a basic need for culture, beauty, and purpose. Below, oracle bone and bronze characters for tree.

The elegant foliage of bamboo
and the grace with which it
moves have made it an indispensable part of the Chinese
garden, not least in rock gardens, where its gentle beauty
contrasts with the weight of the
rough stones. Garden in Suzhou.
Below, the character for
bamboo.

Han dynasty grave sculptures in the form of houses. Above is a roundhouse of the kind ordinary people lived in over thousands of years — compare it with the first oracle bone character for roof to the left, above. Below is a grain store with tiled roof, raised from the ground to avoid dampness and vermin.

Chinese houses are their roofs. Nowhere can this be seen so clearly as on the roofs of Beijing, most of all in the Forbidden City, above. Covered with glazed yellow tiles in the colors of ripe grain, the roofs glow with quiet luster against the frosty blue of winter and the white sky of summer. One of their predecessors is the little 782 Nanchansi temple below, still in its place in the Wutai Mountains.

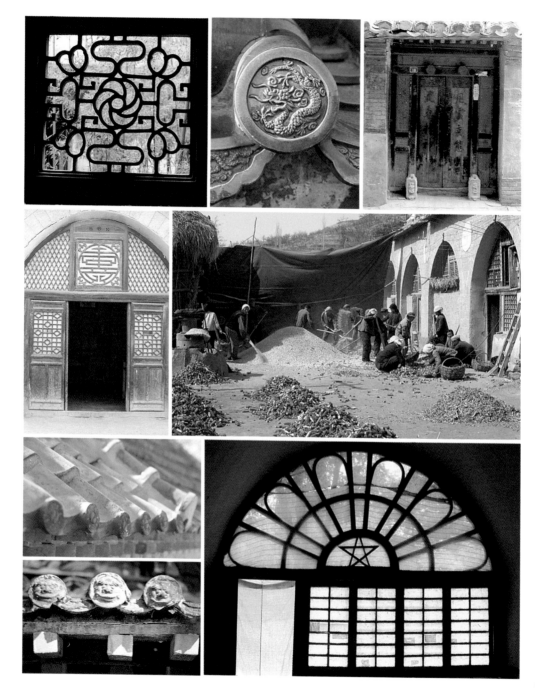

Since the Han period, great care has been taken with minor details within Chinese domestic architecture — in ordinary people's houses as well — the street entrance, the windows with their delicate wooden latticework, the light glowing through white rice paper, and the roof tiles, the ends often reliefs of swirling dragons or grinning masks. Above, the character for doorway, below for window.

On the right, a traditional northern Chinese courtyard, closed outside, open inside, the threshing area at the south end.

Above, schoolchildren in the village of Dayudao practicing the drum dance for National Day, and the man-high drum on the right used in religious ceremonies in the temple of Yongzuozi in Taiyuan—two examples of the central part the drum has played and still plays in China's dances and rituals. To the left of the drum, its character.

On the left, worn fragments of a silk book from 179 B.C.—excavated in 1973—one of the most important early historic finds made in China during this century. The text is the oldest known version of Laozi, the leading Taoist work. The characters are written in ink in vertical lines on the same principle as used on the oracle bones, which can also be seen in the character for documents, volume.

Nine times nine glowing bronze knobs decorate the heavy red double doors of the entrance to the Temple of Heaven in Beijing. The beams, painted in bright blue and green with contours in gold, are visible in the dim light beneath the roof.

Character stroke order

Just as when we learn to write the letters of the alphabet, to be able to learn to write a Chinese character properly, one has to observe certain elementary rules for the formation of the strokes and the order in which they are to be written. Thirty or so different strokes are used in the characters, but of them all, only eight are basic strokes, the others being variants or combinations of them.

Chinese children start learning to write by copying page after page of these eight basic strokes. They fill in printed model strokes with pen and ink in their exercise books, and as they work, they become familiar with horizontal strokes always being written from left to right, and vertical strokes always from above downward, and so on. The children are not allowed to begin writing characters consisting of combinations of different strokes until they have mastered the eight basic strokes so well that they no longer think about how they should be formed. At this stage there is no room for improvisation or personal likes and dislikes.

Adult Chinese write with fountain pens or ballpoints for everyday purposes, but as soon as the slightest aesthetic quality is required of the text, they use brush and ink. It is an art that really requires lifelong practice. Not only schoolchildren but also innumerable adults constantly practice to improve their handwriting.

The strokes are carried out by a complex interplay between greater and weaker pressure of the brush on the paper and the swift or slow movements from one point to another. The brush is outstandingly flexible, but with the slightest uncertainty of hand, the brush becomes willful—the hairs easily splay out in different directions, and the strokes are not given the force and tension they require.

When the brush is put to the paper, the point must be gathered into a nice tip and straightened. As writing continues, the tip must be stroked again and again with a rolling motion against the smooth surface of the ink-stone to regain its form. This also gives

the writer a brief moment for thought and preparation for the next brush stroke—a much-needed pause.

Just writing the simple character for *one*—a single horizontal stroke—is a whole enterprise in itself. There are two possibilities. In one case (1), with some determination one lowers the brush straight onto the paper, waits a moment, then with a steady hand one takes the brush to the right toward the end of the stroke, waits again for a moment, then lifts the brush slantwise backward–upward. Then one has a stroke that starts and ends with a straight, taut, slightly slanting line.

In the other case (2), one approaches the beginning of the stroke from the right with a circular movement that binds the brush point, then lowers the brush even further onto the paper, waits for a moment, then carries it on to the end of the stroke. There one waits yet another moment before taking the brush a fraction downward and returning back in the stroke one has just completed, at the same time carefully lifting the brush off the paper. One then has a stroke with a softly rounded beginning and ending.

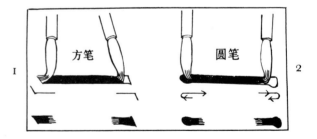

Which of these two writing methods one chooses depends on the sort of expression for which one is striving and the calligraphic style to which one adheres.

To carry this out correctly requires a great deal of practice. But that is not all. The stroke must also be full of vital force and must not sag at both ends like a carrying pole, weighed down by heavy burdens, nor must it look like a swaying suspension bridge. Well-assembled, firm, and vigorous, it should rest on the paper with a light floating lift to the right.

There are similar rules for the other seven basic strokes. A sketch in a 1983 calligraphy textbook shows how they are to be carried out.

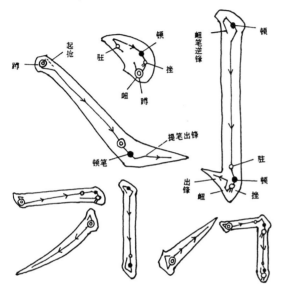

→ indicates the direction of the brush

◎ indicates the stage at the beginning of the stroke, when for a brief, concentrated moment, one presses the brush fairly far down toward the paper and lets the ink slowly well out of the interior of the brush, before again lessening the pressure and taking the ink across the paper to form the rest of the stroke.

● indicates the pause and the strong pressure down used when one wishes to reinforce a part of the stroke—give it 'more bone,' as the term goes—at the beginning or the end of a stroke or at the 'joint' where two merging strokes meet.

o indicates a brief pause.

ρ indicates the completion of a stroke, in which the brush at last returns back into the stroke or is lifted

slanting upward–backward to the left and there forms a point before finally leaving the paper.

It is hard enough to write the eight basic strokes, but the real difficulty is yet to come—putting together the various strokes included in a character and making them form a well-balanced unit in which every part is given as much space as it deserves.

Every character is to be written as if it were standing calmly and harmoniously within a square. This is a convention that began in the Han dynasty or earlier, then became the general norm over the following centuries. To make the characters of equal size, they used to fold the paper first, into squares of appropriate size. That method is still common, but nowadays there is printed exercise paper on which squares are divided into smaller units—often four or nine—an even greater help in placing the character correctly. In many cases, the diagonals are also indicated.

Writing the character for *one* into a prepared square of this kind does not cause much trouble. The only thing to look out for—apart from the stroke being in the form prescribed by the rules of the art—is that it lands in the middle of the square, inclining to the right. The ideal is that the upper left and lower right corner of the stroke should touch on the horizontal middle line and that equal parts of the stroke are on each side of the vertical line. This gives the stroke the free rhythm it should have.

When a character consists of several strokes, new difficulties arise. Before one can even begin to think about where they are to be placed in their square, one has to be quite sure in which order the different strokes are to be written. There are basic rules for this, too.

一 十

First horizontal, then vertical—as in the character for *ten*.

一 二 三

First above, then below—as in the character for *three*.

丿 人

First to the left, then to the right—as in the character for *man*, *person*.

亅 小 小

First in the middle, then on the sides—as in the character for *small*.

丿 几 月

First outer, then inner—as in the character for *moon*.

丨 冂 日 日

But if the outer stroke, as in the character for *sun*, forms a closed square, the lower stroke is written last. 'First go in, then shut the door,' as the saying goes for this type of character.

Neither *sun* nor *moon* is particularly hard to write. The strokes are clear and well demarcated from each other. But if one is to achieve balance in the character for *clear, brilliant*, which consists of *sun* and *moon* together, both must renounce their original form. In principle, the different strokes are carried out in the same way as when the characters stand independently, but in the compound character they have to be modified in length and width for the new unit to have the right proportions.

The more strokes in a character, the more necessary it is that the calligrapher has a clear mental picture of the character in all its detail before lowering the brush onto the paper to make the first stroke. He must feel the tension and interplay between the various parts, know where to hold back and where to extend the gesture. This is a matter of millimeters, and most of all of rhythm. All strokes are dependent on one another. They must be adjusted to each other, accommodate each other, and give way to each other. The harmony of the whole is the first principle, and everything is subordinate to that.

One is reminded of the tens of thousands of ingeniously constructed pieces of wood that bear and support a Chinese temple building and allow the high roof to soar without a single nail holding the parts together. In Chinese society, as well, since the dawn of time, individuals have subordinated themselves to the demands of the larger whole—the family and the state—a loyalty that goes so far beyond the boundaries with which we are familiar that we find it difficult to see the security that may lie in this interdependence.

Handwriting exercises in Chinese schools are thorough and time-consuming, but through them the children learn not only how to write correctly and beautifully but also how to practice patience and endurance. Indirectly, they probably also learn a good deal about the realities of life when it comes to interdependence, adaptation, relations between part and whole, and the values prevailing in society.

The texts of the exercises themselves are an important part of this schooling. For all junior schoolchildren, they often contain practical or moralistic exhortations. Through them, the children become aware of what is regarded as right and wrong, and what adults and society expect of them: 'Study hard and make progress every day.' 'Don't drink unboiled water.' 'Think about your eyes: Don't read in bad light or on a shaking bus.'

Older children practice their writing on texts from well-known, often moral tales, on the beloved poems of the past, and on philosophical aphorisms. In the middle of the Cultural Revolution, the children filled their exercise books with forceful slogans such as 'Serve the people,' 'Trust your own strength,' and 'Long live unity between the peoples of the world.' The content was political, but the handwriting was based on the very best classical models such as Wang Xizhi (307–365), Ouyang Xun (557–641), and Yan Zhenqing (709–785), which have functioned for over a thousand years as guidelines and inspiration for everyone concerned with calligraphy. The care taken with the formation of the characters even during that stormy period was just as minute as during times with quite different political intentions.

Writing training continues all through school; regular lessons are still given in the most senior classes, with the teacher still correcting characters in exercise books. Really well-written characters are rewarded with a red circle, the color of joy, and every year the schools compete in calligraphy, exhibiting the best work for general discussion and meditation.

What I have described so far are the first introductory stages when one learns to master *kaishu*, the regular script, up to a reasonable level. For the more expressive forms *xingshu* and *caoshu*, there are other rules; but without being first fully familiar with the regular script, it is meaningless to try them. The result simply becomes painful.

Anyone wishing to go further into calligraphy will in time be faced with a difficult decision: Shall I choose Wang's free, quite elegant style as my model, or Ouyang's taut, manly style, or Yang's rich, mature, but somewhat humorless style? Or are my hand and feelings more suited to Su Dongpo's or Zhao Mengfu's ways of writing? The choice is not easy, for the differences are great. But anyone who wishes to develop has to decide.

As aids to further study, there are the works of famous calligraphers, which are constantly republished in new editions and are available in any bookstore for a sum corresponding to the price of a pack of cigarettes. A solemn moment in life is when one comes across a work in that calligrapher's own hand—an inscription on a stone in Beilin in Xi'an, a painting in a museum—and with one's own eyes can follow the bold interplay and vital rhythm of the lines.

The freedom an experienced calligrapher can in time allow himself has its roots in many years of training, in which each element is practiced until the hand moves as freely as a skilled pianist's, without having to reflect on individual strokes or the composition of the characters. When everything one has learned at school has merged with experiences of following in detail in the tracks of the great master and the student has become one with the tradition—then and then only is the way open for anyone wishing to try something new and of his or her own. The way to that point is long, and there are no shortcuts.

For anyone wishing to start writing some of the fundamental characters, here is a chart showing how and in which order the strokes are to be made. Don't be frightened by the difficulty—it is great. A day may come when, with profound and unconditional concentration, as in nighttime conversation with a confidant when neither is watching his or her words, you can let the brush dance over the paper and see the characters growing out like parts of your own thoughts and feelings, see the pictures of people's lives and labors, the mountains and fields, the rivers and boats with their straight prows and sterns, and the deer with their tall antlers. One never comes closer to China, the empire of symbols, than one does in her characters.

sun	日	丨	冂	日	日				
moon	月	丿	刀	月	月				
divine	卜	丨	卜						

man, person	人	丿	人						
big, great, large	大	一	ナ	大					
eye	目	丨	冂	目	月	目			
face, surface	面	一	一	厂	丆	而	而	而	面
ear	耳	一	丆	丌	耵	月	耳		
nose, self	自	丿	亻	自	自	自	自		
mouth	口	丨	口	口					
tooth, teeth	齒	丨	丨	止	止	歨	歨	歨	齿 歨 歨
		歨	歨	齒	齒				
heart	心	丶	心	心	心				
hand	手	丿	二	三	手				

to fight, to contest	鬥	l	丨	ﻟ	丨	丨	丨	丨	丨	丨	鬥
foot, stop	止	l	卜	止	止						
body	身	╯	╱	向	自	自	身	身			
woman	女	く	女	女							
mother	母	ㄥ	�	母	母	母					
son, child	子	╯	了	子							

water	水	」	기	水	水				
river	川	)	川	川					
mountain	山	l	止	山					
valley, ravine	谷	╯	八	夕	父	父	谷	谷	
cliff	厂	一	厂						
stone, rock	石	一	厂	不	石	石			
spring, origin	原	一	厂	厂	厂	所	盾	盾	原	原
fire	火	丶	丷	少	火				

fish	魚	ノ	⺈	⺈	召	台	角	鱼	鱼	魚	魚	魚
net	网	l	冂	冈	冈	网	网					
arrowhead	矢	ノ	レ	二	夨	矢						
bow	弓	⼸	⼸	弓								
deer	鹿	丶	一	广	广	庐	庐	庐	鹿	鹿	鹿	鹿
head	首	丶	丷	丷	丷	产	首	首	首			
tortoise, turtle	龜	ノ	⺈	⺈	𠂤	𠂤	龟	龟	龟	龜	龜	
	龜	龜	龜	龜	龜	龜						
elephant	象	ノ	⺈	⺈	凸	凸	甶	免	免	多	象	
	象											
long-tailed bird	鳥	ノ	⺈	勾	鸟	鸟	鳥	鳥	鳥	鳥	鳥	
short-tailed bird	隹	ノ	イ	亻	仁	作	佯	隹	隹			
feathers	羽	フ	㇇	习	羽	羽	羽					
tiger	虎	丶	⼘	上	广	卢	虎	虎	虎			

dragon	龍	丶	二	亠	立	产	斉	斉	斉	斉	斉
		斉	龍	龍	龍	龍					

dog	犬	一	ナ	大	犬				
pig	豕	一	丆	丂	豸	豸	豸	豕	
sheep	羊	丶	ソ	ⅴ	芉	兰	羊		
ox	牛	丿	𠂉	二	牛				
horse	馬	一	二	三	丰	馬	馬	馬	馬	馬
horn	角	丿	ク	严	角	角	角	角	
hide, skin	革	一	十	廿	廿	革	苦	莒	莒	革

chariot, cart	車	一	厂	币	両	百	亘	車
road	行	丿	彳	彳	彳	行	行	
boat	舟	丶	丆	刀	舟	舟	舟	
cowrie shell, valuable	貝	丨	冂	冂	肙	目	貝	貝

field	田	丨	冂	冋	田	田					
strength	力	ノ	力								
plow, digging stick	耒	´	ㆍ二	三	丰	㞢	耒				
earth	土	一	十	土							
rain	雨	一	厂	冂	帀	兩	雨	雨			
air, vapor, regulating principle	气	ノ	㇈	乍	气						
grass	艸	乚	屮	屮	艸	艸	艸				
well	井	一	二	丯	井						
official, minister	臣	一	丆	玍	丐	予	臣				
fresh, raw	生	ノ	𠂉	仁	牛	生					
onion	韭	丨	丨	㸒	刲	刲	非	非	韭		
grain, millet	禾	´	二	千	禾	禾					
millet (panicum)	黍	´	二	千	禾	禾	乑	秂	秂	秂	黍
		黍									
wheat	麥	一	十	圥	朿	帀	夾	夾	夾	麥	麥

rice	米	丶	丷	丷	半	米	米			
melon, pumpkin, gourd	瓜	丿	厂	爪	瓜	瓜				

wine	酉	一	丆	丙	西	酉	酉			
(pot, jug), jar	壺	一	十	士	吂	吉	壴	壴	壴	壷	壷
		壽	壺							
wine vessel	卣	丶	卜	广	卢	卣	卣	卣		
food, eat	食	丿	人	仝	今	今	食	食	食	
shut, close, fit together	合	丿	人	仝	仐	合	合			
together, alike, same	同	丨	冂	冂	同	同	同			
the vessel li	鬲	一	厂	厅	百	戸	鬲	鬲	鬲	鬲
the vessel ding	鼎	丨	冂	冂	目	目	目	目	鼎	鼎	鼎
		鼎	鼎	鼎						
pottery, earthenware	缶	丿	𠂉	二	午	缶	缶			

hemp	麻	丶	宀	广	广	疒	床	床	庥	麻	麻
silk	絲	乚	乡	纟	幺	幺	糸	糹	絲	絲	絲
		絲									
clothing, costume	衣	丶	宀	宀	衣	衣	衣				

bamboo	竹	丿	𠂉	午	竹	竹	竹	
tree	木	一	十	才	木			
basket	其	一	十	卄	卅	甘	其	其
stool	几	丿	几					

knife	刀	刁	刀		
axe	斤	丿	厂	斤	斤
dagger-axe	戈	一	七	戈	戈
ruler, king	王	一	二	干	王
work	工	一	丁	工	

roof	宀	丶	亠	宀							
high	高	丶	亠	亠	亩	古	卢	高	高	高	高
capital	京	丶	亠	亠	亩	古	亨	亨	京		
door	門	丨	𠃌	𠃌	𠃌	𠃌	門	門	門		
household, family	戶	丶	㇌	㇌	戶						
cave	穴	丶	八	宀	宀	穴					
roof tiles	瓦	一	𠃌	瓦	瓦						
enclosure	口	丨	冂	口							

brush	聿	𠃌	肀	肀	彐	彐	聿				
black	黑	丨	冂	冈	四	四	罒	里	里	黑	黑	黑
writing, script, literature	文	丶	亠	宁	文						
speech, word	言	丶	亠	亠	言	言	言	言			
note, sound, tone	音	丶	亠	亠	立	立	产	音	音	音	

flute	龠	ノ	人	入	个	合	合	侖	侖	侖	侖
		龠	龠	龠	龠	龠	龠				
sonorous stone, stone chime	磬	一	十	士	耂	声	吉	声	殸	殸	磬
drum	鼓	一	十	土	吉	吉	吉	吉	壴	壴	鼓
		鼓	鼓								
middle	中	丨	口	口	中						
joy, music	樂	㇑	幺	幺	幻	幻	幼	纠	維	維	樂
		樂	樂	樂	樂						

over	上	丨	卜	上
under	下	一	丁	下
small	小	丿	小	小
one	一	一		
two	二	㇐	二	
three	三	一	二	三

four	四	丶	冂	冈	四	四
five	五	一	丆	歹	五	
six	六	丶	亠	广	六	
seven	七	一	七			
eight	八	丿	八			
nine	九	丿	九			
ten	十	一	十			

Bibliography

Some of the books I have kept constantly on my desk in front of me and consulted when it came to the form, development, and importance of the characters are as follows:

Karlgren, Bernhard. *Grammata Serica Recensa*. Stockholm, 1957.
Sun Haibo. *Jiaguwenbian*. Beijing, (1934), 1965.
Li Xiaoding. *Jiagu wenzi jishi*. Taipei, 1965. (16 vol.)
Shima Kunio. *Inkyo bokuji sōrui*. 2nd revised edition, Tokyo, 1971
Rong Geng. *Jinwenbian*. Beijing, 1959.
Rong Xibai (ed.) *Jinwenbian zheng xübian*. Taipei, 1971.
Zhou Fagao et al., eds. *Jinwen gulin*. Hong Kong, 1974–77. (19 vol.)
Wang Renshou. *Jin shi da zidian*. Hong Kong, 1975. (2 vol.)
Xu Shen. *Shuowen jiezi zhu*. (Annotated edition) Shanghai, 1981.

The book that led me into studies of the origins and development of the Chinese characters was Bernhard Karlgren's dictionary, *Grammata Serica Recensa*, which is an attempt to reconstruct the Chinese language as spoken during the Zhou dynasty in the Wei Valley around the old city of Chang'an, now renamed Xi'an. The book is primarily concerned with the development of sounds, but it also provides characters for the various words involved.

One summer when my daughter, Clara, was still at the sandbox age and always had to have an adult nearby, I was with her in the garden, going through Karlgren's book from various directions. I made a list of all the simple and compound pictographs in it, then went right through the different phonetic series into which Karlgren divides his characters, in order to acquire an overview of the way in which the different phonetic radicals were used as semantic elements. This took up a large part of the summer and is one of the most exciting intellectual experiences I have ever had.

Having come that far, I became more and more interested in the oldest forms of the characters, of which Karlgren gives only a small fraction, and I eventually found the dictionary known as *Jiaguwenbian* (The Composition of the Oracle Bone Characters), which contains 4,672 different characters, of which 1,723 have with more or less certainty had their meanings confirmed. It is a useful and entertaining book, especially because of the many different variants of characters it repro-

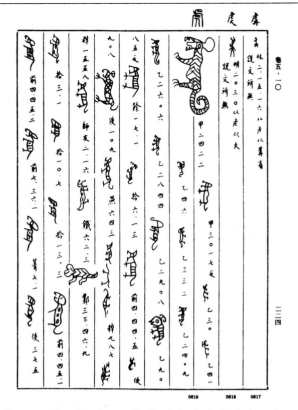

Jiaguwenbian. The character for tiger begins in the third column from the right. Turn the page a quarter way around to see all the beasts with their powerful tails and claws extended.

duces, but unfortunately it rarely includes explanations of the meaning of the characters.

To find out something about the meaning of the characters, I had to go further, primarily to Li Xiaoding's *Jiagu wenzi jishi*. Li starts out from the characters published in *Jiaguwenbian*, deals briefly, but with thorough literary references, with the suggestions for interpretation produced by various scholars, and toward the end of each section, gives his own view. The book is indispensable for anyone requiring a survey of the oldest characters but is sometimes hard to read, as it reproduces Li's handwritten manuscript with its alterations and erasures.

In *Inkyo bokuji sōrui (Concordance of Oracle Records)*, Shima Kunio publishes inscriptions in which over three thousand different oracle bone characters are included. There one finds a survey of the various contexts in which the characters are used, as well as how common they are. In the second edition of the book, there is not only an index—which starts from the modern form of the characters, and from which one can find one's way straight to the corresponding oracle bone character—but also references to the sections in which Li Xiaoding deals with the character in question.

Jiaguwen heji (Complete Collection of Oracle Bone Inscriptions), Beijing, 1978–1982, reproduces in thirteen volumes all the known oracle bone inscriptions. Guo Moruo is given as the editor, but the real work was carried out by the research institute of the Chinese Academy of Science, led by Hu Houxuan. A complementary work with translations and explanations is in preparation. Both works will be invaluable aids to the study of the oracle bone inscriptions.

There is a corresponding dictionary for the bronze inscriptions called *Jinwenbian (Compilation of Bronze Characters)*, which includes the different variants of 1,894 different characters occurring on bronzes from the Shang and Zhou dynasties, as well as the name of the bronze object on which the character is written, making it possible to continue to other publications if a closer study of the character or object is required.

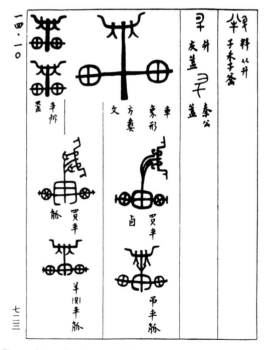

Jinwenbian. First page with the character for chariot, cart.

Explanations of the meaning of the characters are rare in the book. For these it is necessary to go to *Jinwen gulin (Explanations of the Jinwenbian)* which includes long quotes of what various scholars have to say about the characters in *Jinwenbian.*

Wang Renshou, *Jin shi da zidian (Dictionary of Inscriptions on Bronze and Stone)*, apart from many bronze characters, also includes inscriptions—many of them very impressive—on other material such as stone.

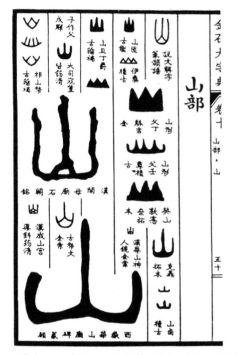

First page with character for mountain in Jin shi da zidian. *The large character at the bottom of the page comes from a stone on Huashan Mountain.*

China's first analytical character dictionary, Xu Shen's *Shuowen jiezi (Explanations of Simple Characters and Analysis of Compound Characters)* was published in the year 121. It includes 9,353 different characters, classified under 540 radicals. This organization became the norm for dictionaries published since then, but over the years the number of radicals has been limited. The interpretations given in the book are naturally often out-of-date, particularly in light of the comprehensive archaeological finds made during the 1900s.

Xu Shen knew that oracle bones were once used to predict the future, but he could hardly have known much about what the inscriptions on the bones looked like. The practice of divining with oracle bones largely ceased with the fall of the Shang dynasty in 1028 B.C., and the thousand years that passed until the time Xu Shen compiled his dictionary contained huge changes in culture and society. The oracle bones in existence were still covered with mud and earth in Anyang.

Xu Shen started out from the form the character had been given in the first standardization during the time of the first emperor, which meant that in many cases the original form of the character was distorted. Interpretations in his dictionary are therefore often misleading. But over the nearly two thousand years since the book was published, it has been regarded as an almost sacred script, and today many older scholars still always refer to *Shuowen* first when it comes to interpretation of different characters, and the book is still widely quoted.

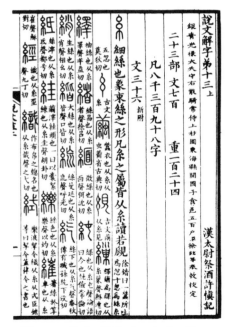

First page of Shuowen jiezi *with the character for silk.*

Some of the outline works in archaeology and science that I have consulted constantly are as follows:

Chang Kwang-chih. *The Archaeology of Ancient China.* Third edition. Revised and enlarged. New Haven and London, 1977.

Shang Civilization. New Haven and London, 1980.

Chêng Tê-k'un. *Archaeology in China.* Cambridge: University of Toronto Press, 1959–66. I. Prehistoric China. II. Shang China. III. Chou China. Suppl. to Vol. I. New Light on Prehistoric China.

Needham, Joseph. *Science and Civilisation in China.* Cambridge: Cambridge University Press, 1954–. One of the most remarkable works of our time, indispensable for everybody who wants to understand the Chinese civilization.

Vol. 1 Introductory Orientations.

Vol. 2 History of Scientific Thought.

Vol. 3 Mathematics and the Sciences of the Heavens and the Earth.

Vol. 4 Physics and Physical Technology. Part I: Physics Part II: Mechanical Engineering. Part III: Civil Engineering and Nautics.

Vol. 5 Chemistry and Chemical Technology. Part I: Paper and Printing (Tsien Tsuen-Hsuin). Part II: Spagyrical Discovery and Invention: Magisteries of Gold and Immortality. Part III: Spagyrical Discovery and Invention: Historical Survey, From Cinnabar Elixirs to Synthetic Insulin. Part IV: Spagyrical Discovery and Invention: Apparatus, Theories and Gifts. Part V: Spagyrical Discovery and Invention: Physiological Alchemy. Part IX: Textile Technology: Spinning and Reeling (Dieter Kuhn).

Vol. 6 Biology and Biological Technology, Part I: Botany. Part II: Agriculture (Francesca Bray).

Next come two books that are very dear to my heart:

Keightley, D. N. *Sources of Shang History, The Oracle-Bone Inscription of Bronze Age China.* University of California Press, Berkeley and Los Angeles, 1978.

This is the standard work for everything having to do with oracle bones. The book is technical but written with affection and goodwill, to help the reader find what is essential. The main text sometimes takes up only half the page and provides a summary of everything known—and not known—about which bones were used, how the holes were made, where the inscriptions were placed, how they were deciphered, and so on. The rest of the page is taken up with very readable notes in which various opinions and facts are compared and discussed.

Hommel, R. P. *China at Work. An illustrated Record of the primitive Industries of China's Masses, whose Life is Toil, and thus an Account of Chinese Civilization.* New York: John Day, 1937. New edition M.I.T. Press, 1969.

This book is a goldmine for anyone wishing to see and read with his or her own eyes about the tools, implements, means, and methods used by the Chinese—which to a great extent still are used—when they build houses, cook food, draw up water, pound clay into pots, spin silk, and make furniture, brushes, candles, rope, and bricks. Everything is there, reproduced in clear photographs and with good descriptions, the whole of daily life described with affection and respect.

Some interesting works for further reading.

Ancient China's Technology and Science. Beijing: Foreign Languages Press, 1983.

Andersson, J. G. *Den gula jordens barn.* Stockholm, 1932. (English translation. *Children of the Yellow Earth. Studies in Prehistoric China.* London, 1934.)

– *Researches into the Prehistory of the Chinese*, BMFEA, no. 15, Stockholm, 1943.

Atlas of Primitive Man in China. Beijing: Science Press, 1980.

Bagley, R. W. *Pan-lung-ch'eng: A Shang City in Hubei*, Artibus Asiae, 39:3/4, 1977.

Ball, J. Dyer. *Things Chinese* (1900). Reprint Hong Kong: Oxford University Press, 1982 (Amusing reference book full of useful and/or exotic facts about ancient Chinese culture and social life.)

Barnard, Noel. The nature of the Ch'in 'Reform of the Script' as reflected in archaeological documents excavated under conditions of control. In David T. Roy and Tsuen-hsuin Tsien (eds.), *Ancient China: Studies in Early Civilization.* Hong Kong: The Chinese University Press, 1978.

Bauernmalerei aus Huxian. Aschaffenburg, 1979. (Exhibition catalogue with thirty essays illuminating the growth, themes, and types of style in peasant paintings.)

Beifang chang yong zhongcaoyao shouce (Manual of often used medicinal plants in northern China). (Anon.) Beijing, 1971.

Blakney, R. B *A Course in the Analysis of the Chinese Characters.* Shanghai, 1926.

Blaser, W. *Chinesische Pavillon Architektur/Chinese Pavilion Architecture.* Niederteufen, 1974.

– *Courtyard House in China/Hofhaus in China.* Basel, Boston, Stuttgart, 1979.

Boyd, A. *Chinese Architecture and Town Planning; 1500 B.C.–A.D. 1911.* University of Chicago Press, 1962.

van Briessen, F. *The Way of the Brush. Painting Techniques of China and Japan.* Rutland, Vt: Tuttle, 1962.

Bunker, Emma C. et al. *Animal Style. Art from East to West.* New York: The Asia Society, 1970.

Burkhardt, V. R. *Chinese Creeds and Customs.* (Hong Kong 1953–1958) Hong Kong, 1982.

Böttiger, W. *Die Ursprünglichen Jagdmethoden der Chinesen nach der alten chinesischen Literatur und einigen paläographischen Schriftzeichen.* Veröffentlichungen des Museums für Völkerkunde zu Leipzig. Vol. 10. Berlin, 1960.

Carter, T. F. *The Invention of Printing and Its Spread Westward.* Second edition, revised by L. Carrington Goodrich. New York, 1955.

Chang Kwang-chih. *Early Chinese Civilization, Anthropological Perspectives*, Harvard-Yenching Institute Monograph Series, Vol. XXIII, 1976.

– *Art, Myth and Ritual. The Path to Political Authority in Ancient China.* Cambridge, Mass.: Harvard University Press, 1983.

– (ed.) *Food in Chinese Culture. Anthropological and Historical Perspectives.* New Haven and London: Yale University Press, 1977.

Changsha Mawangdui yi hao Han mu (Han grave no.1 in Mawangdui, Changsha). (2 vol.) Beijing: Wenwu chubanshe, 1973.

Chang Te-Tzu. The Origins and Early Cultures of the Cereal Grains and Food Legumes. In Keightley, D. N. *The Origins of Chinese Civilization.* London, 1983.

Chang Tsung-tung. *Der Kult der Shang-Dynastie im Spiegel der Orakelinschriften. Eine paläographische Studie zur Religion im archaischen China.* Wiesbaden, 1970.

Chen Mengjia. *Yinxu buci zongshu* (Oracle bone inscriptions from Yin). Beijing: Kexue chubanshe, 1956.

Chatley, H. *The Yellow River as a factor in the development of China.* Asiatic Review, 1939, I.

Chavannes, E. *Mission Archéologique dans la Chine Septentrionale.* Paris, 1909–15.

– *Le T'ai chan. Essai de Monographie d'un Culte Chinois.* Paris, 1910.

Chêng Tê-k'un. *Animal Styles in Prehistoric and Shang China.* BMFEA 35, Stockholm, 1963.

Cheung Kwong-Yue. Recent Archaeological Evidence Relating to the Origin of Chinese Characters. In D. N. Keightley, *The Origins of Chinese Civilization.* University of California Press, London 1983. (The essay provides a survey of all the finds of inscriptions on pottery vessels published up to 1979 and discusses the various suggestions for dating and interpretation.)

Chiang Yee. *Chinese Calligraphy. An Introduction to Its Aesthetic and Technique.* London 1938. Third revised and enlarged edition. Cambridge, Mass., 1973.

Chinese Rubbings. China Publication Centre. (Anon.) Beijing, (s.a.).

Chongqing shi bowuguan. *Sichuan Han huaxiang zhuan xuanji* (Tile reliefs from the Han dynasty in Sichuan province). Beijing, 1957.

Cihai (Sea of words). (Anon.) Shanghai: Shanghai cishu chubanshe, 1979. (3 vol.)

Creel, H. G. *The Birth of China: a survey of the formative period of Chinese Civilization.* London: Jonathan Cape, 1936.

Dawenkou. Xinshiqi shidai muzang fajue baogao (Excavation report regarding Neolithic grave finds in Dawenkou). Beijing: Wenwu chubanshe, 1974.

DeFrancis, J. *The Chinese Language. Fact and Fantasy.* Honolulu: University of Hawaii Press, 1984.

von Dewall, Magdalene. Pferd und Wagen im Frühen China. In *Saarbrücker Beiträge zur Altertumskunde*, Vol. I. Bonn, 1964.

Devloo, E. *An etymological Chinese-English dictionary: a handbook for the systematical study of the most useful 8,000 Chinese Characters with the etymological explanation of the 200 primitives.* Taipei, Hua Ming Press, 1969.

Dong Zuobin, *see* Tung Tso-pin.

Dye, D. S. *Chinese Lattice Designs.* (1937) Reprint New York: Dover, 1974.

Elisseeff, Danielle – V. *New Discoveries in China. Encountering History Through Archaeology.* Shen Zhen, 1983.

Elisseeff, V. *Bronzes Archaïques chinois au Musée Cernuschi.* Paris: L'Asiathèque, 1977.

Farrelly, D. *The Book of Bamboo.* San Francisco, 1984. (Contains all the necessary information required on bamboo and its uses.)

Fazzioli, E. *Caractères Chinois du dessin à l'idée. 214 clés pour comprendre la Chine.* Paris, 1987.

Fenollosa, E. *The Chinese Written Character as a Medium for Poetry.* With a Foreword and Notes by Ezra Pound. London, 1936.

Gaocheng Taixi Shangdai yizhi (Shang dwelling place in Taixi, Gaocheng). Beijing: Wenwu chubanshe, 1985.

Gao Ming. *Guwenzi lei bian* (Various types of ancient characters). Beijing: Zhonghua, 1980. (Dictionary of characters on bone, bronze, and pottery, mostly reduced in size.)

Gao Wen. *Sichuan handai huaxiang zhuan* (Han period sculptured tiles in Sichuan). Shanghai: Shanghai renmin meishu chubanshe, 1987.

Granet, M. *Danses et légendes de la Chine ancienne.* Paris, 1926.

– *The Religion of the Chinese People.* New York, 1977.

Gray, J. H. *China. A History of the Laws, Manners and Customs of the People.* London, 1878. Shannon, 1972.

van Gulik, R. H. *The lore of the Chinese Lute. An essay in Ch'in Ideology.* Tokyo, 1940.

Hager, J. *An explanation of the elementary Characters of the Chinese.* London, 1801.

Hawkes, D. *Ch'u Ts'u. The Songs of the South.* Oxford, 1959.

Hentze, C. *Die Sakralbronzen und ihre Bedeutung in den Frühchinesischen Kulturen.* Antwerpen, 1941.

– Zur ursprünglichen Bedeutung des Chinesischen Zeichens t'ou (= Kopf). *Anthropos.* Vol. XLV, 1950.

– *Bronzegerät, Kultbauten, Religion im ältesten China der Shang-Zeit.* Antwerpen, 1951.

– *Tod, Auferstehung, Weltordnung.* Zürich, 1955.

A History of Chinese Currency (16th Century BC–20th Century AD). (Anon.) Hong Kong: Xinhua Publishing House et al., 1983.

Hoa, L. *Reconstruire la Chine; trente ans d'urbanism, 1949–1979.* Paris, 1981.

Ho Ping-ti. *The Cradle of the East. An Inquiry into the Indigenous Origins of Techniques and Ideas of Neolithic and Early Historic China, 5000–1000 B.C.* Hong Kong: Chinese University of Hong Kong and University of Chicago Press, 1975.

Hsü Chin-hsiung. *The Menzies Collection of Shang Dynasty Oracle Bones.* (2 vol.) Toronto: Royal Ontario Museum, 1971, 1977.

Hubei sheng bowuguan. *Suixian Zeng hou zhi mu* (Grave of Marquis Yi of Zeng in Suixian). (Anon.) Wenwu chubanshe, 1980.

– *Zhanguo Zeng hou zhi mu* (Grave of Marquis Yi of Zeng from the Warring States). (Anon.) Xianning: Changsha wenyi chubanshe, 1984.

Jia Lanpo. *Early Man in China.* Beijing: Foreign Languages Press, 1980.

Jiang Liangfu. *Guwenzixue* (Study of the ancient script). Zhejiang renmin chubanshe, 1984.

Jieziyuan huazhuan (Mustard Seed Garden Manual of Painting). Beijing: Renmin chubanshe, 1960. English translation by Mai-mai Sze. Princeton, New Jersey: Princeton University Press, 1977.

Karlgren, B. *Folk Tales from the Tveta and Mo parishes Written in the Vernacular.* Swedish Dialects, Vol. 2. (in Swedish), 1908.
– *Analytic Dictionary of Chinese and Sino-Japanese,* Paris, 1923.
– *Yin and Chou in Chinese Bronzes,* in BMFEA, no. 8, Stockholm, 1936.
– *New Studies on Chinese Bronzes,* in BMFEA, no. 9, Stockholm, 1937.
– *The Book of Odes.* Göteborg, 1950. (Contains the Chinese texts plus transcription and translation of the *Book of Songs,* or as Karlgren prefers to call it, the *Book of Odes.*)
– *Easy Lessons in Chinese Writing.* Stockholm, 1958.
Keightley, D. N. (ed.) *The Origins of Chinese Civilization.* London: University of California Press, 1983. (Seventeen well-documented, well-written studies of natural circumstances, agriculture, culture, peoples, language and writing, and growth of the first states in civilization.)
Keswich, Maggie. *The Chinese Garden. History, Art & Architecture.* London: Academy Editions, 1978.
Keys, J. D. *Chinese Herbs; Their Botany, Chemistry, and Pharmacodynamics.* Rutland and Tokyo: Tuttle, 1976.
Knapp, R. G. *China's Traditional Rural Architecture, A Cultural Geography of the Common House.* Honolulu: University of Hawaii Press, 1986.
Kunze, R. *Bau und Anordning der chinesischen Zeichen.* Tokyo and Leipzig: Tokyo Deutsche Gesellschaft, 1937.

Leeming, F. Official Landscapes in traditional China. In *Journal of the Economic and Social History of the Orient,* 1980:23.
Liang Donghan. *Hanzide jiegou nai qi liu bian* (Form and development of the Chinese character). Shanghai, 1959.
Li Chi. *The Beginnings of Chinese Civilization.* Seattle: University of Washington Press, 1957.
– *Anyang.* Seattle: University of Washington Press, 1977.
Li Hui-Lin. The Domestication of Plants in China: Ecogeographical Considerations. In Keightley, D. N. *The Origins of Chinese Civilization.* London: University of California Press, 1983.
Li Jie (Li Mingzhong). *Yingzao fashi* (Treatise on Architectual Methods). Printed first in 1103. Reprint: Wujin: Zhuanjing shushe, Minguo 14 (1925).
Li Shizhen. *Bencao gangmu.* Beijing: Renmin weisheng chubanshe, 1981. (Reprint of 'The Great Pharmacopoeia' first published in 1596.)
Li Xueqin. *The Wonder of Chinese Bronzes.* Beijing: Foreign Languages Press, 1980.
– *Eastern Zhou and Qin Civilizations.* Translation: K. C. Chang. New Haven and London: Yale University Press, 1985.

Liu Dunzhen. *La Maison Chinoise.* Paris, 1980.
– et al. *Zhongguo gudai jianzhu shi.* Beijing: Jianzhu kexue yanjiu shi, 1980.
Liu E (Liu Ngo/Liu T'ieh-yün). *T'ieh-yün ts'ang kuei* (Collected finds of turtle shells). 1903. Lithographed edition, 1931.
Liu Guojun-Zheng Rusi. *The story of Chinese Books.* Beijing: Foreign Languages Press, 1985.
Li Yuzheng et al. *Xi'an Beilin Shufa Yishu* (Calligraphic works in Beilin in Xi'an). Xi'an: Shaanxi renmin meishu chubanshe, 1983.
Loehr, M. *Chinese Bronze Age Weapons.* The Werner Jannings collection in the Chinese National Palace Museum, Peking. Ann Arbor, 1956.
– *Ritual Vessels of Bronze Age China.* New York: The Asia Society, 1968.
Loewe, M. Man and Beast, The Hybrid in Early Chinese Art and Literature. In *Numen,* Vol. XXV, Fasc. 2, 1978.
Lowe, H. Y. *The Adventures of Wu. The Life Cycle of a Peking Man.* The Peking Chronicle Press, 1940–41. New edition. Princeton, New Jersey: Princeton University Press, 1983.

Ma Chengyuan. *Zhongguo gudai qing tongqi* (Ancient Chinese bronzes). Shanghai: Shanghai renmin chubanshe, 1982.
Mathews' Chinese-English Dictionary. Cambridge, Mass.: Harvard University Press, 1975.
Mayers, W. F. *The Chinese Reader's Manual. A Handbook of Biographical, Historical, Mythological, and General Literary Reference.* Shanghai, 1924.
Medley, Margaret. *The Chinese Potter, A Practical History of Chinese Ceramics.* Oxford: Phaidon, 1976.
Morrison, Hedda and Eberhard, W. *Hua Shan. The Taoist Sacred Mountain in West China, Its Scenery, Monasteries and Monks.* Hong Kong, 1974.
Mulliken, Mary Augusta and Hotchkis, Anna M. *The Nine Sacred Mountains of China. An illustrated Record of Pilgrimages made in the Years 1935–36.* Hong Kong, 1973.
Museum of Far Eastern Antiquities (ed.) *Archaeological Finds from the People's Republic of China.*
Mustard Seed Garden Manual of Painting. See *Jieziyuan huazhuan.*

Pan Jixing, *Zhongguo zao zhi jishu shigao* (History of Chinese paper production; an outline). Beijing: Wenwu chubanshe, 1979.
Peasant Paintings from Huhsien County. (Anon.) Beijing: Foreign Languages Press, 1974.
Picken, L. E. R. The Music of Far Eastern Asia. Included in *New Oxford History of Music,* Vol. 1. Oxford, 1957.

Qiu Feng. Zhongguo danshui yuye shi hua (History of Chinese cultivation of freshwater fish). In *Nongye kaogu* (Agricultural archaeology), 1982/1.

Qiu Xigui. Hanzi xingcheng wentide chubu tansuo. *Kaogu* 1978:3. (Outline of development of written language in ancient times).

Rawson, Jessica. *Ancient China, Art and Archaeology.* London: British Museum, 1980.

von Richthofen, F. *Tagebücher aus China.* Berlin, 1907.

Ryjik, K. *L'idiot chinois. Initiation élémentaire à la lecture intelligible des caractères chinois.* Paris: Payot, 1980.

– *L'idiot chinois. La promotion de Yu le Grand.* Paris: Payot, 1984.

Shaanxi sheng kaogu yanjiusuo (Shaanxi Province Archaeological Research Institute) *Shaanxi chutu Shang Zhou qing tongqi* (Bronzes from the Shang and Zhou dynasties excavated in Shaanxi). (4 vol.) Beijing, 1979–84. (The first volumes of a pictorial work, intended to comprise ten volumes in which all of the more important Shang and Zhou bronzes found in the province of Shaanxi—one of the prime bronze-producing areas in the country—are presented in large photographs. Detailed information on dimensions, inscriptions, etc.)

Shandong sheng bowuguan (Shandong Provincial Museum) *Shandong hanhua xiangshi xuanji* (Han period stone reliefs from Shandong). Qi lu shushe chuban, 1982.

Shandong Weifang nianhua (New Year pictures from Weifang). Weifang: Renmin chubanshe, 1978.

Shanghai bowuguan cang qingtongqi (Bronzes in Shanghai Museum collections). (2 vol.) Shanghai: Renmin meishu chubanshe, 1964.

Shapiro, H. L., *Peking Man.* New York, 1974.

Shih Sheng-Han. *On 'Fan Shêng-Chih Shu'. An Agriculturist Book of China Written by Fan Shêng-Chih in the first Century B.C.,* Beijing: Science Press, 1959.

– *A Preliminary Survey of the Book Ch'i Min Yao Shu, An Agricultural Encyclopaedia of the 6th Century.* Beijing: Science Press, 1962.

Sichou zhi lu. Han Tang zhizu. (The Silk Road. Silk from Han and Tang.) Beijing: Wenwu chubanshe, 1972.

Sickman, L. and Soper, A. *The Art and Architecture of China.* Third edition. London, 1968.

Sirén, O. *Gardens of China.* New York, 1949.

Sze Mai-Mai (transl.) *The Mustard Seed Garden Manual of Painting. A Facsimile of the 1887–1888 Shanghai Edition.* New Jersey: Princeton University Press, 1977.

Temple, R. *The Genius of China. 3000 years of Science, Discovery and Invention.* New York: Simon and Schuster, 1987.

Tian Enshan. Wangjude qiyuan yu rengong yujiao xiaokao (Account of fish nets and dams). In *Nongye kaogu* (Agricultural archaeology) 1982/1.

Tiangong kaiwu (The exploitation of the works of nature), (1637). Reprint: Hong Kong: Zhonghua shuju, 1983.

Tong Kin-woon. *Shang Musical Instruments.* Ph. D. dissertation. Middletown, Conn.: Wesleyan University, 1983.

Tsien Tsuen-Hsuin. *Written on Bamboo and Silk. The Beginnings of Chinese Books and Inscriptions.* University of Chicago Press, 1962.

Tung Tso-pin. *Fifty Years of Studies in Oracle Bone Inscriptions.* Tokyo, 1950.

Vaccari, O. and Vaccari, Enko Elisa. *Pictorial Chinese-Japanese Characters. A new and fascinating Method to learn Ideographs.* Tokyo, 1950.

Waldenström, P. P. *To China.* Travel accounts (in Swedish). Stockholm, 1907–08.

Waley, A. *The Book of Songs.* London, 1937.

Wang Shucun. *Ancient Chinese Woodblock New Year Prints.* Beijing: Foreign Languages Press, 1985.

Wang Xuezhong. *Shufa juyao* (Introduction to calligraphy). Tianjin: Renmin meishu chubanshe, 1981.

Wang Yongyan. *Loess in China.* Shaanxi People's Art Publishing House, 1980. (Large pictorial work of various types of loess soil formations).

Watson, W. *China Before the Han Dynasty.* London, 1961.

– *The Genius of China.* An Exhibition of Archaeological Finds of the People's Republic of China. London, 1973.

Weber, C. D. *Chinese Pictorial Bronze Vessels of the Late Chou Period.* Ascona, Switzerland: Artibus Asiae, 1968.

Weber, G. W., Jr. *The Ornaments of Late Chou Bronzes: a method of analysis.* New Brunswick, New Jersey, 1973.

Wen Fong (ed.) *The Great Bronze Age of China.* London, 1980. (Four introductory essays by leading scholars and detailed description of ninety-seven objects from the Shang and Zhou dynasties. Over a hundred color photographs and an equal number of detailed pictures and rubbings of inscriptions. Best introduction to the bronzes at present in any Western language.)

Wenwu da geming qijian chutu wenwu, di yi ji (Archaeological finds made during the Cultural Revolution, vol. 1). Beijing: Wenwu chubanshe, 1973.

Wenwu kaogu gongzuo sanshi nian, 1949–1979 (Thirty years of archaeological work, 1949–1979). Beijing: Foreign Languages Press, 1979.

Wheatley, P. *The pivot of the four Quarters: A Preliminary Enquiry into the Origins and Character of the Ancient Chinese City.* Chicago, 1971.

White, W. C. *Tombs of Old Lo-yang.* Shanghai, 1934.

Wieger, L. *Chinese Characters, their Origin, Etymology, History, Classification and Signification. A thorough Study from Chinese Documents.* (1915) New edition. New York: Dover, 1965.

Wilder, G. D. and Ingram J. H. *Analysis of Chinese Characters.* (1934) New York: Dover, 1974.

Willetts, W. *Foundations of Chinese Art, From Neolithic Pottery to Modern Architecture.* London, 1965.

– *Chinese Calligraphy. Its History and Aesthetic Motivation.* Hong Kong: Oxford University Press, 1981.

Williams, C. A. S. *Encyclopedia of Chinese Symbolism and Art Motives.* New York, 1960. New edition of the classic work originally titled *Outlines of Chinese Symbolism and Art Motives.* Shanghai: Kelly and Walsh, 1931.

Wu Haokun and Pan You. *Zhongguo jiagu xue shi* (History of oracle bone studies in China). Shanghai: Renmin chubanshe, 1985. (Includes a fifty-page bibliography covering all important works and essays.)

Wu Qijun. *Zhiwu ming bao tu kao* (Illustrated flora) (1848). Revised edition: Shanghai: Shangwu yinshuguan, 1957.

Xi'an Banpo (Stone Age village in Banpo, Xi'an). Beijing: Wenwu chubanshe, 1963.

Xin Zhongguo chutu wenwu (*Historical Relics Unearthed in New China*). Beijing: Foreign Languages Press, 1972.

Xin Zhongguo de kaogu shouhuo (Archaeology in new China.) Beijing: Wenwu chubanshe, 1961.

Xinyang Chumu (Two Chu graves at Xinyang). Beijing: Wenwu chubanshe, 1986.

Xu Guangqi. *Nong Sheng Quan Shu jiaozhu* (Complete Treatise on Agriculture) 1639. New edition with commentaries by Shi Shenghan. Shanghai: Guji chubanshe, 1979.

Xu Zhongshu. *Hanyu guwenzi xingbiao* (Compilation of different forms of early Chinese characters). Sichuan renmin chubanshe, 1980. (Dictionary of characters on bone, bronze, bamboo, and pottery; some enlarged, others reduced).

Yan'an Papercuts. (Anon.) People's Fine Arts Publishing House. China. (S.l. et s.a.)

Yinxu fuhao mu (Grave of Fu Hao in Yinxu at Anyang). Beijing: Wenwu chubanshe, 1980.

Yu, Ying-shih. *Trade and expansion in Han China.* Berkeley, 1967.

Zhang Dao. *Zhongguo gudai tu an xuan.* (China's ancient pattern forms). Jiangsu meishu chubanshe, 1980.

Zhang Zhongye. Jinyu shi hua (History of goldfish). In *Nongye kaogu* (Agricultural archaeology), 1982/1.

Zhengzhou Erligang. (Excavation report on Erligang outside Zhengzhou). Beijing: Wenwu chubanshe, 1959.

Zhongguo bowuguan (Museums of China). Beijing: Wenwu chubanshe, 1984–1989. (7 vol.)

Zhonghua renmin gongheguo chutu wenwu xuan (Selection of archaeological finds in the People's Republic of China). Beijing: Wenwu chubanshe, 1976.

Zhou Xibao. *Zhongguo gudai fushi shi* (History of Chinese clothing). Shanghai: Zhongguo xiju chubanshe, 1984.

Zhou Xun, Gao Chunming et al. *Zhongguo lidai fushi* (Chinese Clothing and Adornment in various Dynasties). Shanghai: Xuelin chubanshe, 1984.

Zhong Yuanhao (ed.) *History and Development of Ancient Chinese Architecture.* Chinese Academy of Sciences. Beijing: Science Press, 1986. (Monumental work on development, materials, and methods of Chinese architecture. Technical sections somewhat abbreviated compared with the Chinese edition.)

Journals

Artibus Asiae. Ascona, Switzerland 1925–.

Bulletin of the Museum of Far Eastern Antiquities. Stockholm, 1929–.

Early China. Berkeley, California, 1975–.

Harvard Journal of Asiatic Studies. Cambridge, Mass., 1935–.

Kaogu. Beijing 1959–.

Wenwu. Beijing 1959–.

Guwenzi yanjiu 1979–.

Dynasties and Periods in the History of China

Before the year 221 B.C., when the Qin dynasty was established, all dates are uncertain and are continually adjusted as a result of new research and archaeological finds. Thus, the Old Stone Age was moved back a hundred thousand years in time by the finds in Lantian in the 1960s, and the Xia dynasty, until recently regarded as legendary, particularly by Western scholars, now according to archaeologists seems genuinely to have existed, although no exact date has yet been established.

Uncertainty also reigns over the introduction and end of the two following dynasties. Traditional Chinese history has it that the Shang dynasty was introduced in 1766; according to modern scholars it was in 1523. The Zhou dynasty takeover of power, previously said to be in 1122, is now considered to have occurred in 1027, but that date has also been questioned. Nine other dates have been suggested: 1116, 1111, 1070, 1067, 1066, 1050, 1047, 1030 and 1018. The end of the Zhou dynasty is sometimes put at 256, when King Nan died, sometimes at 221, when the Qin dynasty took over power.

The latter part of the Shang period is also often called Yin, but the term was not verified until sometime during the Zhou period.

The year of transition between the Spring and Autumn period and the period of the Warring States during the Zhou dynasty is variously put at 481, 476, 468, 453, or 403.

Below is the division the Chinese use today:

Old Stone Age (Paleolithic) appr. 600,000 B.C.–appr. 7000 B.C.

New Stone Age (Neolithic) appr. 7000 B.C.– appr. 2200 B.C.

Xia (legendary?) appr. 2200 B.C.–1524 B.C.

Shang 1523 B.C.–1028 B.C.

Zhou 1027 B.C.–221 B.C.
    Spring and Autumn Period 770 B.C.–476 B.C.
    Warring States Period 475 B.C.–221 B.C.

Qin 221 B.C.–207 B.C.

Han 206 B.C.–220 A.D.

The Three Kingdoms 221–280

Western Jin 265–316

Eastern Jin 317–420

Northern and Southern Dynasties 420–589

Sui 581–618

Tang 618–906

The Five Dynasties 907–960

Song 960–1279

Yuan 1280–1367

Ming 1368–1644

Qing 1644–1911

Republic of China 1912–1948

People's Republic of China 1949–

Index

Credits

Bonnier, Albert III, Stockholm: 364, 384
British Museum, London: 39
China Pictorial, Beijing: 27, 29, 34, 55, 66, 71, 94 (right), 105, 107 (left), 114, 115, 117, 133, 135, 197, 206 (far left), 222, 260, 277, 279, 285, 304, 314, 315, 316, 317, 318, 319, 344, 368, 387 (bottom), 390
Chinese Academy of Science, Beijing: 80, 139
Freer Gallery of Art, Washington, DC: 90
Institute of History and Philology, Academia Sinica, Taipei, Taiwan, Rep. of China: 84, 251, 362
Kessle, Gun, Mariefred: 292
Lindqvist, Cecilia, Stockholm: 21, 31, 45, 53, 60, 65, 67, 76, 86, 88, 89, 98, 107, 108, 112, 123, 125, 127, 130, 135, 143, 145, 147, 148, 151, 152, 154, 158, 160, 172, 176, 187, 200, 201, 202, 203, 204, 206 (middle), 209, 216, 218, 223, 226, 229, 233, 235, 236, 237, 244, 249, 253, 254, 261, 262, 263, 268, 269, 270, 273, 276, 279, 280, 282, 286, 289, 291, 294, 296, 298, 322, 335, 365, 369, 371, 372, 373, 375, 377, 380, 381, 382 (middle, bottom right), 385, 386 (top), 387, 388, 389, 391, 392
Lindqvist, Cecilia, collection. Rubbings, 41, 58, 86, 122, 144, 166, 187, 217, 221, 320, 321. papercuts, New Year pictures, posters, etc.: 73, 74, 99, 100 (right), 145, 163, 166, 328, 342, 366, 372, 373, 378, 379
Musée Cernuschi, Paris: 109, 370
National Palace Museum, Taipei, Taiwan, Rep. of China: 59, 177, 208, 367
National Archive, Stockholm: 146
Sweden—China Society Archives, Stockholm: 104, 142, 169, 188, 299, 366, 382 (top right)

Ancient Chinese Architecture, Chinese Academy of Architecture, Hong Kong 1982: 271
Brinker, H., Goepper, R., Kunstschätze aus China, Zürich 1980: 17
Chang, K.-C., The Archaeology of Ancient China, New Haven/London 1977: 140 (left)
—— Shang Civilization, New Haven/London 1980: 271
Changsha Mawangdui yi hao Han mu, Beijing 1973: 225, 312, 313, 382 (bottom left)
Chavannes, E., Mission Archéologique dans la Chine Septentrionale, Paris 1909–15: 148
Chêng Tê-k'un, Shang China, Cambridge 1960: 139
——, Zhou China, Cambridge 1963: 272
China—7000 Years of Discovery. A special exhibition by the China Science and Technology Palace Preparatory Committee and the Ontario Science Centre 1982: 219
Chinese Literature 1979/12: 376
Dawenkou, Beijing 1974: 57, 253, 259
Dye, D. S., Chinese Lattice Designs, New York 1974: 295
Francke, O., Keng Tschi T'u, Ackerbau und Seidengewinnung in China, Hamburg 1913: 245
Gaocheng Taixi Shangdai yishi, Beijing 1985: 40, 177, 178, 250
Goodall, J. A., Heaven and Earth, 120 album leaves from a Ming Encyclopedia, London 1979: 132
Jianming zhongguo lishi tuce, Tianjin 1978: 165, 166, 202, 254
Jin shi su, 1821: 73
Kaogu, 1964/9: 163
Keightley, D. N., Sources of Shang History, Berkeley 1978: 18
Li Chi, The Beginnings of Chinese Civilization, Seattle 1957: 110
Li Jie, Yingzao fashi, New Edition, Wujin 1925: 277, 278, 287
Liu Dunzhen (Ed.), Zhongguo gudai jianzhu shi, Beijing 1981: 275, 281
Liu E, (T'ieh-yün ts'ang kuei), Beijing 1931: 19

Mi Su moji san zhong, Shanghai shuhua chubanshe, 1973: 59
Museum of Far Eastern Antiquities, Stockholm (Erik Cornelius): 25, 94 (left), 116, 157, 199, 206 (far right), 207, 249, 256, 308, 363, 382 (top left), 383, 386 (bottom)
Mustard Seed Garden Manual of Painting, Beijing 1960: 33, 64, 155, 230, 231, 237, 283, 284
Needham, J., Science and Civilisation in China, Cambridge 1971: 142, 150, 153, 156
Nongye kaogu 1982/1: 75
Pan Jixing, Zhongguo zao zhi jishu shigao, Beijing 1979: 214
Peasant Paintings from Huhsien County, Beijing 1974: 374
Shaanxi chutu shang zhou qingtongqi I, Beijing 1979: 87
Thomson, J., China and Its People (1873), New York/Dover 1982: 79
Tiangong kaiwu (1637). New Edition, Hong Kong 1983: 222
Wang Xuezhong, Shufa juyao, Tianjin 1981: 306
Weber, C. D., Chinese Pictorial Bronze Vessels of Late Chou Period, Ascona 1968: 77, 83, 101, 103, 257, 315, 323, 326
White, W. C., Tombs of Old Lo-yang, Shanghai 1934: 81–82, 121
Wu Qijun, Zhiwu ming bao tu kao, Shanghai 1957: 185, 186, 193
Xi'an Banpo, Beijing 1963: 71, 77, 267, 268
Xu Guangqi, Nong Zheng Quan Shu Jiaozhu, Shanghai 1979: 147, 173, 175, 179
Yan'an Papercuts (s.l., s.a.): 96–98, 100 (left), 108, 126, 240
Zhanguo hou zhi mu, Xianning 1984: 319 (top)
Zhongguo gudai shi chang shi, Beijing 1980: 79, 140 (right), 145, 196, 242, 303
Zhong Yuanzhao (Ed.), History and Development of Ancient Chinese Architecture, Beijing 1986: 267, 275